AGAINST THE TIDE

NOËL BROWNE

GILL AND MACMILLAN

Published in Ireland by
Gill and Macmillan Ltd
Goldenbridge
Dublin 8
with associated companies in
Auckland, Dallas, Delhi, Hong Kong,
Johannesburg, Lagos, London, Manzini,
Melbourne, Nairobi, New York, Singapore,
Tokyo, Washington
© Noël Browne 1986
7171 1458 9
Print origination in Ireland by
Wellset Limited
Printed in Great Britain by
Richard Clay Ltd, Bungay, Suffolk

Contents

Preface

Being neither a diarist nor a historian, I cannot claim that this book is a definitive history. It was written with some reluctance, and only after long consideration, in order to correct the inaccuracies of other accounts about a number of important incidents. The events recorded in these pages are the recollected memories of an eventful and at times a controversial life, throughout 'the seven ages', from childhood to old age, both in England and in Ireland.

Circumstances ordained that I should lead a nomadic, itinerant existence. I have collected no library, nor have I kept any records. For this reason, for occasional verification, I have had to call on the generosity and memories of my friends, for their recollection of shared events. Equally invaluable were the records of the relevant period in the State Paper Office in Dublin Castle. As so many students have found, I had the willing help at all times of Dr MacGiolla Coille, together with his painstaking staff. Jack McQuillan and his wife, Angela, were characteristically patient and helpfully critical. Jack, a one-time Clann na Poblachta deputy, generously put at my disposal all his memories of our joint experiences, as well as any papers he had kept. George Lawlor, my first Director of Elections, my good friend during all the years, and a onetime member of Clann na Poblachta, happily for both of us possesses a computer-like memory. He could not do too much for me. Fortunately, in his valuable library of books and papers, he had also carefully retained much of the literature put out by Clann na Poblachta at that time. All of this he allowed me to use. The dates, personalities, and events, so meticulously researched and collated by Katie Burns, of Cork in her excellent thesis on the Mother and Child controversies were an enormous help, for which I am very grateful.

In spite of the evidence of bulging libraries and the tens of thousands of authors, I found that, for me, it was not easy to write a book. The memories, so many of them, flood into one's mind, events long forgotten, prised out of the unconscious, are pieced together to complete the resultant jigsaw. At the same time, order, sequence, chronology, need professional skills, so as to add shape and discipline to the story. That there is order, I am grateful to Ciaran Carty, a professional journalist who edited the script. To Deirdre Rennison, editorial secretary at Gill and Macmillan I offer my profound thanks for keeping the peace between myself, Michael Gill, and others. My lack of writing experience to such polished professionals, needed everyone's understanding patience. I am grateful to the original publishers' 'reader' of the manuscript, who, in its very early stage, gave it critical approval, and recommended that it be published.

To the O Fahertha family, our near neighbours on that isolated yet lovely Cloughmore peninsula on the Atlantic, both Phyllis and I would wish to acknowledge in gratitude their acceptance of the wanderers returned at last to their roots in the West and for the peace which made our work on the books and our life there so pleasurable.

In the end, to myself and to that truly remarkable woman Phyllis my wife, remained the task of preparing the text. My manuscript was typed and re-typed repeatedly by Phyllis with, where needed, valuable critical suggestions. With consistent encouragement of my occasionally flagging energies, she was infinitely more than typist.

In the story of a life, of which over fifty years has been lived together, does my wife not become the joint author? In a just world, beneath its title, this book should have subscribed two names, Noël and Phyllis Browne.

1

Childhood in Athlone

CAGED, a sense of claustrophobic entrapment, surrounded by the vertical lines of bar-like legs. Table legs, legs of chairs and stools, legs of grownups, no way out; these are my earliest recollections, crouching under a table in the yellow darkness of an oil-lamp lighted room, entombed among the legs of those grownups who were at work around the table. I was forgotten by them, occupied as they were with their own frenetic manipulations, coiling in circles six blindingly white starched Irish linen collars into boxes, then closing over the pure white paper flaps, slipping on the precisely-fitting lid, adding that filled box to the pile already by the table. This work was done in addition to an already long hard day's work at one of Derry's treadmill shirt factories; keeping collar boxes filled improved baby's chances of being fed.

The boxes I well remember, since I was given what I suppose was a damaged one to play with. They were virgin white inside, with two speckless flaps of white paper at the top. As befits a product of the Emerald Isle, even in the yellow oil-lamp light the outside was a shiny, grass green, a blindingly gay plaything for baby. But for the grownups it was the pretentious, brashly shining cardboard symbol of working class life over eastern and western Europe at that time, soon to be challenged by a socialist revolution.

My earliest daytime memory is of being held in the arms of a frightened woman, behind a half door which looked out into a stony yard. Holding on to me so hard that her arms pained me, she tried to throw a long flat stone — it could have been a whetstone — at the black rats which appeared to be threatening us.

We had moved from Waterford, where I was born on 20 December 1915. My father, unemployed and the unskilled son of a small farming family in Co. Galway, brought us shortly after my birth to Derry, where we lived for a time in the Bogside. He obtained work in one of the shirt factories.

Because my mother was a daily Communicant, and a devout Catholic, I attended daily Mass from an early age. I have come to believe that the notable intensity of religion and devotion to the Sacraments, by Irish and indeed all Catholic peasant women, as opposed to the relative indifference of the men, must have fear among its origins. There is a forlorn hope that the magic miracle of the Mass, or other Sacrament, will fend off that greatest single fear so many working class mothers know, the fear of the next pregnancy.

While I had no choice as a very small child in attending the Mass, I feared the departure of my mother when she left me to go to the Communion rails. Insecure as always, I would then cry my heart out, until fascinated into silence by the rich golden rays of light, which I learned to create with the altar candles seen through my tears. The frivolous futility of these, my private exotic visions, made crying seem to me neither to suit nor to answer my immediate needs, the loss of my mother.

My overt personal scars from Derry are an unreasonable fear of rats together with one permanently deaf ear and one damaged eye, the result of uncared-for measles. I did not return to the Bogside again until 1969, when I formed part of a Labour Party delegation sent to study the emergent violence. There are no happy memories of Derry for me.

In 1920, my father was offered the job of Inspector with the National Society for the Prevention of Cruelty to Children. With no regrets whatsoever we left Derry and arrived in Athlone, where a good-sized house came with the job and where, until the death of my father in 1923, we lived our lives of precarious survival.

In terms of emotional and physical development we grew up in a one-parent family; our father was virtually never at home. Our mother, a lovely, slight-figured country girl, took on the heavy burden of child-bearing and rearing which contributed to her early death at the age of forty-two. The family consisted of Eileen, Jody, Martha, Kitty, myself, Una and Ruth. There was also Annie, who died in infancy of tuberculous meningitis.

My father, Joseph Browne, was, as his marriage picture

shows, a tall moustached handsome man. He was a well-known middle distance runner, and the shelves on our old Victorian whatnot were covered with silver and gold medals, cups and other trophies.

The formal marriage portrait shows my parents as an elegant pair of happy young innocents eager for the years ahead together. They enjoyed amateur acting and ballroom dancing; he was particularly popular for his songs at the piano, and his extrovert personality. He is proud, elaborately coiffed, in a dress suit with a gold chain, wearing the gold medals he had won. My mother Mary Therese wears a circular fur hat framing her lovely face, and a tiny gold and pink enamel watch, a gift from the groom, on its slim gold muff chain. That watch still bears the dents of a teething child. There was, however, a second, later, picture, also taken in Athlone, which shows my father separately, with seven of his children. My mother was probably pregnant with my last sister, Ruth, to be born shortly after his death. Here he is, physically, a completely different man, in the last destructive phase of tuberculosis. Part Spanish on his father's side, he is a dark, bonyfaced, black-eyed, shrunken man. He was to die soon afterwards. My inconsolable mother died some two years later. We children were then left homeless and penniless, as were and are so many unwanted children of primitive peasant societies such as ours was.

Even though the slow destruction of my family took place during our years in Athlone, my experiences there became the most settled and contented part of my young life. Athlone is set in the dead centre of Ireland with the river Shannon running through it. We spent our days playing just below the weir, on the small stony beach. The fluctuant river with its floods and its droughts and the noise of the weir became a constant heartbeat, conditioning my later adult obsession with the sea, its sounds, its tides, its pleasures and its dangers.

For the most part we played down by the Shannon, sailing unmanageable boats made by ourselves. In wet weather we were fortunate to have access to a builder's yard belonging to a friend of ours named Duffy, who lived opposite our house in Irishtown. This became an idyllic world of fantasy within our other world. There were long, low, dark lofts, garrets, workshops, outhouses and what seemed to us children to be great mountains of sand and gravel, which we converted into strong points during our battles. Our play had unlimited scope for our imaginings. When we were tired, we listened to the stylised music of Mr Duffy's old music box. I still recall those times whenever I hear the melody 'La Barcarolle'.

It became the practice for us children to mimic the Civil War then being fought in all its real ferocity around us. We used cata-pults and pea-shooters, or simply threw pebbles at one another, 'Shinners' on one side and 'Staters' (the Duffys were a Free State family) on the other, from sand heap to gravel pit. I recall being in my special uniform, which included a protective steel white knobbed platecover, and receiving a direct hit on my luckily protected head — killed stone dead, no doubt, in real life — even though I was dug into a deep hole in the centre of a great mound of sand.

Athlone was an important garrison town with a substantial force of soldiers, originally British, now Irish, permanently stationed there. The sides taken up by us in our mock civil war — Staters, Republicans, or Irregulars — reflected the divisions of parental loyalties in the struggles all around us. It was the practice for the Irregulars to invade and harass the town, burning down an enemy property or carrying out a hit-and-run assassination. I watched with no understanding the exhilarating sight of the grocery store owned by the Brodericks, some fifty or sixty yards from our house, burning wildly during a winter's night, sparks and smoke curling away on the wind into the night sky. Fear was transmitted to me from the grownups around because of the danger that the fire would spread along the row of tiny houses and include our own in the holocaust.

There had been a night like that long before. I was learning how to walk and was being helped by my father on our way up to Sweeney's general shop a few hundred yards from our house. There was a hurried scattering of frightened men and women, well used by then to the ominous whine of the Black and Tan Crossley lorries. It was the practice for these British auxiliaries, a force of mercenaries who had fought in the 1914-18 war, to sweep through Irish towns and villages in their Crossley tenders, dressed in a motley of uniforms and armed with rifles and revolvers. They were protected from attack by wire cages over the back of the lorry, and by hostages taken from the local community. The hostages sat back to back on their long wooden forms in the centre of the lorry. Frightened, no doubt and often drunk, the Black and Tans shot at civilians out of a macabre sense of fun. My father on this occasion dragged me into his arms and ran up the few steps to reach the safety of Sweeney's shop. There I found myself sitting on a heap of copper and silver coins and paper money in the centre of the small safe.

One night we were awakened abruptly by my father. He was angry, which surprised me since he was a very even-tempered man, and was abusing those outside the house. I recall hearing him mutter 'if only I had a gun myself'. He ordered us all to lie down flat on the floor. We were in the front line in an ambush: an assassination attempt was being carried out by the Irregulars on a car full of Free State officers; these officers, based in Custume Barracks, used to visit Duffy's house, directly opposite to ours. On this occasion, the senior officer and a young lieutenant were ambushed just as they drove away. We were in the heart of the ambush in our first floor bedroom, listening to much shouting and then shooting. Whether I imagined it or not, I recall hearing someone shout 'don't shoot'. This was followed by the sound of shooting, then the sound of men running up the lane beside our house. I heard the distinctive metallic clanging sound of the heavy iron gates to Kane's field at the top of the laneway, and they were away.

The attackers did not 'get' the senior officer for whom they had set the ambush, General Seán MacEoin, known and admired by the rest of us as the 'Blacksmith of Ballinalee'. Instead a young lieutenant lay dead in his own great pool of blood, which was still there on the following morning for us children to see, covered simply by a rough potato sack — Pearse's 'rich red blood, which so enhances the soil'. I was neither frightened nor revolted, but exhilarated.

At school the following day, I went over the sequence of the night's killing again and again for my interested fellow pupils, the centre of attention for having had the front seat at an ambush and a killing, and with the bullet-scarred walls of our house to prove it. This awful example of man's unique capacity to kill cruelly a fellow man, even the wrong man, simply appeared to us like a cinema show. The bodily agony of the wounded and dying was transmuted by a crude potato sack and the faded black patch of blood. Is this all a merciful protection for the young who must live out their lives among the 'grown-up' men and women in control of man's destiny?

Twenty-five years later, an odd sequel was acted out in the Cabinet office in Merrion Street, after the formation of the first coalition government in 1948, when the members of the Cabinet met to be introduced to each other. I introduced myself to Sean MacEoin, who was to be Minister for Justice. The last time I had heard his voice was under the window of our bedroom on the night of the ambush outside Duffy's nearly thirty years before. I told MacEoin that in my account to my schoolfriends I had attributed to him the shouted words, 'don't shoot'. It was generally believed by the public that in spite of being a soldier, with the soldier's awful job of daily learning how to kill other men more cleverly, MacEoin was a gentle peaceful man, who greatly regretted the 'split'. He neither wanted to kill, nor be killed. MacEoin replied that his instinct would have been to try to stop the shooting, but on both sides.

Possibly attempting to obliterate the unhappy memory, he then proceeded to show me how he had disarmed his British Army guard when he was a prisoner in Dublin Castle, during an abortive attempt made by Michael Collins to rescue him. He grabbed my right hand, no doubt what he would have called my revolver hand, and pinned it helplessly behind my back. Even then, in middle age, he was an extremely powerful blacksmith of a man.

I remember too seeing row after row of tricolour-covered coffins, side by side. To me they were just so many colourful outsize parcels, in a great room in some building. In these coffins were the remains of men shot in Custume Barracks by the Free State government as part of massive reprisals for the killing of Dáil deputy Sean Hales; they could not lie before the altar in St Mary's, since the Republicans had been excommunicated. These grim white pine boxes, filled with the bodies of innocent youths who had been murdered, 'the sow devouring her farrow', left no shocked memory on my child's mind. Why not leave the bullet-shattered, terrified, open-eyed, naked corpse exposed for the young such as myself to see, and to learn from it the folly of our 'wiser and older' leaders of church and state?

This flag which we looked at was the same national flag run

up over the castle in Athlone, after the Union Jack was lowered, to signify our new freedom from the British Army. Standing with my father on Custume Bridge, I had happily watched them tramp out of our lives, to be replaced by our new Free State army. But had this freedom not been won by these same young men, now boxed carcases, shot by their own, not by the British? Incomprehensible grownups; a child must learn to accept without question or explanation the enigmatic contradictions of adult life.

Much later in a diary kept by Peadar Cowan, an officer in the Free State army in Custume Barracks, I read of the blindingly whimsical system whereby the victims were chosen for death: it was a simple process of taking a group of prisoners from each county. Between November 1922 and May 1923, seventy-seven Republican prisoners in all were to be executed without trial. Since these men had all been in custody at the time of the shooting of Hales and were known to be innocent of the assassination for which the reprisals were being carried out, their killing was indefensible. The most stunning experience for me was to read how Peadar, a parliamentary colleague of mine in later life, recounted the incident of the mass executions without showing any sense of horror, shock, guilt or concern whatever for the whole process or his own part in it. Yet Peadar was what is known in Ireland as 'a devoutly religious man'.

During the British period of occupation there were many raids for arms and hostages were taken to clear the barricades or ambushed roads outside the town. Our houses were searched for men 'on the run'. Armed soldiers took over total control. The fear was instant and freezing. 'Please God, let them go away, and leave us alone.' I'm afraid that there was always the emphasis on that 'us'; let them torment someone else. The awful selfish self-preservation of the hunger camps affects us all.

The child of a large family, such as ours was, is nearly inevitably deprived of the emotional nurturing found in the stable small family. In the large family neither the mother nor the father can make the time needed to socialise with the children. Children are deprived of the personality moulding, formative process of intensive or casual intelligently-directed conversation with the parents. It is not surprising that we understood little except the crude differences between pleasure and pain.

There was one comforting feature in our family's life. This happened at near five o'clock on a summer's evening when our tea, bread and butter was ready. It was my mother's practice, a strange one for the shy country girl she was, to stand outside at the front door of our house on the step. Then, no doubt to the neighbours' surprise since no-one else did it, she proceeded to whistle us all home. This distinctive slow rising and falling whistle was the 'exclusive' Browne sound. Wherever we were playing, in Begley's or Duffy's yard, by the Shannon or in Kane's field at the back of the house, playing hopscotch, rolling hoops, or smashing our champion chestnuts against our rivals' we would all, like the sunflower turning to the sun, wend our way towards home, and our waiting mother, and tea. She would remain at the door and continue to whistle until she could count all of us safely home at last. Such was a child's life in the town of Athlone in spite of the Civil War we played. We found that her fragmented love for us was sufficient.

I became a pupil at the Marist Brothers' school. I served Mass at St Mary's throughout my life there and could be depended on to turn up in time in all weathers. (My mother was pleased to see me involved even at this remove in church services; she hoped that I would one day become a priest, like all Irish Catholic mothers of her time.) It was there that I was subjected to the torment of copper-plate handwriting. We were compelled to copy the headline copy books with our right hands, and I was naturally left-handed, a 'citeóg'. In those times a person who wrote with their left hand was considered to be in some way in league with the devil. The Marist Brothers' solution, of compelling me to write exclusively with my right hand, was intended to solve the problem of my becoming the devil's child. It left me unable to write legibly to this day, with either hand.

I have happy memories of a patient young lay teacher, Mr Handley, who spoke Irish and gave us plasticine to play with. There was also a harassed and unhappy-looking older man, Mr Roper, whose appearance was somewhat intimidating. He lived in a pretty rose-covered cottage outside the town. Small in size and figure, he wore grey knickerbockers with long grey stockings and brightly-polished black kid laced boots. He was nearly bald, with a few wisps of what had been red hair brushed carefully across his head, and had small eyes. His face was that of an

impatient man with a short temper yet I do not recall his being
unduly angry at any time.

This was the time when the new native government, under
Marcus O'Sullivan, the Minister for Education, was enthusias-
tically, and not very wisely, pressing forward with their insistence that we should all speak Gaelic, irrespective of whether the
language of the home was Gaelic or English. This was just one
example of the non-Irish speaking enthusiast's impractical and
bizarre belief that he could, irrespective of its results on others,
achieve the impossible. Do what I say, but not what I do. I
understood that Mr Roper, who appeared to be in his late
forties, was submitted to a brief 'crash' course in the Irish language. Understandably, it was impossible for him to learn the
language, in such a short time, and consequently to teach it to
us. He himself neither knew nor spoke, and possibly did not even
like the language. He certainly did not appear to share his
Minister's love of it.

In the infant's class I had the sole unhappy experience of my
childhood with either of my parents. It was the custom in the
school, following the First Communion ceremony, for the
brothers to celebrate the day by giving the children a fine breakfast. Very few of us had any such breakfast at home. Somehow I
happened to be at the school one morning on the boys' return
from their First Communion. They were dressed as was the
custom in shiny black boots, short pants, spotlessly washed white
shirts, and grey socks, knees pink with the cold, and carried with
pride their red-ribboned Holy Communion medals. As they
filed into the converted classroom for breakfast, Mr Handley
told me to join the others at the breakfast table. I can still recall
the large fried egg, placed on the centre of a piece of fried bread,
tea, bread and butter unlimited. On the completion of the meal
I returned home, and was astonished to find my gentle mother
very angry with me. Alas, she was over-sensitive, and afraid that
the breakfast I had been given by a kindly Mr Handley was intended as a charitable gesture to her 'hungry poverty-stricken
child'. She came from a proud village family home in Co Mayo
and was deeply hurt by the implications of charity, a common
false pride in such Irish homes then.

Following release from infants' class, I made my First
Communion, and the now famous breakfast was rightly earned

and eaten. I passed into Brother John's class: he was known to his colleagues as 'Snowball'. He was a small, neatly-dressed man, with well cared-for white crinkly hair, and the most delicately-shaped hands and fingers I have ever seen on man or woman. He had clever blue eyes and a finely-formed nose; his mouth was small, firm and mean. When his clever eyes became brighter, and his face cherry-coloured, we knew he was angry, and that we would soon see the brisk swinging action of his springy yellow cane. He had only one serious interest in life, Gregorian chant. The miscellaneous nondescript room, full of boys poorly but cleanly dressed, with no vestige of culture, inexplicably presented to Brother John a collection of potential songbirds. From these he found it possible, in time, to extract beautiful musical sounds. He would simply persist and pray, and maybe cane a few of us if need be, in order to relieve his frustration and improve our singing. He appeared to me to look over us, to look through us, to look around us, but never at us. Were we there at all for him? I cannot recall having any formal classes about academic subjects during his classes. The cane, with the traditional incongruous tiny handle, protruded like a 'shooter' in a Western cowboy picture from his cassock pocket, always at the ready.

Because I was punctual, predictable, and never missed school, Brother John chose to rely on me to run messages. I was given the money needed to fetch jotters and school books from the shop opposite the Prince of Wales Hotel in the centre of the town. I knew how to count and bring back the correct change. The most important message, for which I was dispatched early in the morning, was a large roll of shiny black paper, about the size of a roll of wallpaper. On my return with this black roll and a large box of drawing pins, Brother John would tell us all to be silent. It was then I would notice his thin, nimble, wax-like fingers. He would unroll the shiny black paper and attach it with fine precision to the left-hand side of the blackboard, then unroll the paper and pin it to the board until it crossed to the outer edge, where he pinned it again. This transformed the school blackboard into a shiny rectangle, like black glass. We watched in silence, not a word from anyone. Brother John had that effect on all of us: he rarely, if ever, spoke to us.

Having provided himself with this enormous sheet of black

glass, he would then bring out a manual and begin to write musical notes, his fingers as controlled as precision instruments. We would then be told to climb up on our seats, for all the world like clumsy blackbirds on the branches of a tree, and singing lessons would begin. We sang and sang all day long. The odd thing is that I do not recollect that we ever acted as a choir in St Mary's church, which would have justified the time spent on the lessons.

Brother Maher, my teacher when I passed into the higher class, was a tall powerfully-built, curly-haired, bright-eyed young man, who took his teaching very seriously and was good at it. Unfortunately, he also liked to support his methods with the free use of the cane. To us he was a giant and although he never beat me — indeed I was not beaten by anyone during my time in Athlone or Ballinrobe — being beaten by these men must have been a truly shocking experience for a child.

During school breaks from the classroom we played in the stony playground. Few of us escaped a visit to the local District Hospital with torn knees and hands, results of our falls. With three other boys I was once caught taking apples from the Marist Brothers' orchard. I can remember the threat of the Brother, 'I should take you down to the station', but he did not carry it out.

The most enjoyable part of my life in Athlone was when, aged about seven, I was taken on as helper by the (to me) enormous Mr Molloy, our milkman, who delivered milk in his donkey cart to his customers at a decidedly leisurely pace every morning. The poor donkey, heavily laden, could not be blamed for taking its time. The warm milk, straight from the newly-milked cow in the cowshed, was contained in a truly grand brassbound steel churn about four feet high. A brass tap delivered the milk into a classic triangular pint measure. The donkey cart was the regulation Reckitt's blue, with red shafts and red wheels. Even though I was small, there were just about nine inches for me beside Mr Molloy on the seat, a long flat plank placed across the sides of the cart.

We meandered along upper and lower Irishtown, delivering the milk. Then, in the pub near the bridge over the Shannon, Mr Molloy, who was a quiet, redfaced moustached man — he had been a rowing man in his youth but had badly 'gone to

seed' — would take a ritual mid-morning pint. I minded the
donkey. After I had 'served my time' and learned how to drive,
to regulate the tap and to fill the measure (once or twice
according to the customer's needs with always the small extra
drop for luck or for the cat) it became Mr Molloy's practice to
dismount slowly and solemnly outside the pub, enter a sweet
shop, and bring me out a small twist of brown paper, filled with
a pennyworth of sweets. We never said anything to one another.
I knew real happiness for the first time in my life when he would
hand me the reins of the donkey. I had absolute freedom and
responsibility to drive the cart back to Molloy's farm at
Ballymahon. I was a Roman charioteer in full flight with my
fine, intelligent, speedy donkey and we trotted home just this
side of a gallop. I learnt the well-known truth that the sprightly
willing horse or donkey, on the way home, is an entirely different
animal from the same perpetually exhausted creature on its way
into town, to the market. They lose years, and develop a new
spring, power and speed in their legs and feet, on their way back
to the stable and a feed of hay in the manger. Mrs Molloy, a kind
and gentle English lady, hearing us thundering down the hill on
our way to the farm would caution me of the danger of a fall and
the consequence of injury to myself. But I enjoyed standing up in
the centre of the cart, aflame with the excitement, the clinking
noise of the harness, and the iron clatter of the wheels on the
road.

Mrs Molloy probably rendered all of us in the family a very
special service, for she always insisted that I take a can of milk
home to my mother to make rice puddings and porridge and use
for the tea. It became the only worthwhile feature of the otherwise bread-and-rhubarb jam diet of our class.

Our kitchen had a single cold tap, and an open Stanley range
on which was a giant iron black kettle. My mother continually
organised our spotlessly clean and ironed clothes. The iron was a
flat, solid contraption, heated on the red coals of the fire; she
would spit on it to judge the heat by the sizzle. She boiled the
black kettle endlessly on the range, making tea, washing dishes,
or laundering the family's clothes. She made our bread, cooked
puddings and porridge and, thanks to Mrs Molloy's kind gift of
milk, occasionally baked a raisin-filled rice pudding in the oven.
She sweated and scorched herself over the old bastable pot oven

making the large cartwheels of soda bread needed to keep her growing family nourished. One persistent memory I have of my mother is her hands, her thin hands, stoking the coals with the tongs on to the top of the lid and under the pot itself in order to raise the heat enough for cooking bread well into the night. Her face and forehead would be wet with sweat, the lines of her black hair clinging to her harassed face, pink with heat. Always it was 'for the will of God and His Holy Mother', as she would tell us to the end of her life.

From my mother I learned an assortment of semi-religious secular sayings for every disaster, every dilemma: 'age is honourable', 'show me your friends, and I'll tell you what you are', 'the mills of God grind slow but sure'. Most things were 'a sign from God'. Throughout the many disasters which affected herself and the rest of us until her lonely death in a London workhouse, she kept this unquestioning childlike faith, trusting in a kindly God. Progressively, slowly, but in her memory regretfully, I ceased to share it.

Long after our homework was completed under the yellow light of the oil lamp and our rosary had been said, lying in bed upstairs we were lulled to sleep by the rhythmic swish and stop and swish again of my mother's foot treadle Singer sewing machine. A dressmaker before her marriage, she made all our clothes as well as knitting our pullovers and socks. My father, in spite of his own exhaustion, still managed to mend our boots on the oldtime last, inseparable from any workingclass home.

A member of the Murphy family, a Republican, with whom my mother had worked in Ballinrobe before her marriage, stayed with us on his release from Custume Barracks. He had been imprisoned by the Free State forces.

My recollections of my father are slight. He was out virtually all day and home later, dead tired with little to say to us. When I could I stood beside him, watching and following him like a tail on a high-flying kite. With the exception of the incident of the ambush outside our home, I cannot recall him showing anger or displeasure with anyone. My mother and my father appeared to find peace and tranquillity in their loving relationship. I recall on one occasion seeing him sitting by the evening lamplight in a great galvanised iron bath by the fireside, his back being washed by my mother, following a truly horrendous day in mid-winter in which he had had to cycle through many miles of rain and cold. His income of £5 a week remained static as he slowly destroyed himself working long and late hours.

On Sundays my father derived much pleasure from singing and accompanying himself on the piano in the parlour, surrounded by all his prizes for athletic success. His songs were old Victorian ballads, such as 'The snowy-breasted pearl' and 'I dreamt that I dwelt in marble halls'. He had a pleasant light tenor voice and we children greatly enjoyed listening to him. He took us for walks in the surrounding country-side, but they were largely silent, though pleasant, excursions.

Being from a rural family, he used to cultivate our garden. He'd slice the potatoes and show me the 'eyes', which he then placed at regular distances, pointing upwards, in the straight neat ridges of rich black clay. There was no babble of information. We planted a seed pip from an apple which became the fine apple tree that still grew in that garden the last time I looked for it.

My father's work was concerned with the protection of children in the surrounding counties, who were at risk from deliberate cruelty. On an old-fashioned high-framed bicycle he cycled virtually everywhere, covering great distances in all weathers. The usual causes for cruelty to children were widespread poverty and the fact that most families were too large to manage. Because of his somewhat distasteful job, taking children from their homes on court orders in cases where, in his view, they were enduring needless suffering, my father's activities were frequently greatly resented. He was assaulted on one occasion outside the courts and on another was shot at on his way home towards Athlone. But the most awesome demonstration of hostility happened one afternoon in mid-summer. We children were playing with our tops outside our house when we heard the sounds of wailing women, crying and shouting. They came from the direction of Lower Irishtown and were heading our way.

Amongst the crowd there was a distinctive lady, the centre of the cursing, jeering and shouting crowd which continued to gather outside our house. She was a distinctly frightening, powerfully-built, very old woman. We children scattered up the land and into the house by the back door to watch her and the crowd from a safe distance, behind the curtains of the parlour windows. This old lady had long, tangled, rusty-grey, curly hair, which reached down to her shoulders and around her neck. Her loose wrinkled skin had the awful yellow dirty colour which is sometimes seen on the aged who have lived their lives indoors, in semi-darkness. Her clothes were simply an old skirt, green with age, and her once black shawl. Her eyes were of a watery blue, washed with tears of anger or distress. Her mouth had long since lost all its teeth.

Like a great Diva playing a sequence in grand opera, she sank slowly to her knees. She then opened her powerful lungs and in a mighty voice, and with great feeling, called on God, his angels, and his saints, to curse and damn for ever my father, with all 'his breed and seed'. She then turned to each of us children, and wished us unending disasters and unhappiness to all our children, and to their children throughout their lives, with a death in the end for all of us of great agony and pain, to be followed by never-ending torment by the devils in a deepest hell.

Her curses on our house and home completed, exhausted but happy, she slowly rose and, with imposing dignity, moved away, the crowd following her. Whatever my father's real or imagined crime had been against her family, horror and damnation were facing us in reprisal. Looking at the life of each one of us since, much of it tragic, the peasant in me sometimes wonders about the power of an old lady's maledictions.

A country child's introduction to life and death is rough, direct and inescapable. Infants are born and animals die, cruelly, deliberately, slowly or for whimsical reasons of sport. My father was a purposeful and pre-occupied man who made little attempt to detail or explain what he was doing. There might be a short conversation with my mother in the kitchen around the table at tea-time. . . . 'She's old, and hasn't laid an egg for months', he'd argue. Later came the action. He cornered a hen at the back in the dark black turf house, frightened, squawking, feathers flying as if she knew.

He'd already made the preparation — the old dependable bone-handled hacksaw-edged knife; the preliminary sharpening; backwards-reverse-forward, backwards-reverse-forward, no explanation, just the business-like sounds of steel on the worn stone edge of the smooth back doorstep.

Over to the blackened brass cold-water tap in the corner of the yard, now turned on, wastefully gushing down into the trap. I would see the reason for that soon. He wore his black trousers and countryman's white striped shirt, open at the neck with its brass stud, the shirt sleeves rolled up. He had the hen clutched between his knees. There was a last glimpse of shining, terrified, tiny amber eyes. Her head was gripped tight, bent into a feathery half circle rainbow of copper red, pressed to the shining edge of the knife. A shudder, a strangled scream for freedom, the kicking yellow claws protesting hopelessly. Her neck was tougher than he expected, the knife blade not as sharp. He made a desperate sawing action. He surely disliked what he was doing. The pumping flood of crimson burst at last from the heart of the red feathers, held now quivering under the gushing tap. For years she had strutted the yard, behind the lordly cock, scratching and clucking over her little ones, tearing at the newly wet black soil for what she might fall on to kill and eat. With that blood down the trap flowed my childhood innocence.

Beside us lived a widow called Mrs Bracken, who had already reared her own large grownup family. She had grey hair with a wisp that always seemed to straggle out, a reminder of a handsome curly-haired young woman; she was brisk and vigorous, with a Junoesque figure. It was difficult to understand her speech because she had so few teeth. She didn't talk much, but smiled continuously, above all with her eyes. Her sleeves were always rolled up, revealing plump powerful arms, ready for action on her washing board, scrubbing a tubful of washing and wringing out heavy sheets or blankets on a permanently waving multi-coloured line of washing. As each of the Brownes came into the world Mrs Bracken would take over our house and family. So gentle and natural was her presence that we hardly noticed the loss of our mother, who was yet again committed to bed to add to our growing family.

Mrs Bracken acted as mid-wife; we had no money for a doctor. As a new life took its place among us, we asked no questions and were told nothing. Blood-stained cotton wool in a corner waiting to be burned, and a new tiny voice crying at night; later my mother, pacing the floor with the ailing child. In our 'big bed' all of us, boys and girls, top and toed, would lie awake, tired and puzzled. There was a noiseless burst of violet blue flame as my mother lit the metal, spider-legged, methylated spirit lamp on the small side table, illuminating her white face, broad forehead and black hair. She would pace the room as she waited for the small saucepan to warm the milk needed to pacify the infant. Peace restored, the small metal cap dropped on the violet flame, darkness returned, and we all slept. My mother would go back to her cold bed, with its broken sleep. Was it we men who invented that mocking phrase, 'the gift of a child?'

Mrs Bracken had a daughter named Lizzie, who had the pale lemon skin of someone always indoors, and the bulging eyes of a goitre. Her voice was shrill, she smoked incessantly, and had greying hair. She was married to gentle, diffident Pat McKegue, but had no children. Poor Pat got the blame; it simply couldn't be the fault of a Bracken. Pat was a nondescript man with putty-coloured grey skin, grey eyes, and uncared-for tousled grey hair.

His great love was a sleek, well-fed, biscuit-coloured greyhound named Siki. Though he said little, and talked to no one, he once invited me to join him in exercising and hunting the dog. We walked down through the shanty part of lower Irishtown, over the railway bridge and out the Moate road until we came to the lanes and fields of the countryside. Behind us came the racing machine, Siki.

As far as I was concerned this was an exciting change from marbles, conkers, hoop rolling and mock civil war battles, or sailing our toy boats on the Shannon. But there was a sinister purpose in our Indian file with Siki at the tail end. So quick was the movement behind me that I saw nothing, only the tiny screech of a death agony and a dog wagging its tail, delighted by the rabbit between its teeth. The deliberate movement of Pat ahead had led the creature to break cover and run straight into the ivory trap of Siki's jaws. Death came in an instant of pain. The walk had lost me more of my childhood innocence. Unaware of my shock, Pat kindly showed me how to slice a hole with a knife in the heel tendon of the rabbit's leg. Then he put the other foot through that slit and slung the rabbit over the walking stick, carried for just such a purpose. He brought home four dead rabbits; Siki had paid for her keep.

Pat once invited me to go with him to a place just outside Athlone called Horseleap, where there was to be a coursing match. There were so many new experiences that day which bombarded my small child's mind, but only one remains with me clearly, that of a man with a long leather lead with two collars in which were strapped the necks of a pair of quivering greyhounds. A silence fell on the crowd. All of us turned to watch the man as he ran backwards, tugging on the double leash. This had the effect of releasing the hounds. Together they burst after the hopeless scurrying puff ball of fur, twenty yards ahead, flying for its life. Two yelping hounds eager for the kill. Just as eager were the on-lookers with their own animal sounds, only deeper: they were men. The hounds reached the hare together, each furious at the other and mad for that spoonful of blood in the small body, as indeed were the baying human beings around me. There was a long death scream of pain that rode to a crescendo, and died in my ear. Like acid on a glass, that memory of the primeval ritual of a coursing meeting remains etched on my mind.

Other country rituals would take their annual course. In the late summer and autumn, each farmer's wife would churn the surplus milk and make butter to bring to Athlone for sale. The day would start for her at dawn with the long drive into town with her husband seated on the narrow plank in the horse and cart. The humiliating trail from door to door, where she was not always well received, would begin. The oblong basket, made from sally rods, could also hold eggs, a pair of bright-eyed pullets, or old hens past their best and meant for the pot. My mother enjoyed reviving memories of the butter-cup yellow country butter associated with her childhood, but we children were not as fond of the butter as she. It tended to be salty and go rancid easily.

The bargaining was intricate and slow. The farmer's wife was torn between anxiety to get a good price and the desire not to have to face another stranger at a door. She might even have to bring the butter home. Much depended on the price, but the taste was even more crucial. Many a farmer's wife had a heavy hand with the salt; it depended on what she and her family liked. My mother would use the third finger of her right hand to scoop a shallow line in the soft surface of the narrow block of butter; this small fragment of butter she put to her lips. If the taste suited her family, then the haggling began; the usual price was around a shilling a pound. If a deal was closed I was sent into the kitchen to get a big clean white dinner plate. The butter was placed in the centre and brought into the kitchen. Sometimes it was marked by the wooden thistle-mould used by the more artistic farmers' wives.

Living in the centre of Ireland we were beside the Bog of Allen. Farmers, their own fuel needs looked to, would earn extra money by loading turf into the horse cart to be sold in Athlone. The usual shallow two-foot-high sides of the cart were increased in height by the addition of creels on all four sides, made of light timber slats and shaped like a cage. The turf was built up beyond the top of the creels and shaped inwards like a cock of hay, held in place by another cage made from ash or birch slips.

The turf loaded the previous night was ready to start for town shortly after dawn and timed to arrive as early as possible. Prospective purchasers, such as my father, started their watch early also. Most of them first generation small-holders, they knew a load of good turf — coal black, heavy and stone-hard in a well-filled high creel cart. It burned long and gave out great heat. No one wanted the light auburn turf that burned quickly with little heat.

The practice was for farmers to parade the streets with their loads. Some might stand in the broad market place in front of St Mary's Church, or just under the castle, near Custume Bridge. The purchaser went from one to the next, trying to beat down the price. The bargaining began as soon as my father was satisfied that he had the best turf. It was a sad picture, two desperately poor heads of families each trying to outwit the other for a matter of pence. Such were the imperatives of our competitive society; the farmers could not afford to agree among themselves on a fair price. The price usually was between five and seven shillings a load.

With the deal made, the farmer wearily turned his tired horse into the short narrow lane up a slight hill that led to the yard at the back of our house. It needed skill and care to turn off the main street with the delicate load. The steel pins that held the tailgate in were knocked out, the belly band under the horse unshackled, the shafts of the cart tipped up and the black turf bricks tumbled out of the cart and through the gate. My father fed the turf into canvas sacks to be carried by us into the turf house. We were prepared for the worst that winter could do to us; at least we'd be warm.

Out of all these memories looms the day my father bought a young kid goat. The austere spare lines of the body, the angular head with its amber slit eyes, the sharp spikes for ears and the emergent horns: to me a kid goat has all the fineness and purity of a Dresden figure. We treasured the new pet, troubled by the plaintive cries for its mother which we were unable to still.

Then came the shock which blacked out all feeling. This lovely creature was not meant to be our pet but was to be butchered by our father and eaten by the rest of us. Any remaining figment of childhood innocence was at an end. My father prepared to cut its throat, skin it, and eat it. Loyally, we gathered for the butchering ceremony at the blackened brass tap in the corner of the yard. Memories crowded back of the old red hen. The infant-like scream from the kid goat strangled in its own blood seared my ears. I remember nothing more. In the end, though hungry, none of us ate it.

Outside St Mary's Catholic Church there is a spacious square with the national school and the secondary school, both run by the Marist Brothers, on one side, and the red ticket dispensary on a raised site directly opposite. In front of the dispensary on this raised site, visiting politicians would speak. Astride my father's shoulders, I first heard Eamon de Valera speaking there on one of his visits to Athlone in the twenties. I could remember the man, so distinctive was he; I understood nothing of what he said.

Directly below was a recessed site under the high wall, and with the low wall into Kane's field on one side and the main road on the other, here would sit the stone-breaker, a small black-haired moustached man with a hungry sullen-looking face. It was his job to sit there all day in all weathers, and break stones. He rarely looked up from his work, which no doubt was assessed on 'piece' rates, and had a can of cold tea and a bread sandwich wrapped in paper beside him. Over his eyes he wore a pair of black fine wire mesh protective goggles. All day his hammers busily cracked and broke the stones, big hammers for the rocks, and small gracefully shaped light-handled hammers chosen to suit the size of the stones as they were broken down. He was like a mammoth snail, moving his sack seat inch by inch back along the heap of newly quarried granite rocks continually fed to him by horse and cart. There was no satisfying the appetite of the newly-made roads. Behind him stretched a three-inch high and three-inch wide miniature roadway of rough diamond-shaped newly cobbled stones. Thankless job, primeval artist, he sculptured miles of country roads with his hammers.

Monthly Fair Days in Athlone were grey and wet. Streets lined with huddled horses, cattle, sheep, calves in rough pens, heads all turned away from their tormentors. Under-foot, the road was fouled with animal waste, straw and mud. The pungent smells; a pig's scream; the questing moan of a cow newly separated from its calf; the distinctive metallic sound of solid steel cartwheel shafts on the well-worn oaken wheel hub slowly trundling through the rutted streets, all return to my memory. Wildly swaying masses of animals tried to stay together, to escape prods and slashes on undefended backs. Men's voices, occasional noisy meetings and partings among bright-eyed weathered faces, each new fair day formless in shape, sounds and behaviour of animals and men. Few women to be seen. A cross between theatre and circus. The low-sided horse or ass carts had high creels and no tail gate. Young bonhams and calves slept uneasily in a straw bed. When it was needed the pig, its hind leg grabbed by the farmer, was dragged to the edge of the cart on its back. Held upside down by the leg, as if already a flitch of bacon in a grocer's shop, it screamed helplessly.

A huddle of men stood around three young calves penned in a corner. As with the cow, except louder, the calves protested miserably. They had no hope of being pitied in that company of farmers, dealers, horse copers, and cattle tanglers. Farm animals, for the most part fed only for slaughter, learn to fear the wanton cruelty of their farmer owner. Uncharacteristically, a calf on weak young legs staggered across to one big farmer to be comforted. Possibly surprised, the man drew back the bony knuckles of his closed fist and struck it across what he knew to be its tender nose and mouth. As he did so, he muttered, 'someone's oul' pet'. With the calf I felt the pain, and I wondered how long does it take a farm child to grow up and become like that. As children we were not restricted to the house on fair days until late afternoon when the streets could become dangerous, not because of the farmers, drinking to their pain and pleasure in shiny black pint glasses, but because if tinkers flush with money made from selling tin cans had too much drink taken there could be a flare-up of old faction fights; the Joyce clan, I recall, right or not, was often blamed. These I watched from the safety of our front parlour window, listening to the wild cursings of tormented unhappy men, hopelessly trying to exorcise the frustration of the empty wasteland of their lives; ragged trousers tied at the middle, bare hairy chests slashed with streaks of blood made with knives as they battled up and down the now empty street.

I never tired of watching the formalised transactions of the sale of an animal. It was one of the features of an Irish country town that children were unnoticed on such occasions, and saw a lot more than was intended. I once witnessed the strange pre-sale preparation of a sleepy-looking chestnut gelding that took place up the street from our house. While one man held the head, the owner mixed a succession of substances in the palm of his hand. I don't know whether I overheard or was told that among the ingredients were mustard, well-chewed black cut plug tobacco and ginger. He worked the mixture into a paste, using spit as lubricant, and rolled it between his palms until a hazelnut-sized chocolate-coloured ball was ready. The second man lifted the horse's tail, allowing his friend to push the concoction into its rear end. Before long the onetime drowsy horse was transformed; head up, he became as sprightly and restless as any young cob.

Soon a purchaser arrived. The horse's teeth were examined; from its knees down to its hooves and upwards the prospective buyer thumbed and fingered for rings, curbs, spavins, signs of 'firing' or old injuries or scars. Then the horse must show its paces. Its owner tugged at its head and surreptitiously tapped its flanks with his ashplant. He had no need to. This horse was vibrant with life, trotting up and down the centre of the street. Then there was the ritual walk away in disgust by the buyer at the price expected, and the equally disgusted attempt by the owner to drag his horse home because of the miserable price offered. At last both were brought together by the 'tangler'. With a continuous quick patter he groped anxiously for each man's semi-reluctant but readily available wrist. Raising his voice to attract nearby witnesses to his skill and success, he shouted the price, then violently slapped his hands into each of the other two men's open palms. Luck money is paid over as the tangler gets his cut; the innocent victim, the horse, has a new owner. No doubt the horse, rid of the irritant at its rear end, soon became once again the tired old animal that had been dragged to the fair.

As children we spent a lot of our time on the Ballymahon Road, which encircled the fair green where we played football and where Duffy's Circus pitched its tents every year. Speechless with excitement, for I had never done it before, I once led the small giddy circus pony down from the railway goods yard where the animals had arrived — 'Hold her by the ring, in the bit, and you'll be alright'. She was so different from Molloy's donkey, frisky even after a day's work; unsure of myself and the pony, I was relieved to be rid of her. Promised a ticket for the circus on the morrow, credulous child, I learned not to believe grownups always — there was no ticket.

On the fair green on summer nights Toft's roundabouts trumpeted out the distinctive hurdy-gurdy sounds of the steam organ into the normally silent night of Athlone's residential area. Round and around gyrated and galloped the wide-eyed hobby horses, with flaring blood red nostrils, and streaming and flying white tails behind, racing into nowhere. At that fair my mother, a recluse by her avocation of housewife and mother, broke the rules to bring us to the roundabouts, and delighted us all and herself by winning a china teaset playing 'hoopla'.

It was on the Ballymahon Road that I suffered an unexpected humiliation. Eileen, my eldest sister, had taught me to ride her heavy ladies' iron bike. Still too small to reach the pedals and sit in the saddle, except when freewheeling precariously down the hill, I'd ride the bike standing on the pedals with an up and down hobby-horse movement, elbows higher than the hands on the handlebars, out to Molloys' farm. I would leave it there while delivering the milk, and then ride it home again. This already precarious journey was further complicated by the can of skimmed milk Mrs Molloy would give me for my mother.

On my way down a small incline under the bridge I mistimed the follow through up-hill on the other side and was sent sprawling across the middle of the road, covered with milk. A man passing by came over to me, enquired how I was, helped me to pick up the bike and the empty can, and led me to the side of the road. My gentle soft-voiced friend murmured through my tears this information: 'If you are patient, very patient, and take great care, the easiest way for you to catch a blackbird is to reach out with a pinch of salt in your fingers and carefully place the salt on his tail'. For some years I continued to wonder how this could be true. I learnt from this man that a lie like this in a good cause is sometimes permissible. At the same time, he contributed to my growing awareness about the fallibility of grownups.

Also on this road, I encountered for the first time the oppressor's contempt for the oppressed. Myself and my sister Una were walking close to a high demesne wall. Seated on top of this wall were a boy and a girl, belonging to the big house. They must have seen us from a long way off, but they remained dead silent and unmoving. Because of the height of the wall, as well as our own tiny size, we did not see them until we were directly under where they sat. I looked up just in time to see a big outsize drop of spit spiralling down, impossible to avoid, onto my head and shoulders. For its infinitesimal size, it was a disproportionally painful experience wiping the spit away. We knew the name of the family, and as is the way on our tiny island I was to meet the boy years later when I was a medical student in Dublin's Rotunda Maternity Hospital, where he had become an assistant master.

About a mile further along that Ballymahon Road, passing friends in a donkey cart gave me a lift home from Molloy's one day. We meandered slowly home towards Athlone. On the pathway ahead of us came into sight a child-sized man, striding clumsily along, with long arms, long legs, and the short ugly twisted body of a hunchback. It was my brother Jody. There were already three of us on the narrow plank, stretched between the sides of the donkey cart. The ineradicable pain from which ever since I have suffered is my failure to leave my two friends and their donkey cart so that I should walk home with Jody or, better still, give him my seat in that cart.

2

Growing up in Ballinrobe

LIFE in Athlone was orderly and uninterrupted until the dread day when, surprisingly, both of our parents took the train to Dublin, leaving us in the care of our eldest sister, Eileen. An expression of total desolation on both their faces as we met them at the station made it clear to all of us that something dreadful had happened. A Dublin medical specialist had confirmed that our father suffered from severe pulmonary tuberculosis. Although they did not know it at the time, my mother was also infected by the same disease. They in turn could have infected their children. I recall an infant sister, Annie, leaving our house in a tiny white coffin. She had died of massive pneumonic miliary tuberculosis. My eldest brother, Jody, in addition to a serious speech defect caused by an untreated cleft palate and a hare lip, developed a grossly deformed hunchbacked spine, infected by tuberculosis. He never grew taller than between three and four feet in height. Though he was intelligent, he could never attend school. Schoolchildren then would harass and jeer at the crippled and the disabled. Surprisingly my father, disappointed no doubt that his eldest son was deformed, was impatient with him. Jody was unwanted, crippled, and unable to fend for himself or communicate his simplest needs, except to the family; he was unable to mix with his peers. It is impossible to imagine the awesome humiliation and desperation of his life. I have never understood its purpose.

In addition to Jody and the infant who died, my mother, myself and two sisters became infected with tuberculosis and, with the exception of myself, all have since died. There was at that time no known worthwhile treatment. My father's hardworking conditions had led to the infection in the first place, and with no light work available there was little prospect for his survival. It was simply a matter of months. He was sent away to Newcastle Sanatorium in Co. Wicklow where, as medical officer many years later, I read of the hopelessness of his case in his clinical notes.

Because there was no free tuberculosis service then, hospital care had to be paid for. Since there was no hope that the out-of-work patient could pay as his income had stopped with his work, or was simply inadequate, he would be sent home to die. In the process he would infect one or more of his loved ones. Discharge home from a sanatorium was, in effect, a sentence of death for the patient, and possibly for many members of his family. There were frequent examples of families, in desperate hope of saving the life of a loved husband, wife or child, being compelled to sell off their small farm or business in order to pay for medical expenses or hospital care. Consultants would agree to treat patients only so long as they had money; as soon as the money stopped, the treatment also stopped.

There is a tombstone in a graveyard by Newcastle Hospital, on which the names of nine young children of the same family are inscribed. Not one of the children was more than three years of age at death. Each name is recorded — Michael, Patrick, Mary, etc. It is of interest to note that the last name on this tombstone is the father's name; he died at the age of eighty years. It is more than probable that this man, unwittingly, was responsible for the deaths of all his children.

From the day on which the consultant gave his diagnosis on my father, life for the Browne family followed a pattern which was a prototype for tens of thousands of families in our class in many countries. There was only the most rudimentary concept of what became known as welfare socialism throughout Europe. There was little or none in Ireland, where influential religious teaching rejected the 'creeping socialism' of state intervention in time of family need. I recall a curate in Newtownmountkennedy informing his flock from the pulpit on one occasion, when he had thundered 'communism' because of the local people's attempt to feed the school children a hot mid-day meal in winter: 'They can come to my back door and ask for it, if they need it'.

At times of impending disaster, young people appear to be preserved from understanding and appreciating the facts of what lies ahead for them. I continued to go to school and to deliver milk on my wonderful donkey-drawn equipage. My father had to stop work. Later still he was no longer seen around the house and was compelled to stay in bed. He was visited once by a doctor, and by a Franciscan priest on a number of occasions. Our aunt Bridie, a nurse, appeared more frequently at the house, and I began to notice a sad subdued mood within the family. I still had no idea that my father was dying.

Late one summer evening, in August, 1925, I was called to his bedroom. There was a crowd of people whom I did not know outside the room and around his bed. Though a son of the house I was unable to get to him, being crushed on the landing outside, too timid or unwilling to push my way in. There was an air of great solemnity among the grownups who, in the dark of my father's room, murmured prayers in the awful rhythmic sing-song ritual for those about to die. Someone had made him hold a lighted candle, and called for prayers for his soul and his happy death.

My father raised himself and, in a falsely strong voice, claimed 'Joe Browne is not going to die'; then he sank back. Sometime during that night he must have died. It was possible that I was sent off to bed and had gone to sleep. I recited the Hail Marys with the others, not knowing why; I had not been conscious that he was dying or about to die. I did not know or understand about death. Later, in a dark corner in our big outhouse, I studied the oblong yellow pine coffin lid with its brass plate bearing the words, in black print, 'Joseph Browne, aged fifty-four, R.I.P.' The inexorable breaking up of the family had begun.

I sought to avoid walking behind the black horse-drawn hearse on its way to St. Mary's Church, although Jody did. I have no idea why I felt this reluctance. Possibly I wished to deny his death or to recall him from the dead. He was buried the next day, as he had requested, in his family plot in Craughwell, Co. Galway. This was the first occasion on which I had met his brothers and sisters; I stayed with them for about a week and then returned home to Athlone.

The families of my parents had disapproved of their marriage and each of them had given up their own in order to be together and live out what came to be a tragically short life of mixed happiness and tragedy with each other. There was never to be a reconciliation. My father's devoutly religious family would accept no responsibility for helping his young widow and her seven young children. My mother, who had absolutely no experience whatever to help her cope with the immense financial difficulties facing her, was compelled to try to make a home for her young family on a total of £100 insurance. There were no widow's or orphan's pensions, or children's allowances. Our house belonged to the NSPCC, and the next inspector would need it when he took over.

My mother applied with no success for a local authority house in Athlone. For all her faith in God and his blessed Mother, she would send one of us children nearly every night with a drained teacup inside which the tea leaves lay, wrapped in a brown paper bag, to a local woman in Irishtown who would 'read the cups'. She hoped that this woman would one day see a house for us in the tealeaves. Such a house never materialised, and she realised that she would have to take her family away.

She decided to return to Ballinrobe, under the commonly-held illusion that she could live out her life where she had happy memories of her young days. She had been born in Hollymount, just outside Ballinrobe, and moved into the town after her schooldays to work as a seamstress with a Mrs. Murphy, who owned a newspaper shop and dressmaker business. It was here that she, an exceptionally attractive country girl, met and fell in love with my father, a 'comer-in' from Athenry.

My mother was to find, on her return to Ballinrobe in her time of great need and deep distress, that she had not yet been forgiven. Other than the rent collector, I do not believe that anyone ever called or crossed the threshold of that newly-built small house except our childhood friends. They came, it is true, to the final auction sale some two years later, in order to bid for the remnants of her furniture and family possessions which were for sale. So, they divided up her few belongings between them.

The auction signalled the end of an Irish widow's hopeless two-year struggle with her orphans, after my father's death, in the new and pitiless Irish Free State. But that disillusionment was yet to come. Meanwhile, we packed up our possessions, and prepared to leave Athlone.

My memory of moving is of being seated beside Jody on the front cab seat of a lorry driven by a small Athlone man, whose face remains with me — black bushy eyebrows, sallow healthily-tanned skin, intelligent sturdy face, jet-black kindly eyes and a head of black curly hair on which he wore a cap. My particularly detailed memory of this man stems from the fact that he lost the way on our journey to Ballinrobe. It was a wintry night and we became very frightened. We had been sent on with the lorry driver to save train fares, and had travelled through the day with all our worldly possessions behind us in the lorry. It started to snow and the whole countryside was soon covered in snow. The worried look of the driver's face is my last memory of that journey; through weariness I must have gone to sleep in spite of my fears. This journey was a momentous occasion, since it was the first time we had been separated from our mother in our lives.

Finally we reached Church Lane, Ballinrobe and helped one another to settle into our new home. The lack of welcoming visits from neighbours should have had its own ominous warning for my mother that she had seriously misjudged her people. All the members of her immediate family, the Cooneys, had long since left Hollymount for America on the emigrant ship, part of the great diaspora in the 1920s and 1930s. In her hopes for compassion, forgiveness or sympathy, my mother could have more usefully chosen the Sahara Desert for her last refuge.

I went to school, to the local Christian Brothers. They certainly taught us with great diligence, and with some effect, but for the most part they were enthusiastic religious zealots, whose sole purpose was to win young Irish boys and girls to Roman Catholicism in a united Ireland. They did not see any contradiction in fighting fiercely and winning partial sovereignty from the English while still proclaiming total subservence on all issues of serious social or political importance to a different faraway foreign ruler in Rome. 'We will be true to thee 'til death', they'd bellow at Croke Park.

These deeply religious men and women, using the word 'religious' in its loosest sense, had represented a remarkable phenomenon during the nineteenth century in Ireland, giving up their lives to promote a most powerful renaissance of Catholicism while at the same time sending hundreds of their numbers throughout the continents of Africa, Asia, the

Americas and elsewhere as missionaries for the Catholic faith. They recognised the simple truth: 'give us the child, and we will answer for the man'. Those who control education control minds, and thus control society.

There was no Gregorian chant in Ballinrobe. The general ethos was a powerful sense of angry nationalism and the demand that in all of us there must be inculcated a self-sacrificing patriotism. Singing classes were occupied with emotive patriotic songs mixed with the sweet laments for Ireland's wrongs. A militant republicanism replaced the bland Free State ambience of Athlone. We knew and admired men 'on the run'; unconsciously we braced ourselves for future sacrifice and struggle, probably even prison or death, 'for Ireland's freedom'. We played exclusively Gaelic games. I never possessed a hurling stick, since my mother could not afford to buy one, so I played Gaelic football.

This driving obsessive hatred for and of the English was systematically inculcated into our consciousness and rationalised for us into an embittered set of convictions. Hatred for Protestants, because their faith was of English origin, became an unpleasant feature of our young lives. A little jingle summed it all up for us — 'Proddy, Woddy, ring the bell, when you die, you go to hell'. The hatred derived not solely from the occupation of our country but, according to the teaching of the Christian Brothers, from the destruction by the English of our Catholic faith.

Our history taught us to mourn, with intent to revenge, the savage torture by pitchcap and the rack of our patriot martyrs. Cromwell was simply a heartfelt curse word. As if to reinforce our introverted exclusive Irish nationalism, we had the 'advantage' of learning to speak the true Irish of the Gael.

While nearly all of us in the school were of poor English-speaking family background, already class distinctions were evolving. The children of successful business men or gombeens left early on to enter residential secondary schools. Some found their way into the diocesan colleges, the forcing ground for the Catholic priesthood. These church links between the Irish middle class and the priesthood help to explain the deeply conservative nature of the Irish Catholic church and of the new Irish state.

The children from the Gaeltacht areas were even more

impoverished than ourselves, dressed in ragged misfitting clothes. They walked long distances bare-footed to school, with their hair uncombed and laden with lice, unwashed and dirty. Their teeth were rotten, their skin pockmarked with flea bites. In spite of the fact that here was the true repository of the cherished native language, they were not favoured by our militant nationalist Christian Brothers but treated with contempt as members of a lower order as the British had once treated all of us native Irish. I do not recall that they were shown any patience, concern, or understanding because of their illiteracy in English and their understandable difficulties in keeping up with the rest of us. At least one of them appeared to be chosen with little reason for the cruelly unbridled beatings which constituted Christian Brother discipline.

The brother who taught me first was a tall white-faced man, with thin bony shoulder blades protruding beneath his black cassock. He coughed violently and convulsively, and held to his mouth a white handkerchief which came away with fresh red bloodstains, all signs of tuberculosis. In the front row, I was unpleasantly close to the execution ceremony and truly dreaded the shock of it, though I myself was never a victim. The brother would grip my desk tightly with his hand until his fingers were blanched white in order to give himself support and added power. Then he carefully took hold of the visibly trembling fingertips of the defenceless victim and opened the dirty hand firmly. He took careful aim, and slashed out without restraint or pity. Each time, increasingly excited, beads of sweat gathering on his pale forehead, he raised the cane higher over his shoulder like an old-time thrashing flail; down it came again and again, increasing in speed and ferocity until it seemed to us that the tip of the cane appeared to whistle around in a full circle.

We could not understand how any of us could have fomented such an irrational anger or deserve such punishment. Yet I never saw any one of the beaten boys make any response, certainly no visible protest. The beaten mutilated hands were simply pushed up underneath the armpits, the sole concession to this savage and insensitive public assault on their bodies and on their self-esteem. Surely there was some private pain which the brother thereby tried to exorcise within himself. My greatest sympathy lay with the Irish speakers who could not have understood why they were so often chosen for punishment. For them there was an added isolation, the rest of us being unable to sympathise because of our inability to speak with them.

Even more scandalous was the Christian Brothers' behaviour to a young boy named Paddy Power, who lived with his mother, a widow since the first world war. They were a respected, quiet family, the eldest boy building up his own hairdressing business in the town. Perhaps because the father had fought and died for the British, the young son was chosen as a safe whipping boy, particularly by one of the senior brothers, a fearsome-looking redfaced bull of a man with a closecut convict haircut, who would take Power out to the garden shed at what appeared to be regular intervals. We could hear the screams of the helpless captive child, yells and cries for pity and release from his vicious tormentor.

One winter's day in the school yard, snowball fights began among the boys. This harmless fun suddenly changed with the appearance of one of the brothers, who normally made full use of the cane. An onlooker would have seen a gradual but concerted disintegration of the multiplicity of fights around the school yard. With a strange spontanaeity, like a flight of starlings as they turn together, all the boys flew around the brother, cornering him against a school wall. The snowball fight took on a vicious intensity and seriousness as they sought to pound him with their snowball weapons, all of them against one. It was then that I acted independently of the mass of those around me. I went in beside the brother to help him fight back.

This was a completely spontaneous action on my part, as I had no need to fear him myself, or to look for his favour. Instinctively I disliked the idea of the hopeless odds against him, and at the same time wondered and worried about the uncontrolled futile ferocity of the children. Clearly they hated the brother, whom they now believed they had cornered and helpless. Of course they were wrong. He was unhurt and would still bully them individually.

A brother in one of the higher classes was even more intimidating. He was a powerfully built blond man, feared by all of us, who not only used the cane frequently and freely, but was a practising pederast as well. No young boy in his class was safe from his attentions. It was his practice to sit down at the desk and purport to be anxious to help whatever child he chose to sexually assault. What could the terrified child do, so young that he hardly knew what was happening to him? What mother or father in the Ballinrobe of those times would listen, or understand, or dare to take action, even if the child were to report the incident to them? Happily for myself, I left Ballinrobe before being admitted to that class.

I had come across this sort of thing before. Once, in the school in Athlone, Brother John had asked me to guide a visiting member of the order who was inspecting classes in the school. I collected him from downstairs, where he had been talking to a class, and brought him upstairs to Brother John. The two of us had just arrived on the landing outside the classroom when he indicated that we should pause. The next thing I knew, the brother had convulsively thrown his arms around me and was kissing me passionately on the mouth. I was astonished and overwhelmed by a mixture of shame and shock that this assault should have been inflicted on me by a cleric. My mother had inculcated in all of us a sense of devout reverence for the 'cloth'. We were taught to tip our forelock when we passed a priest in the street. It was my first experience of this kind with man or woman, since my mother never kissed or fondled me. The brother then moved away from me and with complete self-assurance and aplomb, opened the door to Brother John's class, marched in with all the syrupy unction of his kind and proceeded to behave as if nothing had happened between us. My innocence was such that I simply accepted his behaviour as another adult aberration, surprising, peculiar and unpleasant.

I stayed a time with my uncle Jack in Hollypark, near Craughwell, when I was about ten years of age. One day, my aunt Isabelle sent me with my young cousin to visit a curate friend of hers who lived some miles away from my uncle's home. Shortly after our arrival at the curate's residence I felt that there was something strange about him. Though I knew little of these things except what I had unexpectedly learned from the Marist Brother in Athlone, it was not long before I gathered that this middle-aged priest also had an affection for young boys. There was no bus until the following morning. Effectively, we were at the mercy of this middle-aged curate. I was deeply disturbed, and very upset at the prospect of having to stay the night. It was a small house with only two bedrooms, the curate sleeping in one and his housekeeper in the other.

Bedtime arrived. While my cousin without demur agreed to stay the night with the curate and sleep in his bed, I blankly refused to join them. The night ended for me with a comic opera solution: I agreed that I would sleep in the bed of the priest's house-keeper. I have distinct memories of some arrangement of a blanket partition between myself and the housekeeper. She need not have been worried, even if I had known of the possibilities and wished to avail myself of them. I fell asleep at once, totally exhausted by the struggle to keep away from the curate's bed.

Our home life in Ballinrobe was a mixture of happiness such as is found where the mother is especially gentle and loving, and of deadly fear. It had become apparent that our mother was very seriously ill. As the days went by, though she never complained to us, her discomfort and distress forced unavoidable cries from the intensity of her pain. She lay on the small sofa in the corner of our kitchen and moaned quietly between spasms. She never looked for medical care since she knew she could not afford it, or else, I suspect, she was unable to bring herself to take the charity of Poor Law medical services, even if she in fact knew of their existence. My mother may well have been the original source of the family infection; she had always suffered from an incessant, productive cough, and was a delicate woman.

She now became the child, to be nursed, protected and cared for. It was our delight to be permitted to look after her. We would 'gladly put our hands under her feet'. There were five of us at home all under twelve years of age. We did all the work in the house, washing dishes and making the fire. (I was severely burnt on the face with the explosion of the paraffin oil which I had unwisely used to light it — there was no call to the doctor on that occasion either). I carried in the turf, went down to the River Robe with a small home-made four-wheeled contraption for the water, and dug the garden to plant potatoes as I had seen my father do in Athlone. We kept the house bright, clean and shiny.

My eldest brother, crippled Jody, got a job as a messenger boy in a local grocery shop. It was a truly shaming sight to watch this pitifully small hunchbacked figure, with his heavily laden messenger-boy's bicycle, pushing through the hilly streets of Ballin-

robe delivering groceries to the big houses. He was paid a pittance each week-end, together with a white paper bag full of the
torn bacon slices which had fallen beneath the bacon-slicing
machine.

Neither in Athlone nor in Ballinrobe were we at any time
visited by any public official or person of substance other than
the rent collector. No member of a religious order, nun, priest,
or brother, came near the house to see if we needed help. Life in
Ireland then was completely unconcerned with and uncaring
for the poor. It was in Ballinrobe that a very hurtful remark was
made to me by one of the children with whom I was playing. My
young friend had simply repeated what he had heard at home
from his parents. Angry about something I had said or done to
him, he jeered, 'you had to come to Ballinrobe to be fed'. When I
told my mother, she cried.

My mother had found that she was unwelcome in Ballinrobe.
She must also have concluded that she was suffering from an
illness from which she would shortly die. As orphans and
paupers we could be sent to a workhouse or an industrial school.
As a boy, I would be sent to either Artane in Dublin or Letter-
frack in Co. Galway, each of which had a justifiably grim
reputation. In desperation, she decided to take us to our eldest
sister, Eileen, who had emigrated to London in 1926, aged
sixteen. Unable to pay for medical treatment or care, she would
not leave us to go to a sanatorium. Because she had no money
with which she could pay our fares to London, she must first sell
all that she had.

In the way of children, I did not know of the impending
tragedy. School was tolerable, the pleasures of boys in rural
Ireland were enjoyable: football, fishing, street games, and the
competitive Sunday sports in nearby villages. One day I was
shocked to see the blank walls of the town covered with the local
auctioneer's small yellow posters, telling those who cared to read
them that everything the Brownes had in their small terraced
house was up for sale by auction. My mother was forced to sell
everything, the few personal possessions which she had chosen
and bought with my father for use in their hoped-for years of
married life together.

On auction day she sat through the ordeal, watching the
people of the town where she was brought up and had worked as

a young woman bidding for her possessions. The people knew that 'everything had to be sold', regardless of its price. She must have wondered about these strange creatures, now on their first and only visit to her home, who were prepared to strip her and her orphan children of all they had.

Having gathered our few clothes, we made our way to Ballinrobe railway station. There we took the train for Dublin, Kingstown, and finally London. My mother had had no experience whatever in arranging such matters as travel, even inside Ireland. She now faced her *via dolorosa*, the long, tiring, journey to London into an unknown future with all her children, one of whom was a cripple.

Before leaving Ballinrobe she was compelled to take one more cruel decision. She had to part with her young daughter Una, nine years of age, whom she loved as much as she did the rest of us. Our aunt, Martha Jennings, a sister who had emigrated to New York when young, had offered to take Una to live with her. My mother believed that it would be a wonderful opportunity for Una to be free from the threat of an Irish workhouse; there was hope for a life in America, away from the hard-faced society in which she lived. Unaccompanied, Una was sent to the States in an emigrant ship which sailed from Galway. To the end of her life, Una was embittered by this apparent rejection by her mother. Inexplicably, for she was too young to understand, she had been sent on that long fearful journey to America to live with someone whom she did not know. Worse still, the aunt exploited her as cheap domestic labour. In spite of this, Una finally managed to complete her training as a state registered nurse. Married, she knew much happiness for a few years, and made a life for herself and her family, who loved her dearly. In the end she was afflicted with a rare form of tuberculosis, Addison's disease, from which she died at an early age, having previously suffered the loss of her eldest son, Paddy, in a car accident.

There is reason to believe that a subordinate cause of death arose from the shock of Paddy's death. He had completed his military service with the US Navy, and with his discharge bounty had bought himself a sports car, popular with the 'young bloods' in the United States. He had taken it onto a busy highway while still unused to it. Shortly after midnight Una heard the telephone ring to give the message most feared by all mothers — 'There's been an accident'. Paddy was dead. Una worshipped her Paddy, a red-blooded Irish-American, full of a sardonic wit and charm inherited from his mother.

After Una had left the house with my mother in a car, I can recall myself, my brother Jody and my sister Martha sitting on the top of the stairs with our arms around one another, crying our eyes out. Because my mother had had to leave us to travel with Una to Galway, we wrongly believed that we too had been abandoned by her. Between self-pity and the loss of Una we endured our own 'American wake' for our tiny emigrant sister. I was not to meet her again for forty years.

But what of the agony of my mother? Una had simply become one of the many hundreds of thousands of rejected Irish unwanted by their own society. In the words spoken for all of them by my young school friend in Ballinrobe, 'It's no use coming to us to be fed'; this would be an apt epithet for our Irish ethos.

The carriage doors slammed, with no-one to wave us farewell. Surrounded by her young family, my mother finally broke down, and wept quietly. The train steamed out, on its way to the emigrant boat, and London.

Eileen found a temporary home for us with an English family in Herne Hill near London. My mother had saved us just in time; within days of our arrival, she lay in a coma. My final memory of this unique woman is when we children were each called into the hallway where she lay on a stretcher to bid her 'good-bye'. I was twelve years old. I recall leaning down across the stretcher to kiss her on the forehead. It was moist and sallow in colour, a single bead of sweat on it. Her eyes were closed, as if in a sleep of deep exhaustion. She did not acknowledge our farewells. Shortly afterwards she was moved to the waiting ambulance outside, and brought to a public ward in a London hospital. Within a few days she was dead. The final humiliation of this proud, brave Mayo country girl still awaited her; she was buried in an unknown pauper's grave in London because Eileen could not afford anything better for the mother she so dearly loved.

Recently I made a visit to Ballinrobe with my wife. I walked through the streets for the first time since I had been there as a child. It had changed little. On our way home I was surprised to find myself being overcome by a sudden overwhelming black depression. I was compelled to stop the car and get out, in an attempt to conceal my emotions from my wife. Somewhat to my embarrassment and surprise I was overcome by waves of uncontrollable tears. I leant on the car roof until these had passed, a bit ashamed of myself at this unusual happening; I then got back into the car and we continued on our journey. The contrast between my two lives in, Athlone and then in Ballinrobe, and the memories of my family, had left their own mark.

Eileen's agony was now about to begin. In her early twenties, she was to endure a succession of crushing ordeals that led to her lonely death in a tuberculosis sanatorium in Italy.

Eileen was cast in the mould of my mother. I could not pay her a higher tribute. She had a quality which led people to admire her courage and, if at all possible, to help her. She was good-humoured, charming and highly intelligent, and much admired for her classic black-haired blue-eyed Celtic colouring. So that she could take care of us all, she chose to remain unmarried, never even to enjoy the fleeting happiness experienced by my mother and father during their tragic years together.

Before our arrival Eileen, a first-class administrator, had found work in a holiday home, owned by a Miss Salter, in Worthing. It was one of those institutions found in England during its colonial period, the only homes known by the children of the colonial administrators. For reasons of health or education, the children could not join their parents in the colonies, so children and parents were deprived of each other's company and of any family life together; the children went from the unloving life of the public school to the equally uncaring life of the holiday home. Miss Salter's generosity made it possible for all of our family to live in this home, where Eileen acted as manager, administrator and housekeeper.

By a fortunate coincidence Miss Salter had a sister who was joint proprietor of St Anthony's school in Eastbourne, a small Catholic preparatory school, and she had me admitted to this exclusive school, free of charge. Once again I was to be rescued from my frighteningly insecure future. In spite of the harrowing experiences through which we had just lived, with the resilience of a child I became occupied with my next new experience and in October 1929 I set out for St. Anthony's from London in the buggy seat of an open sports car driven by an actress friend of Eileen's named Eve.

3

Education in England

UNDER the teaching of the Christian Brothers in Ballinrobe I had come to believe that the English were a race to be hated, the nation which had tormented and persecuted our people for many centuries. I had become a militant Irish republican, waiting for the day when I could join those others now in jail or 'on the run' and, if need be, die for Ireland. I was also deeply committed to a particularly paranoid, militant brand of Catholicism, which condemned the Protestant faith of the British people.

On my arrival in Britain, the discovery that the grass grew green, the sun shone and the swallows flew freely above was a real surprise to me. But this phase of my aggressive republicanism, and certainly my anti-British convictions, obstinately survived my stay in St Anthony's. Other misconceptions about the British could not survive against their astonishing hospitality and generosity and their acceptance and care for many of our family, and for tens of thousands of strangers from Ireland such as us, rejected by their own.

St Anthony's was a preparatory school intended exclusively for the education of the sons of wealthy Catholic families. However, since there were not sufficient English Catholics to keep it filled, it had become pleasantly cosmopolitan, with a high proportion of Central and South American pupils, as well as French, Central European, and American. French and Spanish were spoken nearly as widely as English.

Though I had passed through a distressing family tragedy, I appeared to have developed a tough emotional patina with a growing imperviousness to personal distress. I was a healthy young boy who had astonishingly been transmuted, from an emotionally painful and physically impoverished home, into

being a member of the pampered class. It was impossible to
remain unmoved or unchanged. At St Anthony's we had small
classes, with university graduates to teach all subjects; we had a
fine gymnasium, spacious playing fields and, in summer, access
to a full-sized heated swimming pool. Our food seemed, to my
impoverished tastes, like a series of state banquets. The
dormitories were large, clean, and served by sumptuous bath and
washroom facilities. In Ballinrobe we had carried water by the
bucket from the River Robe.

The contrast inevitably muted my other personal depri-
vations. The shock of my transition from Athlone and
Ballinrobe, with conventions, beliefs, and practices so different
from those now around me; the trauma of my splintered family
life; the loss of my father and my mother; all these experiences
brought about an inevitable continuous emotional conflict, with
all that that implied for a child of my age. Yet the contrast of life
patterns was greatly mitigated by the fact that there were a large
number of boys who, for quite other reasons, were feeling just as
isolated as I was. It appeared to me that we foreigners dominated the school. We recognised our common links of alienation
from English life, and this created in us a spontaneous camaraderie. The school had this remarkable distinction: there was
absolutely no bullying of anyone by anyone else, either by
teachers or boys.

One of the teachers I remember best was Mr Tibetts. He had
carroty untidy hair, a very red face and a bulbous nose, through
which he spoke in short, nasal, and for a long time to me unintelligible bursts of sentences, spattered with spittle. The end of
his nose was constricted by his enormous hornrimmed
spectacles, which appeared to rest permanently there. Even
with the thick-lensed spectacles he was still nearly blind. He was
both gentle and patient; rarely exasperated, he would call out a
boy, ask him for one of his house shoes and, then having told him
to bend over, inexpertly try to find the target and beat it in-
effectually. Mr Tibetts gave the impression of hating his job of
Latin teacher.

The French master, M. Talibart, disliked both us and his
teaching. He would read the newspaper throughout the class,
taking the precaution to prod a hole through the centre with his
fat index finger to give us the impression that he was watching

us. He tended when exasperated to cuff a boy on the right ear, then on the left, and kick him on the shins, muttering to himself, 'take dis, and dat, and dose', 'those' being the kicks given under the desk. I also remember Mr Harding, a blindingly handsome black-eyed crinkly-haired teacher who, I suspect, was illiterate. He was an awe-inspiring person, as it was said that he had at one time played cricket for Sussex. Like Brother John in Athlone, his educational concern was limited to just one subject: sport.

Although we were aged only between ten and fourteen years, Mr Harding took our training with extraordinary enthusiasm and seriousness. All our classes were illustrated with drawings on the blackboard and taken up with discussions about tactical formations in the game of soccer, which he expected us to absorb and practice for the coming Saturday's football game. We took part in a lot of inter-school games, as there were many other preparatory schools in and around Eastbourne. Luckily I enjoyed games. From Gaelic football I now turned to cricket and soccer. Mr Harding for some reason called me 'Tishy', perhaps after the Strube cartoon horse with the funny legs. Being a good athlete is a magic passport to popularity in any English public school.

Mr Lowndes had grey hair, cropped close, was obsessionally clean and lived with his mother in a fine red-brick house opposite the school. He seemed to be the only serious teacher we had. His manner was somewhat brusque and impatient. He wore a grey Norfolk jacket with peeping white shirt cuffs. His pink hands were carefully manicured, his shoes always shining black, and clever blue eyes shone from his scrubbed face. He always seemed to be at his happiest leaving through the front door of the school; to him, I suspect, we were simply a tiresome collection of morons whose wealthy social origins presaged a life of never-ending decadent entertainment and recreation. There was no purpose in casting any cultural or intellectual pearls before us. I remember him taking the trouble on one occasion to show us how to brush our nails; he did not aspire to anything more testing for our pampered lives.

There was also Mr Robinson, a big, jolly ex-Naval man with blazing blue eyes. He wore enormous ill-fitting plus-four suits of light grey, and shiny brown leather shoes with great finger-shaped leather flaps to them. We liked to listen when he played rollicking music-hall songs and sea shanties at the piano for us. Because of his ill-fitting false teeth, he spat a lot as he sang, but he must once have given great pleasure to his shipmates, for his voice was soft, pleasant and musical. He made no attempt to teach us anything.

The wife of the proprietor, known as 'Maw P' because her husband's name was Patton, was a particularly well cared-for, dumpy, knock-kneed lady always dressed as befitted her position, complete with a shining necklace of pearls and a gold wrist watch. She was the sole person of whom all of us went in some fear, though she did not harass or try to interfere with us. She had a strait-laced severe appearance which we found intimidating, but it was said that she was a compulsive gambler on the horses. Her husband, 'Paw P', was a charming, self-effacing, equally knock-kneed tubby little man, who appeared to enjoy life uninhibited by his managerial cares. He took his pleasures where he found them; even we young children could see that. I understand that the school no longer exists. Whether this is in any way related to the gambling proclivities of his wife or not, I do not know.

In the school holidays I would return to Miss Salter's holiday home in Worthing. A number of the boys whose homes were too distant to justify travelling home during the shorter vacations lived with us there. Life for all of us in the home was very spartan — a bread and margarine existence. Since we were near the sea, I swam continuously and in all weathers. My distracted sister Kitty, whose job it was to mind us at the beach, continually pleaded with me 'not to go out too far'. The South American boys were unhappy about the food, the crowded dormitory conditions and above all, the winter cold. Julian Romero from Peru even attempted to heat his bed by putting a lighted candle beneath it.

Kitty and my youngest sister Ruth, aged four, were accepted as boarders in a convent run by the Notre Dame Sisters in Worthing. Kitty was happy there but for the infant Ruth convent life was no substitute for her broken home and the loss of both parents. Ruth stayed there until she was eighteen, then took up a secretarial job in Sussex. When she and I met again, during the Second World War, we had to carry specific newspapers to be sure of recognising one another. Ruth later returned to Ireland to live with us for some years, but is now happily married in Tennessee.

With the closure of Miss Salter's home in the late 1920s, following her death, the medical mafia of Irish doctors all over England helped Eileen by taking me to live with them during holiday times. Sometimes I stayed with limitlessly wealthy aristocratic friends in their stately homes and castles in England or in France; at other times Eileen could afford to pay for a home with working-class families, where I was a 'lodger' or paying guest. I never knew from one holiday to the next where my next home would be. For a time one of Eileen's friends, Martin Coughlan from Clare, took me to live where he worked in Whitechapel, near London's Chinatown. We lived in the workhouse but enjoyed free access to the local cinema and the music halls. My cosmopolitan experience in St Anthony's was consolidated in the class sense by the wide variations of social surroundings in which from time to time I found myself. I can say that I was never tempted to defect from my own class origins by what I saw within the wealthy and privileged houses I visited. My class instincts are deeply rooted.

Though brief, my years at St Anthony's were the most enjoyable of all my school life. The school had a cheerful universal tolerance which developed in me a balanced non-partisan view of the world. Race, colour or nationality became to me as unimportant as the colour of a boy's hair or eyes. I had no understanding of the chauvinist, political or religious differences which separate the peoples of the world. My short spell at St. Anthony's counteracted the introverted neo-racialism of the Ballinrobe Christian Brothers' vision of Irishness.

However, the clearly entertaining but academically useless education which I received had its disadvantages. These were shown clearly when I was given to understand that, were I educationally suitable, I might qualify for a scholarship to Beaumont College near Windsor. It was found that the educational process, as far as I was concerned, had virtually ceased when I left Ballinrobe and the Christian Brothers, and there was not much that I had learned there which would be of help to me in being admitted to the intensely chauvinist Jesuit College. Once again I was to be rescued.

The wife of M. Talibart was a large pleasant French lady, and she heard of the wonderful possibilities which would open up to me were I to pass the scholarship examination into Beaumont. She kindly agreed that if I would co-operate and work hard, she would 'cram' me with the subjects needed to pass the examination. I was glad to work hard at academic subjects for a change. I won the scholarship to Beaumont, for which St Anthony's was one of the recognised preparatory schools.

Beaumont College was run by the Jesuits, and intended for the education of the small number of middle-and upper-class elite Catholic families who had survived the Reformation and the confiscation of the great estates in Britain, the Howards, the Throgmortons, the Russells, the Cliffords, the Ponsonbys. Many of these families had been associated throughout English history with the defence of the values of the Roman Catholic religion. There were also a few boys from wealthy Irish Catholic families.

Schooldays at Beaumont were very different from St Anthony's, but happily they shared one important feature which is common to Catholic schools within the British public school system. There was none of the ugly bullying that is an integral part of the infamous 'fagging' system, that is the exploitation of the younger boys of the school in carrying out menial and often humiliating services for the older boys who subject them to arbitrary, unpredictable and often cruel punishment.

The long-term hopes of the Jesuits for Beaumont were trenchantly expressed in the reply said to have been sent by the Headmaster of Beaumont to Eton College, situated nearby. The occasion was an invitation by Beaumont to play football; the Etonian authorities were said to have queried 'What is Beaumont?', in response to which Beaumont's Father Rector stated his vision for his school. He wrote, 'Beaumont is what Eton College once was, a Catholic school for the sons of gentlemen'. Whatever the truth of that story, we in fact regularly played games with Eton College, as we did with many other schools in the area.

It was intended at Beaumont that the sons of English Catholics could receive instruction in their own religion in order to develop informed grounding in the purpose and objectives of their faith. It was the practice for the older students to be sent out to London at week-ends with the Catholic Evidence Guild which held public meetings and discussed the general subject of Catholic apologetics. (I was never to be sent on these sorties.) The majority of our teachers in Beaumont were either professed Jesuits or students of the Order. We were educated to believe that we were quite rightly a privileged class, the generally accepted belief of the English public school system. Because of my education in Ballinrobe, where I was taught another version of the British historical mission, I found myself in some trouble concerning this question. As with so many schools, we held debates on subjects of public interest. There was discussion about the unquestioned 'right' of the British armies to 'civilise' the Irish just as they had civilised the Indians, the Africans, and a host of other nations in the world. As with the Christian Brother's defence of his heroes, so did the British teacher preach his own special version of the 'just war'. We had been taught in Ballinrobe that we might with justice kill violently our British fellow-man so that we could free Ireland. But in Beaumont the Jesuits of the same faith taught me that it was 'just' that the Irish had been murdered in the process of the subjugation. It made me question the casuistry of all the great religions, especially my own.

In the course of the acquisition of their Irish colony the British had also, according to my Christian Brother, continued to suppress and destroy Roman Catholicism in many demonstrably cruel ways. It occurred to me that this fact created a serious dilemma for the English Catholic. I set out to make this point at a subsequent debate, and so disturb their complacency. My simple case was that we Irish were the sole defenders of the one true Roman Catholic faith and that the British Catholic was both a renegade and a coward. The consequences of my use of this debating point were both absurd and serious for me, and for my sister Eileen.

I was called to the Rector's room. There was a double door, green baize outside, to be negotiated before gaining entrance for the interview. This proved to be an intimidating experience: on one hand the aristocratic headmaster of a leading English Catholic public school and on the other an unlearned child who was in that same school on sufferance. There was the added fear of the consequences of some misdemeanour of which I was quite unaware. The Rector, a Wellesley, was as always courteous.

Sorrowfully he intoned that he had been approached by a young boy named Clifford, now Lord Clifford, a member of the distinguished aristocratic recusant clifford family which had governed England under Charles II. They had a long and honourable history in British politics and in the defence of Roman Catholic values. It appeared that Hugh, who was, and still is a good friend of mine, had complained to the Rector that during a debate I had been particularly hurtful to him and his family. My case was that they had failed to sacrifice their land, their home, their property, and everything they had, for their faith, as we Irish had done. 'We Brownes had owned great estates in County Meath before Cromwell came to rob us'.

Father Weld gently chided me, explaining that the Cliffords had been a source of powerful support to the Catholic Church in British history. I had also questioned such issues as the indissolubility of marriage and the right to divorce, unusual for that time. I appeared to question religious practice generally; it had been noticed that I had declined to join the society known as the Apostleship of Prayer, of which every other boy in the school was a member. Father Weld had written to a distracted Eileen to tell her that I had 'anarchistic tendencies'. If I could not change them, then I must leave Beaumont. Eileen, shocked at the possibility of my being expelled, could not help being amused by such an absurd conflict between the distinguished Rector and his child pupil. Happily I was not expelled, nor did I change my beliefs about the virtues of Catholicism until much later. I acted for the rest of my stay at Beaumont as an acolyte at all the religious services.

At the great church feast of Whitsun, in the midsummer sun, the presiding priest wore blindingly white silk vestments, bejewelled with semi-precious stones. While the priest and acolytes recited between them the great drama of the Mass, the choir supported by the congregation of boys sang Gregorian Chant, or one of the many resounding anthems or hymns, swelled by the thunder of the organ, surprisingly played to such effect by the tiny jockey-figured, Cockney-accented choirmaster, Mr Clayton.

Services were in every way and on all occasions pure theatre. The light splintered on the solid gold chalice. There was the gold monstrance, carrying its snow white host in the centre of the shimmering golden sunray cruciform stand. Great scented clouds of incense rolled upwards towards the ceiling, from the gilded and jewelled thurifers which we swung from side to side, held in our spotlessly white kid-gloved hands. Upwards, languidly, they climbed in multi-coloured amber, scarlet, amethyst, and emerald balloons, of incense, scented fumes, changing colour as they passed before the saintly population of heavenly figures in the stained glass windows over the high altar. The faint dim light was intensified by the soaring banks of dark yellow candles on their heavily ornate, gilt, flower-bedecked candle holders. In total contrast, at Requiem Mass, the overall deep orange yellow, and black and white motif unrelieved by flowers, colour or jewels, in the Mass for the Dead, effected its own profound macabre evocation of loss, mourning and death.

I was never to extinguish those candles, by means of the long black delicate slim pole on the end of which was the tiny triangular clown's hat-shaped snuffer, or use the slim lighted taper needed to light them, without the worrying fear that some evening I might inadvertently bring tumbling down the whole great carnival of scents, sounds and colours, and so shatter the dreaming mesmeric quality of their effect on us all.

We boys depended on one another emotionally; the homosexual, as in prisons, greatly enjoyed himself. Each of us had friendships based on our special educational or sporting interests. There was a continuous programme of intellectual and physical activities all through the day, and the educational process was promoted through a competitive dynamic. The classes were evenly divided into two groups; we were marked for achievement and these marks were noted at the end of the week. Classes were interrupted by meals, prayers, and various recreations or training sessions. I started the day with a swim in a cold swimming pool. This saved washing in the equally cold basin and ewer, and splashing my feet in cold water. We played all the usual games, cricket, tennis, football and squash. The playing fields, tennis courts and amenities of every kind were superb. Our rugby fields were on the historic Runnymede where the great British charter of democratic freedom and individual rights, the Magna Carta, was signed. We had the mildly intimidating function of reading to the priests during their meals. I was chosen to read books by Irish authors having, in the view of the priests, a noticeably Irish accent.

The English public school has its many functions. In Victorian times, it relieved the moderately wealthy parents of the emotional and physical demands of bringing up a succession of children. They believed that it was their function to produce loyal subjects who, if need be, would fight and die for His Majesty's military adventures and expeditions. Convictions about elitist rights and privileges were indelibly imprinted. As members of a leader class, we were heirs to a code of social and political practice and behaviour which was identical throughout the public school system. The thin veneer of superficial good manners and concern concealed a diamond-hard obsession with the pitilessly efficient accumulation of wealth, regardless of the cost in terms of human suffering.

We were to man the highest ranks of the Tory party and the civil service. What would the pauper Jesus have said, if he were consulted? English public schoolboys are educated to equate wealth with authority and privilege. These 'rights' and privileges are reserved for themselves and for their families. They are taught to believe in and to commit themselves to an uncompromising defence of those rights. They are prepared to defend them against either an equally greedy enemy from abroad or another class within their own society. They are on permanent call to mobilisation for war through the Officers' Training Corps.

This unique apparatus of compulsory military training involves children in serious manoeuvres by day and by night, frightened beyond belief by the lonely darkness and the sense of an 'enemy' out there attacking their 'lines'. We were trained as a battle reserve in annual summer camp on Salisbury Plain. Drilling, marching manoeuvres, machine gun, rifle and bayonet practice were all inculcated with considerable efficiency.

No conscientious objectors were tolerated. We were subjected to a curriculum of military training throughout our school lives, from recruit through the ranks to the small handful of officer class. The sole virtue of the officer class to me was that they wore a pleasantly smooth uniform, unlike that of privates which was made from a particularly irritating barbed wire-like cloth known as 'bull's wool'. Most of us wore our pyjamas under our trousers to protect our legs.

With the tight, high-collared uniform we wore First World War-style puttees. To a new recruit, these were the most infernal arrangement, thick, long, very irritating woollen bandages, about five inches wide. They were either too long or too short, depending on how the recruit had misjudged the process of winding them around his legs; they were intended to fit perfectly, reaching from the ankle to the knee. After much trial, it was not too difficult to achieve the ideal distribution of the puttee over the leg, but there was then the problem of keeping it in place. Since I had long thin legs, I always had the dread feel that during marching and counter-marching exercises the puttees might begin to slip until down and down they came so that, like great inert snakes, the long khaki bandages trailed out behind. They then became a danger both to oneself and to those in the pursuing ranks of child soldiers. There followed the pitying, scathing voice of sergeant-major Percy Martin, Irish First World War veteran, bellowing at you, with the whole world looking on, 'Corporal Browne, fall out and dress yourself!'

There was no mistaking the seriousness of our training with full service-size 303 rifles. In order to accustom us to the sound of battle and rifle fire as we sought to kill the enemy — Germans today, Soviet citizens tomorrow, unfortunate African or Irish wog anytime — we would fire noisy blank bullets. The machine-gun fire was simulated by enormous wooden rattles. They omitted to simulate the screams of men in their death agonies. We were also taught how to fix foot-long lethal steel knives to the end of our rifles. This knife was, we understood, to be dug into the enemy's body. Sometimes, we were told, the long knife might go right through your enemy and come out on the other side, perhaps becoming stuck in the body when you tried to withdraw it. In these circumstances it would be necessary to put a foot on the dying man's chest to lever out that great long knife and prepare to stick it into another human being. No one reminded us that French or German or Russian boys were being taught at the same time the same brutal techniques.

On a cleverly-arranged rifle practice range an apparatus created, as realistically as possible, a succession of moving targets, pictures of a man standing, a man running, and a man lying down. It was quite clear that we were not forbidden to kill a man, even if he was trying to run away from us. So much for our public school code of honour: 'Never hit a man when he's down'. We competed with one another in scoring the highest

number of men killed. For the squeamish, this was described as
'bull's eyes'. The riflemen who were not so successful were the
ones who left the enemy painfully maimed, wounded or dis-
figured for life. We were not reminded that other inept marks-
men would take mutilating pot-shots at us.

Doctored versions of the recent history of colonial wars were
used to rationalise to us child soldiers our killer role. Boys with
whom I had stood before the fine Giles Gilbert Scott War
Memorial on Remembrance Day could read the names of their
own fathers who had died in the 'war to end all wars'. In time,
many were to have their own names inscribed on the 'scroll of
honour' — the Mackenzie Bells, the Dixies, and many others
whom I remember with deep affection.

Few of us understood that we were destined to become well-
cut gilded names on a granite war memorial. Yet the adults
knew. The men and the women, the parents who bred us,
remained silent about it. Only the fact that I developed
tuberculosis was to save me from that fate.

How could the parents justify the metamorphosis of the child
into the soldier-to-be within the OTC? Was it lack of
imagination, callousness, indifference, moral cowardice, or the
fear of protest or dissent in public, especially the mothers?
Regrettably, there were no Greenham women then, no peace
movement.

I do not believe that there has ever been a woman, a mother, a
sister, known to call out against the obscenity of children, rifle-
and bayonet-carrying, marching, and countermarching, being
made ready for war. Many of them, even then, had already lost
their husbands, the fathers of their children, their brothers, in the
First World War. How did these mothers tolerate the convention
that their boy children must, in their turn, be trained to kill, or be
killed or maimed, in defence of their forcibly-acquired colonial
Empire abroad, or their social or financial position in society on
the home front? It is something of which we may be proud that
ours is the first generation which has at last provided the first
powerful peace movement, 'Women for Peace'.

I would like to think that I made my own simple protest against
it all. At the conclusion of the period of OTC training in the 'art' of
war we would sit for an examination known as Certificate A,
which automatically qualified the holder to become a com-

missioned Officer in the regular British army on the country's mobilisation in time of war. The questions were simple intelligence tests: 'What is to be done by an officer whose platoon had just received a consignment of two hundred left-footed only army boots from CQMS?' There were also practical military tactical problems: where would you site your machine guns so as to kill and maim the most men possible in an enemy force approaching your position through an area of hilly countryside?

In spite of its simplicity, and the fact that I was never to have any trouble with academic or medical examinations, I succeeded in failing Certificate A a record twelve times. On my thirteenth time, in mercy no doubt, I was finally graded as officer, leader and gentleman material, and was awarded my certificate.

I was considered to be a good athlete. This unfailing prerequisite to acceptance in an English school assured me of a largely untroubled life. I progressed up the ladder to become one of the school's captains. The underlying dynamic of life at Beaumont was simply competition — at games, in the OTC, and in the classroom. Classes were divided into teams, each given the name of respected Jesuit churchmen. We began all our tasks with the words 'Ad majorem Dei gloriam' (to the greater glory of God), at the corner of the page, and concluded the work with 'Laus Deo Semper' (praise God always).

Weekly assessment was made mainly by the religious teachers; lay teachers did not participate. There was an annual Shakespearian school play, and a variety show in which, to my family's disbelief, I was once encouraged to sing, face blackened, 'My ole black mammy'. While classes in art were available, there was little or no evidence of interest in music. I recall only one boy who played the piano. Neither was there great interest in the theatre. But there was a well-stocked library in a large, comfortable, warm room, in which it was possible to find peace from the gramophone, billiard ball and 'ping-pong' noises and chatter of a boys' school. I became quite an authority on the New Testament.

All of the teachers were conscientious educators, and the level of formal education was high. We passed our outside examinations with case. There was a branch of the British Union of Fascists, Oswald Mosley's organisation, in the school, but it is only fair to say that there was a succession of other organisations and societies, including the intensely chauvinist Tudor Rose League Society, with its colourful red rose emblem, which many of us found particularly attractive.

I was most impressed of all by the fundamental principle of Jesuit life, which they made no attempt whatever to inculcate in us, and which was the direct antithesis to the elitist beliefs which we were encouraged by them to hold. This was the pattern of personal self-imposed discipline observed by the Jesuit fathers, the novices, and the brothers of the Society.

I watched this way of life and was moved by it. Their lives exemplified thé capacity for self-discipline, the qualities of humility and self-abnegation, the impressive ability to submerge themselves 'ad majorem Dei gloriam' for the welfare of the Order and the success of their life's mission, i.e. the final triumph of Roman Catholicism and the perpetuation of their own power under the 'Black Pope' (the Jesuit Superior).

The Jesuits appeared to accept honours and demotion unemotionally, without question or complaint. They showed all the discipline of their soldier founder, St Ignatius of Loyola. Each pursued his vocation, whether at the aristocratic Farm Street Church, the London house of the Jesuits, or as simple storekeeper in a provincial school. A solitary rootless life was implicit in unexpected moves and transfers from one institution to another. There was also real poverty — pittance tobacco money, threadbare clothes, frayed cuffs. We had one priest who had forsaken great estates and a peerage for his vocation. We saw the bare tables within the linoleum-covered and uncurtained rooms, the breviary with a few books, the simple crucifix above the priedieu. They owned no personal possessions; comfort was a small fire and a ration of tobacco or cigarettes.

I found these features of the Jesuit life easily the most impressive part of my education at Beaumont. On many occasions throughout my troubled life of illness, humiliation, disappointment, and occasional success, I like to believe that to some extent I was prepared for it while watching them, though not necessarily by what I heard in formal classes. It has puzzled me that the great institution of the Society of Jesus would appear to have concluded that only a very few are fitted to adopt the values and practices of selfless self-denial in relationships which they choose for themselves, and within whose boundaries they live out their austere lives.

At Beaumont I was subjected, for the only time in the whole of my school life, to corporal punishment. The system adopted by the Jesuits eliminated the possibility that the person angered by the pupil's behaviour could indulge his personal anger on a child. A specially-designated priest executed the strokes on the palm of the hand, using a whalebone-lined stiff leather contraption. My punishment had been awarded for some trivial offence. At a specified time, I went to the room of Father Furness, a member of an old aristocratic Irish family. He read the piece of paper which I presented to him, in which was recorded by the teacher the sentence which was to be carried out. Proceedings were completed briskly and without comment by Father Furness. My memories of this occasion are a mixture of surprise and shame that a grown man could demean himself by assaulting another human being, especially one who was smaller, weaker, and totally defenceless.

The effect of my beating was possibly the very opposite to that which was expected. There was no question of my being intimidated into obeying laws which I might have chosen to ignore. I simply resolved that there would be no 'next time', since I would take extra care that they should not come to know what I had done. Nor was there: the capacity to create superficially conforming little humbugs is to my mind the most disagreeable feature of corporal punishment. The child-adult relationship ceases to be one of respect, mutual trust and love. It becomes infused with fear, and alienation must form and develop in what is in effect a deceitful and lying relationship.

The public school encapsulates a safe, blinkered microcosmic inner world, remote from life and the wider world outside. While we read the *Illustrated London News*, *Country Life*, and *Punch*, I do not recollect ever reading a daily paper or a Sunday paper except occasionally to consult the Club Rugby results and to find out how our 'old boys' team did on their weekend match. Within our society, there was a non-elected governing authority, with its nominated officers, which devised the code of behaviour and rules. We were not exposed to any experience of the electoral process. The Notice Board was used to inform us about everything, from membership of the school football team to the names of the new school captains. It is not surprising that the disciplines of army life came readily to those who chose to enter Woolwich or Sandhurst from Beaumont.

There was a general lack of interest in elections. Change depended on the need to replace those who had graduated elsewhere, just as in the great world those who grow old, fall ill, or die help us to realise our ambitions by their replacement. We were not encouraged to believe that we could be in any way masters of our own environment. The public school creates a two-dimensional stereotype member of a mutually supportive freemasonry designed to protect and perpetuate a privileged position in society at whatever cost. A remarkable feature of the moulding process is the mutual acceptance by both adult and child of the nearly total absence of family life. This becomes a normal facet of their lives. The child has no choice but to rationalise the implicit parental rejection with an assumption of unwantedness: an ideal recipe for the well-known public school psychopath.

My education could not have more unfitted me for my prospective role in life. The protection provided by the public school system was dependent on a moderately wealthy home background to facilitate an easy transition from public school to business, to industry, the services, to the university. I listened with a sense of irony to our pre-graduation talk by Father Rector, who told us of our good fortune on entering the glittering world outside where we must take care to guard the good name of Jesuit education and the Catholic Church. He concluded, 'Do not forget that, in a turbulent world, you belong to the leader class in society'. Unlike the rest of them, I was both penniless and homeless.

Because of lack of vocations Beaumont has since been compelled to close. It is no longer the 'Catholic school for Catholic gentlemen' for which it was intended; its garish ornamentation, gilt and gilding, has given way to a computer factory.

4

Student Days

WHEN I left Beaumont in 1934, I had no money, no home, and nowhere to go. Eileen was seriously ill with tuberculosis and completely incapacitated. She realised more fully than I did the hopelessness of my position. I had nothing whatever except the clothes that I had on me. There was talk of a job in the bank, or the desperate last resort of the penniless public school youngster, the army. Luckily for the bank, the army, and above all, myself, none of these desperate remedies was needed.

Father Weld had once asked me to befriend a new boy coming from Ireland, Neville Chance, and help him in any way that I could. He confided in me that while the boy came from Clongowes Wood College, 'the ways of Irish public schools are not our ways', implying that they tended to be somewhat rough and uncouth. It would be up to 'us' to help young Chance unlearn his ways — he hesitated here — and though he naturally did not use the word he clearly meant 'culchie' ways. I readily agreed to do whatever I could, but he did not need my help.

Neville was very good company, and readily settled into school life. It transpired that my friendship with him was to change the whole direction and purpose of my life. Possibly appreciating my home and financial dilemma, Neville now asked me to spend the summer holidays with his family in Dublin.

Neville's mother was Lady Eileen Chance, widow of a distinguished Dublin surgeon at the Mater Hospital, Sir Arthur Chance. She had been his second wife. I spent a wonderfully happy summer in Dublin with Neville and his brothers and sisters and at the end of the summer I returned to Worthing to stay with two elderly ladies, the Misses Stephenson. They had spent much of their lives in India, where their brother had been a provincial governor. I went with them in their antique Trojan car to the bazaars, tea parties, and Morris dancing in which they were interested. On my arrival in my new 'home', I sat down and wrote a conventional but deeply felt 'thank you' letter to Lady Chance for her many kindnesses to me during the holidays. This turned out to be probably the most important letter I have ever written in my life.

The three unmarried members of the first Chance family, Percy, Arthur and Norman, and their sister Alice, had felt sympathy for me because of my bleak future. Now, in a gesture of great generosity, they together agreed to finance my education at Trinity College medical school so that I could become a doctor. Lady Chance and her remarkable family agreed that I should live with them at their home, Nullamore, just outside Dublin, until my qualification as a doctor. It was an extraordinarily selfless decision to take. There was only one difficulty in carrying through their proposal; since I was literally 'of no fixed abode' they did not know where I was. Luckily my 'thank-you' letter arrived soon afterwards. Immediately a letter was sent inviting me to travel to London to meet Percy Chance at the United Services Club where, in the course of lunch, he outlined the proposal.

It was completely unexpected. I had never presumed to aspire to a university education, let alone become a doctor. It was difficult to assimilate the incredible news and all its implications at once, but I agreed gratefully to return to Dublin to begin a new life. I had passed the School Certificate matriculation examinations with many credits, so I was unafraid of the new challenge on that point.

The ephemeral, roller-coaster existence of continually appearing and then disappearing people, landmarks, and relationships had dismantled my relatively stable old world, with its constant warm and loving mother 'whistling us home'. While very young, I had had to learn to form instantaneous, superficially warm relationships with total strangers, and a succession of friendships in different families. My own identity as a member of the Browne family merged into all of these sensations and was no more.

Each of those whom I had known and loved had disappeared and left me. I had lost the belief that I could ever again form permanent friendships or lasting relationships. My always limited capacity to believe in or to trust anyone I only regained much later, and with great difficulty. Yet I had known nothing but support and kindness from everyone. It was the suffering of others and of my own family which I could not ignore. I had learned to expect that each new encounter must end.

On the loss of our temporary home in Worthing, after the death of Miss Salter in the late 1920s, it was my brother Jody who was to suffer most. Eileen was told that she also had advanced tuberculosis. I recall the evening on which she returned to the tiny single-room flat in Bayswater where we both lived. She threw herself on the bed and wept bitterly, not for herself I am sure, but for the rest of us who had been entrusted to her care by my mother. It was now the turn of my sister Kitty to take on that role. She has since told me about her hopeless trek from door to door, to convents, orphanages, institutions, hospitals for the disabled throughout London, looking for shelter and help for Jody. Finally in great distress she had to decide to have him admitted to a London workhouse. So was finally smashed Jody's last vestige of a sheltered life, empty, miserable, purposeless though it had been.

It was then, and in my own experience in hospital still is, the practice for surgeons, in pursuit of experimental material on which to perfect a new surgical procedure, to scour the wards of non-paying patients for individuals needing such a procedure. Such was to be the fate of my brother in the London workhouse. His cleft palate and hare lip greatly interfered with his speech, adding to the humiliation and discomfort of his hunched back. He was a pitiable, totally dependent creature. A surgeon decided to operate on his hopelessly inoperable cleft palate and hare lip. Jody died on his twenty-first birthday, in great distress and pain, following the operation. He had made one friend in that workhouse, a nursing sister. On the day preceding his operation he went out to a florist and bought her a small bouquet of flowers, in gratitude to her for her kindness to him. He is buried in a pauper's grave in the heart of London, as our mother was.

In September 1933 I passed the entrance examination to Trinity College medical school and began my course as a medical student. This was to be the first occasion on which, without any malicious intent, I ignored the dictat of the Archbishop of Dublin. It was forbidden at the time, if one was a Catholic, to attend Trinity College. My attitude stemmed from my experience as a Catholic in England, where the easy attitude to religion had been noticeable throughout my stay. Catholics there were grateful if they were permitted to live their lives in uninterrupted peace with their fellowmen, very much as do Protestants behave in Ireland. English Catholicism had none of the hectoring arrogant triumphalist contempt of other religions which I later came to associate with Irish Catholicism.

A Trinity degree brought its own inbuilt disadvantages. In pursuit of employment I was to find that there were occasions when I was passed over in favour of younger doctors. I know of only one other Trinity doctor of my year who survived this boycott by the public service of Trinity medical graduates in Ireland, other than by succession to a father's practice.

Yet bigotry was not confined to the Catholic side. Mainly because he was our professor of surgery and we would later meet him in our examinations, I attended the clinic held by Professor William Pearson at the Adelaide Hospital. Just before it began he told us that he did not 'lecture to Jews, niggers, or Papists', and asked those of us in these categories to get out of his ward. He would not begin to teach until we did so. There were some African and Jewish students present. Shocked by the bigotry of this declaration we had no choice but to leave.

Religion was to enter into my life once again in the North of England after I had qualified. The Superintendent of the Cheshire Joint Sanatorium where I had been working in a non-permanent capacity, declined to appoint me to a permanent post because I was a Catholic. This doctor, a Methodist lay preacher and a fine physician, appointed instead a young man with no post-graduate experience, but a graduate of Queen's University, Belfast and, no doubt, a Protestant. The pleasant irony, which both myself and the young Queen's doctor enjoyed, was that he was one of the few Catholics who had studied at Queen's to become a doctor.

With the Chance family I was to enjoy a modicum of stability in my new home. Sensitive, compassionate, tolerant, and infinitely patient, Lady Chance had nurtured the merger of her two families; she had watched grow into adulthood her three stepsons and one stepdaughter, as well as her own four sons, and three daughters. She now welcomed myself, a total stranger, into her home, as if I were one of her own, and I was effortlessly assimilated by them. Any awkwardness that might arise stemmed from the projection of my own intense dislike of any outside intrusion into my own inner life. How could they uncomplainingly tolerate my intrusion on the privacy of their home life?

It was this realisation of my intrusive presence that conditioned my own inclination to withdraw. One defence was to escape into my own bedroom at Nullamore. There was always plenty of reading to be done. With the breakup of the family following the death of Lady Chance, I went to live with the two bachelor brothers, Norman and Arthur, who lived in one of Dublin's elegant historic Georgian houses, 90 Merrion Square.

The maid, Mary, who cared for us, was a remarkable specimen of early Victorian domestic servant. She was a tall, heavily rouged woman, and wore a white frilly apron, over a full ankle length black cotton dress, dropping down over her black well polished heavy brogue shoes. She effected a deceptively demure and austere demeanour. As with a Grenadier Guardsman's Busby, she added greatly to her stature and presence by a bulky florid red wig, carefully balanced on her head. The clever use of a narrow black velvet ribbon, puckered into the antique shape of a beautifully white, old-fashioned mop cap sat atop the wig. In spite of her demure appearance, Mary was an obsessional gambler. She bet mainly on horses, and had a wide knowledge of the skills of riding and racing, with a rich easy flow of betting jargon, reminiscent of a character in a Damon Runyon novel. 'He started at threes, but by the off, was back down to odds on', sounded strange coming from this uniquely Victorian vision.

I later went into residence in Trinity College rooms, where I learned to cater, alas inadequately, for myself. My health was to suffer in consequence. A bottle of milk snatched from the doorstep, and swallowed running across the front square on my way to a nine o'clock clinic, was no substitute for a 'full Irish breakfast'.

Student life had not at that time entered the intensely competitive pressures of the present. The short terms, crammed with lectures and clinics, and the long vacations created an exhilarating pattern of study of man's body and mind, in health and sickness, interspersed with the limitless permutations of recreations and pleasures to be found in Dublin. There was tennis, sailing, horse riding, squash, canoeing, skiing, and swimming.

For the public school student leaving the cloistered order of a Jesuit college, university life was a welcome experience of personal liberty. There was virtually no limit to the scale of my enjoyment. At one time I part-owned a young brown mare, named Araminta, which I hunted with the Bray Harriers. I even rode, unsuccessfully it is true, in the old Calary Point to Point race meeting.

With Dick Sandys, I helped to form the Trinity College Squash Club, build the squash courts, act as secretary, and play for the team. Reluctantly, and mainly for the companionship, I played rugby. With George Anderson, whose father was the formidable head of Mountjoy School, I borrowed a donkey and cart and, with a tent, in mid-February, set out to tour the Liffey Basin. I recall a week later walking home alone through the night, from the bottom of Sallygap Hill, over the Military Road, and down into the dawn, to Rathfarnham village, arriving home to Nullamore, just in time for breakfast. From there I took an early train into Harcourt Street and Trinity College so that I might finish my last important 'half' anatomy examinations.

Very reluctantly, to please a fanatical boxing enthusiast friend Jack Dennehy from Kerry, I might 'fill in' on the Trinity boxing team when Jack had an unexpected defection. My tolerance for such a silly and dangerous sport ended when, to my surprise, at the Jewish Boxing Club in South Circular Road, I knocked out a young Jewish boxer. His mother, present at the contest, was understandably distressed to see her unconscious son. Filled with remorse, I never boxed again.

Oliver Atkinson, known as 'George', became a close friend of mine. In the early thirties, we joined the newly formed 'An Oige' organisation. Our first walk together, in mid-winter, took us from Ballinclea Hostel, a tiny one-roomed cottage, across Table Mountain, down into the Devil's Glen, and across Glenmalure, to the An Oige Hostel at Laragh. This walk was important for two reasons. For the first time I learned to value the hypnotic attractions of the Wicklow and Dublin mountains; later I walked, rode on horseback, cycled, travelled by car or donkey cart over every inch of them, and came to know them as well as my own back garden. For the ill-fated George Atkinson, our long and lovely walk was recalled together when he was struck down, with a massive infection of the spinal column, by infantile paralysis.

When I visited him at home, he was totally paralysed; his eyes alone signalled his pitiful determination to survive this disaster. He struggled on patiently yet hopelessly, helped by his devoted mother and sister. At one time, desperately, he tried to replace his now useless arms and back muscles by having himself strapped to a plain crucifix-shaped splint. He was intellectually gifted beyond the average, and a special dispensation had been needed to admit him into medical school because of his youth. His brilliance and talents were, in time, all squandered on his early death.

Another friend of mine, Pat Martin, was the son of a country rector in Cavan. He liked to claim that the Martins had their origins in 'good British yeoman stock'. He had joined the British Royal Navy and was a Pay-Master Lieutenant, but had been invalided out and had chosen to do medicine in Trinity.

Pat had a small car, which greatly facilitated our enjoyment of Dublin's entertainments. While we were both conscientious about attending lectures and passing examinations, we did not allow work to interfere with our indulgence in the bizarre night-life available to us under the peculiar licensing laws of the time, the 'bona fides'. These had originally been related to the exigencies of travel by saddle and horse cars, but a visiting English journalist once wrote of the wild chariot race of cars that now left the city as the pubs closed each night. Circling Dublin was a ring of euphoniously-named places, such as The Golden Ball, The Lamb Doyle's, The Wren's Nest, The Igo Inn, The Hole in the Wall, The Stepaside Inn. Entry was gained into a totally darkened establishment simply by whispering the magic word, 'traveller'. These dimly-lit places were peopled by small private groups, earnestly talking well into the dawn. They were for the most part refugees from unhappy homes or marriages or money worries, or students such as ourselves.

Pat had much natural charm, and could talk the cross off an ass's back. He would wheedle a late-night meal for us in some sleazy nighttown cafe by temporarily trading his presentation gold watch or his superb black serge naval overcoat. Sometimes he might cash his cheque from the Indigent Protestant Fund through the good graces of John, the curate, or Davy Byrne himself, in the famous 'back room'. On one occasion, while we had a fish-and-chip supper in Fenian Street, behind the old Holles Street hospital, I found myself remembering the previous night's banquet at Nullamore — the gold plate, the gold cutlery, the museum-specimen Waterford glass. My appreciation of the kindness and generosity of the Chance family, which left me free to choose my own path without any sense of indebtedness, has grown and deepened with the years.

Pat subsequently qualified as a doctor in England, and ended up back in the navy helping to man the guns at a Dieppe beachhead, saving the lives of wounded army and navy personnel during a disastrous Allied commando raid. He was awarded a DSO.

Although it was becoming apparent that a war was approaching, I was lucky in being able to travel, although in conditions of austerity, through many countries of Europe. Many of these trips were by canoe, the most memorable one taking place in the summer of 1938 when Peter Denham and I travelled down the Danube. We had met by chance during holiday time at the front gate of Trinity and he suggested that I join him. Two years later, struck down by tuberculosis and confined to bed at Midhurst, I read in a travel book by an English canoeist that he was still wondering what had happened to the two young Irish canoeists he had met as they gingerly put their canoe into the water on their thousand-mile passage. Since he could see that neither of us knew very much about canoeing, he wondered if we had survived that ambitious journey.

The main dangers came where the already powerful flow of water in the river was compressed upwards and narrowed by its passage through the narrow sections of the medieval bridges of south Germany and Austria, creating a torrential rush of water. With water up to and over the spray cover and around our waists, we found that it was best to hold our paddles horizontally while sitting still and await an eventual projectile-like exit through the narrow arches of the bridges. A good sense of balance and a steady nerve was all that we needed. We capsized on one occasion, but with the help of the lifeline, managed to manoeuvre the canoe into the bank, where we dried out our clothes. We lived nearly exclusively on black rye bread and cheese, and the incomparable Bavarian lager. In time we arrived at Vienna, where we rested at a pleasant swimming pool at Klosterneuburg. From there, folding our canvas canoe, we travelled by train to the medieval city of Prague. In Prague I was given attention for a dangerously poisoned foot, and a kindly steursmann gave us shelter and money, while we waited for money from home. Membership of An Oige permitted us to use the many fine youth hostels; more frequently we camped on the bank. We ended that enjoyable journey with a ticket home, otherwise penniless, in the cathedral city of Cologne. I had one small orange, and a bar of chocolate, total sustenance until I reached Dublin.

My wife carefully kept the address of the Hamburg steursmann of the barge who had been so helpful to us in Prague. At the end of the war, with little hope, she wrote to that address, and offered him and his family whatever help he needed. Gladly we sent food parcels which helped them through the hungry immediate post-war years in Germany.

On my return from one of these European trips, in 1937, Lady Chance gently took me aside to say that a telegram had arrived in my absence with the sad news that my sister Eileen's last struggle to live had ended, at the age of twenty-nine. She had died in an Italian sanatorium near Lake Maggiore. As with my parents, she had continued to work on long after she should have accepted defeat and called for medical help. Because of the extent of the disease, no serious attempt could be made to treat it.

In addition to her medical friends, who continued to visit her faithfully to the end, Eileen had been befriended by an Italian priest who worked in the Italian community church in Soho. He pitied her distress, her tangled family life, and her hopeless condition and arranged for her to be sent out to the sanatorium in Italy with which his Order had links. Yet even in Italy, where they had developed hopeful new techniques, she was beyond help.

Just before her death the Soho priest enabled Kitty, now aged twenty, to visit her. It was to be a last meeting of pure torment for both of them, for they had always had a very close relationship. Kitty worshipped and loved Eileen deeply, and she never fully recovered from her loss.

Kitty was a kind and gentle person who loved children. Despite caring for all of us, she put herself through teacher-training college. Emigrating to the USA after the war, she became a teacher in the United Nations School in New York. She did not share Eileen's keen wit or administrative talent, but she was successful and happy in her chosen profession and enjoyed, for a few years, the deep and loving care of her dear friend of twenty-five years, Lois Coy. Lois nursed Kitty through her long ordeal with Parkinson's disease, treating her with dedicated concern and self-sacrifice. Relentlessly, Kitty became a helpless, dependent cripple; I have never known greater love and dedication than Lois showed her. In 1980 Kitty died, following a fall that resulted in an impacted shoulder fracture that was not recognized in the hospital. In their happy earlier lives together, Lois and Kitty had planned to live out their retirement in the quiet American county town of Harrison on the Ohio river, at Lois's family home. Instead, because of Kitty's tragic death, these plans are no more. Lois flew Kitty's remains for burial in the family grave in the cemetery near their home. In time Lois intends to rejoin her friend, and share their last resting-place together.

My other surviving sister, Martha, two years older than I, is now retired, and lives in south-west England. She worked with an anti-aircraft battery during the war, and was invalided out after an accident. A deeply religious Catholic, she has always been shocked by my activities.

This was a period in medical training when we could use the excellent apprenticeship system for medical students. The custom was for a student to live and work in hospital and gain practical experience. On leaving Trinity in 1942, I went to the historic eighteenth-century Dr Steevens's Hospital, which had associations with the great Dean Swift. We slept in tiny bedrooms under the ancient roof in a place known as the 'cockloft'. At that time a student served an apprenticeship in all aspects of medicine and pharmacology in the hospital, constantly on call on a rota system to attend at the wards and out-patients department. There were incidents of all kinds day and night, trivial or fatal accidents and sometimes suicides. One of our senior physicians, Dr Winder, was of the generation which still used the original wooden stethoscope, normally stored in a top hat, for diagnosing chest and heart diseases. The stethoscope was about nine inches long and had a flat wooden disc at each end. Understandably, it was a very crude instrument; if the unhappy patient had sounds in his chest which could be heard through that stethoscope, there was not much hope for his survival.

As a student I was presented with the need to make a judgement on the issue of euthanasia. Possibly many will accept as wisest and most humane the attitude adopted by the physician with whom I was caring for a newly-admitted case, which was that the decision should be left to the discretion of the experienced medical attendant. Our patient was a young motor mechanic, who had been working on a car. He needed petrol and, thoughtless about its dangers, had struck a match to light a cigarette. The petrol can exploded all over him and he was drenched with flaming liquid. All that remained of the skin of his body was a nearly invisible narrow red slit, the remains of his lip, covering the inner edges of his mouth. His whole body was now an excruciatingly painful, jet black, smouldering, quivering cinder.

I was astonished to see that in spite of the appalling damage to his body those residual lips still moved in low moans of pain. Clearly there was no hope for the man's recovery. Nothing could be done for him by us. I believe that the physician was right in deciding to inject a massive overdose of morphia into the man's body. At the time I was shocked by the awesome finality of that Godlike act. There is little doubt that, in time, society as a whole will come to accept the need to share with the profession such grave responsibilities which many now accept in lonely isolation on society's behalf.

While I was at Dr Steevens's hospital a strange fatal accident case was admitted about which I am still puzzled. This man had survived the 1914-18 war, and had volunteered as a rifle shooting instructor. It was the practice for the instructor to lie flat on the ground, faced by his pupil, also lying flat on the ground, just a few inches away. The pupil held his .303 rifle to his shoulder in the conventional way and took aim. The hairline front sight had to be at the bottom of the rear 'V' sight. The

instructor held a four-inch fine wire circle in the centre of which
there were two dead straight wires of equal length, crossed as in
a crucifix.

It was the instructor's function to educate the pupil to fix the
front hairline sight in the bottom of the rear 'V' sight of his rifle,
then to fix these two at the exact point at which the two wires
crossed at the centre of the wire circle. The instructor then had
to verify the correct position of all of these components of the
exercise.

On this occasion, during a nightime instruction, the
instructor, with one open eye, judged all this to be correct. He
advised the pupil to make his first gentle pressure, then the
second longer pressure on the trigger, so as to fire the rifle. Then
he shouted his command, 'Fire!' The instructor was dead, shot
through the brain. We recovered the bullet from the pelvis. All
my life since I have wondered about that death. It was an incredibly unlikely accident. Was it murder? Was it a thoughtful
suicide? The coroner's verdict was the usual anodyne and
meaningless one, 'death by misadventure'.

While in Steevens's hospital, I became involved in my first
struggle against what I believed to be an injustice by authority.
The matron of the hospital was a Miss Reeves, a fine lady, with
strict Victorian attitudes to individual behaviour. She was a
first-class matron and had built up a training school with such
standards of skill that the nursing in the hospital was quite
superb.

Miss Reeves believed that only by exercising a nearly penitential pattern of discipline could she achieve and maintain those
high standards with the raw young girls who came from all parts
of Ireland for training. The Nurses' Home was run like a
Carmelite monastery. Absolutely no fraternisation was permitted between the young girls and the medical students on the
staff, or indeed, any male companion. Diet was spartan, the last
meal possibly sardines on toast at five o'clock in the afternoon.

It was the practice then to treat consumptives suffering from
tuberculosis of all forms with many strange, painful, even at
times lethal procedures. The truth was that we did not know the
cure for the disease. One of the principles of treatment was the
belief that fresh pure air, ideally like that of Switzerland, would
help to kill the germs, but there was no scientific proof that this

was so. The Swiss hoteliers were delighted with their continuously filled rooms. Yet a desperate disease merited desperate remedies and the patients were encouraged to sleep out of doors on open verandas. Sanatoria were invariably built with such verandas in the heart of the country, and the unfortunate patient, winter and summer, slept in the open air, depending on the whim of his doctor or his particular nostrum for this frightening disease.

The nurses were compelled to work through the night in short-sleeved uniforms, and became more and more perished with cold as the night wore on. I shared their belief that this was unreasonable and that a sweater, cardigan or pullover should be permitted. At that time, the overall leadership of the nursing profession was particularly obsequious and deferential to the members of the medical profession, especially to the consultants. They successfully promoted the idea that nurses belonged to an angelic sector of society who must dedicate themselves entirely to the sick, as though they had a religious vocation. Nurses were led to believe that membership of a trade union or preoccupation with terms of employment and living conditions in hospital was improper and certainly not to be considered as subject for public protest. They accepted with awesome docility the discrepancies between the doctors' income and their own in their separate vocations.

I agreed to approach the matron on their behalf to win more reasonable treatment for their grievances. It was agreed that I would act as spokesman for the group and that they too would come with me to the matron's office. We assembled in the TB ward at the top of the hospital, about twelve to fifteen nurses to start with, and I led the way down the long winding stairs. There were desertions on every floor. The sad end to the story is that by the time I arrived at the matron's office and pressed the bell on her door, not a single nurse was left with me. Lamely I made the case, which was listened to with obvious impatience by the matron. Nothing was done to change the harsh conditions of the nurses. It was Miss Reeves who 'tut-tutted' and sent back to work a gentle vivacious young nurse, who complained to me of not feeling well and of having headaches. Clandestinely, I had an X-ray taken of the girl. To our dismay, and I choose the word deliberately, the picture showed the dreaded 'snowstorm' effect of galloping consumption or miliary tuberculosis. The unfortunate girl had between six weeks and three months to live. Her death was a truly terrible one, slow and intensely painful. She went totally blind before the end.

In urban areas such as Dublin in the 1930s and 1940s, the two most consistent killers of infants were gastro-enteritis and diphtheria. The gastro-enteritis was largely due to the fact that the milk supply was dirty: the effect of poor hygiene on the farm and in the home of the consumer. With low educational standards, a lack of proper water supply and inadequate sanitary conditions and domestic facilities, bad hygienic conditions were inevitable. Any of these factors could contribute to the spread of this lethal condition through the infant population of the community, and many babies died needlessly.

I recall my sense of total helplessness when I was 'on the district' as a Rotunda medical student. With another student, as inexperienced as I was, I had been called out to what turned out to be a perfectly normal birth. A fine, well-formed infant lay on the bed, delivered nearly spontaneously by the mother. Yet the child did not breathe freely and suddenly ceased to breathe altogether, rapidly losing consciousness. He died before our eyes. The mother was distraught at her loss, and we knew in some way we had been at fault. The incident was what is known as the 'white baby' syndrome, and the remedy is simple to the initiated. There is an instrument, nearly as old as the practice of midwifery, which, if used promptly, can extract the plug of mucus that could have saved that child's life for its mother. Death was the result of my inadequacy. That child should not have died. Yet surely those who devised a system where inexperienced students could be sent out in a state of ignorance were also to blame? Though I persuaded myself of this, it was of little comfort to me.

On another occasion I was called out 'on the district' to a back street near Belvedere College, to a loft over a stable. In order to get to the loft where the lady was about to have her baby, I found it necessary to climb a nearly vertical ladder. Light was provided by an oil lamp. A large black iron brass-bound bed, complete with feather mattress, stood in the centre of an otherwise empty room. There was no running water. While the unfortunate woman lay in labour, a hen sat perched asleep on the top rung at the foot of the bed. How did that pregnant woman get to that loft? What was to be the fate of that child, brought up in those conditions? The woman at one stage was compelled to leave her bed and, like a horse at a fair, void her urine on the floor. Could a woman have been more humiliated? She then returned to her bed and, with little help from me, went on to have her baby.

In the last summer before the Second World War broke out, I sailed to the west coast of France in an old luxurious gaff- rigged yawl, the *Samphire*, once owned by Lord Lloyd. My companions were Bill Chance, Robert Stoney, William Pike and Major Bob Clements. Bill Pike, a second-row rugby forward stood on the narrow edge of the yacht's dinghy, which was laden to the gunwales with stores, and, in an attempt to climb aboard the *Samphire*, upended everything into Dun Laoghaire harbour. This was an inauspicious start to a voyage which for me would prove disastrous.

Within hours the engine stopped and refused to work thereafter, in spite of being vigorously coaxed into action with red-hot plugs, fried in the pan by Bill Chance. Later, shortly after midnight, dozing uneasily in heaving, soaking-wet bunks, we were all routed out by the ominous cry, 'All hands on deck!' We were in the heart of a storm and the mainsail halyards had been carried away. I stumbled on deck in my pyjama trousers into the wind and rain, to see the intermittent light on the stark black Tuskar Rock. Later, near Brest, when it seemed we would have to abandon the yacht with only four life-jackets, it fell to my lot as the youngest unmarried crew-member to swim for my life to the shore, which seemed about a mile away. Happily, the emergency passed.

Our troubles were not yet over. As we cruised in the inland waters around Concarneau, I noticed a bubbling straight line in the water, coming directly towards us. It was through below and away astern before we realised what it was; we had been torpedoed. Foolishly, we had strayed on to a French naval torpedo range, and a peculiarly humourless matelot had decided to practice his lethal skills on us. The torpedo head was a dummy, but even a dummy torpedo at the wrong depth could easily have sunk our old timber yawl.

We finally left the yacht at Southampton in September 1939, just as Britain's young men, humping their duffle-bags, mobilised for war. (The yacht, I understand, was later destroyed by German bombing.) We had had nearly continuous rain, with never-ending gales. In nearly all the photographs of the journey I can be seen with my head down on my arms, sleeping; because I suffer from seasickness, I found it difficult to sleep below.

However, when I returned to Dublin the sleepiness and continual weariness, no matter how much I rested, together with the loss of weight, compelled me to look for medical advice. A chest X-ray confirmed that I had quite serious tuberculosis on both lungs which would require immediate hospital care.

Suddenly the possibility of years in bed lay ahead. In spite of my experience of the disease I did not appreciate that there was no certain cure for tuberculosis and that death was relatively common. I was more concerned at the abrupt end to my pleasant student life, my lectures, clinics, sporting and social activities. In addition, there was one other disappointment to be faced; I had already passed two parts of my three final examinations, but if a Trinity student did not complete the three examinations within eighteen months, he had to forfeit the examinations he had passed and start all over again.

This was one of the very few occasions on which I missed my own family. I wanted them to share and, no doubt, comfort me in my misery. The Chance family, as always, were uncritically kind, concerned only to console me, but the two doctors among them had some idea of the testing prospect of months in bed for a young man of whose family so many had already died of the disease.

It is difficult now to comprehend the sense of shocked disbelief with which one heard of a friend's misfortune in contracting tuberculosis. People faced not only personal isolation but also nearly inevitable residual physical disability or even death. Possibly the most chilling experience occurred when I was kindly taken into the Chance home, to await hospital accommodation. Some time later I learned that the woman who acted as domestic help declined to come near the room in which I lay to assist me or bring me my food. She was simply frightened of contracting the disease. Overnight I had joined the ghetto of the tuberculosis lepers in Irish life.

This is not an unfair description of the public attitude to tuberculosis; sanatoria were built when possible in the country, some distance from the urban areas. It was the common practice to send off the servants of the 'big houses' immediately they contracted the disease, the further away the better. A nearly hysterical fear of tuberculosis was universal. It affected all classes, because there was no certain cure, and as death took a long time and could be painful, this fear was understandable. A bus conductor once told me that many passengers, in fear of their lives from tuberculosis, would hold their breath when passing Newcastle Sanatorium in case they caught the germ.

Yet the terror of tuberculosis was not confined to the 'illiterate peasant'. I remember being called to a very sick woman in a sanatorium where I worked. She had undergone a new and experimental operation on the previous day which had, unfortunately, gone badly wrong. Her lung had been perforated. As a result of the strange structure of the lung coverings, she continued to exhale air with each breath into her surrounding tissues. Her whole chest was grotesquely distended with air, and crackled like tissue paper to the touch. Nothing could be done for her. Pitiably, she gasped out that simplest of all wishes, 'If I could only breathe'. Since she could not live, I had called for the Catholic curate, so that she might have the last comforts of her religion.

The priest, a fine robust man, a brave rider to hounds and *bon viveur*, strode into the ward in which lay my dying patient. He was unrecognisable until he spoke, and even then was almost unintelligible. He could not see too well. All that was to be seen of his face were his two bright black eyes. To my amazement, he wore an enormous snow-white surgical gown, strapped around his great circular frame. On his head was an operating theatre skullcap; on his face the nearly totally concealing surgical mask. The ward could have been a surrealist set for a dream sequence by an avant garde Scandinavian film producer. This was one soul to be saved that was not worth the priestly risk of contracting tuberculosis. Here was one 'brave' man who did not intend to risk his health to help this dying woman 'make her peace with God'.

The disease could show itself by a cough, followed by the appearance of blood in the mouth, then the dramatic scarlet on the white handkerchief which I had first noticed in the case of the Christian Brother in Ballinrobe. It was a peculiarity of the disease, never explained, that if it first showed itself by the coughing of fresh red blood from the lungs, then every succeeding recurrence, if the patient survived the first attack, showed itself with bleeding from the lungs. The real importance of this distinction was that onset by haemorrhage usually meant that the unfortunate patient would finally die in conditions of uncontrolled bleeding. Since the outpouring of blood from the ruptured vessel could not be removed fast enough from the lungs, the victim drowned in his own blood.

After some consoling visits, I now had to face the loss of my friends, and my happy life with them. I had just come to know Phyllis Harrison, who was to become my wife; we had met at a Trinity Boat Club dance by the Liffey. Common sense dictated that for her own protection she should forget our friendship; remarkably and happily for me, this she did not do.

I was an exception to the general rule that while the wealthy were treated under ideal conditions, so long as they could pay, the rest of the population were compelled to wait at least one year before being admitted to a badly-equipped, slum standard sanatorium where the staff could do little or nothing for the unlucky patient. It was my good fortune to have the support of the Chance family, without whom I would not have been able to pay for treatment. When it was accepted that there was no effective treatment for me in Dublin, I was sent to the King Edward VII Sanatorium in Midhurst, Sussex, in the summer of 1940.

I had one natural asset, evident on the night on which my father died and again when I was so full of fear on the lorry near Ballinrobe: I could always sleep. On wonderful summer nights in Midhurst, in my moon-filled room, I would weep in angry self-pity, but then I slept, blessed relief. My second asset, which I developed with time and practice, was reading. In all my waking hours I can safely say that I rarely took my eyes off the printed page. I read through the hospital libraries, and then more.

I also bought a tiny radio, costing £4, and so enjoyed the pleasure of listening to talks, debates, theatre, discussions on virtually everything. My new life in bed became peopled with new friends, ideas, new perspectives on human relationships and society hitherto untouched in my mind, and I began to question the many easily-assimilated verities of my old world as part of a more serious attitude to a life purpose. This was probably greatly helped by the eclectic nature of my reading. This constant reading and listening, with all the time in the world to dwell on what I had newly come to know, emphasised for me the barren muscle-bound shoddiness of a formal English or Irish education. A young Guards officer, Mike Bolitho, later killed in North Africa, introduced me to the great pleasures of classical music. The walls of my prison had ceased to some extent to press in and suffocate me.

Midhurst was a beautifully situated hospital, well run by an Australian, Dr Geoffrey Todd. The visiting surgeon was Dr Wynne Edwards, one of the many Welsh doctors who completely dominated chest surgery and medicine at that time in Britain. With the best possible intentions I was subjected to many extraordinary drugs, some of them positively dangerous, and all useless. At least one of them, a gold preparation named Sanocrycin, damaged my blood cells by inducing a blood disorder and I became very ill. All else having failed, it was decided in 1942 to operate on my right lung.

The disease in both of my lungs being so advanced, it was not possible for the surgeon to use the conventional mutilating but fairly safe thorocoplasty operation, under which four, six, or even eight ribs were removed in their entirety. My disease was too unstable and too unpredictable, so an entirely new and relatively untried operation called extra-pleural pneumothorax was proposed. Part of two ribs would be removed and air would then be injected under pressure into the space created. It was later shown to be a dangerous and impractical procedure and was rapidly discontinued, but the doctors did not tell me quite how new and dangerous it was.

The reality was that there was no choice. A slow and painful death was otherwise inevitable. It was quite common for patients to be told that because of the extent of their disease, there was simply nothing that could be done for them. I suspect that I was in this category, but my two physicians courageously refused to concede it. My distressing symptoms of drenching night sweats and sleeplessness became exacerbated, and I had lost over two stone. I had never seriously contemplated the possibility of dying from the disease, but now for the first time I became frightened, and agreed to have the operation.

Because of the state of my chest, the operation had to be carried out under a local anaesthetic; a general anaesthetic would have been too dangerous. In spite of the cotton wool in my ears, I could hear the terrifying sound of my ribs being cracked painlessly by the giant shears which I was later to come to know so well, when working on my own patients. My fear stemmed not only from the unpleasantness of the operation, or of the operating theatre; sedation and anasthesia were not as effective then as they are now, but there was yet another reason for my fears.

I had been invited to go to Mass with the Irish nurses in the nearby village of Midhurst on the Sunday prior to my operation. Though I had given up the practice of my religion, I went lest I should hurt their feelings, and met the priest. I am sure that the sermon which he gave about the beauties of Heaven and the angels was a good one, but understandably, it seemed to me peculiarly inappropriate at a time when the air was full of German fighters and bombers. Damage in cities was widespread, and sudden death was frequent. The Battle of Britain was being fought out over our heads, for weeks on end. Because of pilot losses and shortages, our sanatorium was scoured for men who though ill might be fit enough to fly. We were warned daily not to walk around the hospital grounds, lest we be machine-gunned by the German fighters. Death was near to so many of us, in so many ways.

The priest had been told of my operation. On the night before it was to take place he came to offer me the Last Rites. I happened to believe that I did not want his kindly help and, as gently as I could, told him so. Somewhat brutally, he told me what the surgeons had thoughtfully kept to themselves — that the operation which I was to have on the following day was a dangerous and virtually untried procedure, which I already knew, and that the same operation had recently been carried out at Midhurst on a young Dublin doctor, who had bled to death. Shocked by this revelation, I was above all else repelled by his unfeeling timing. It did not have the hoped-for effect; I sent him away. I entered the operating theatre on the following day a very fearful soul indeed, frightened not by hellfire but of dying painfully like my young predecessor.

I survived the operation, though for technical reasons the procedure was a failure. I had bled copiously; when the bleeding stopped, the space which had been intended to be occupied by air was now filled with blood. So it remains to this day.

There was little else that could be done for me. Dr Nicholson, Dr Todd and the nursing staff with great care and skill helped me over the operation itself. I still marvel at the generosity of a society which, in the middle of a war of such ferocity, could have turned aside to concern itself with saving the life of an unimportant outsider, whose own country had chosen not to concern itself with the struggle.

5

Medical Practice

AS SOON as I became fit to do so, I completed my final examinations in 1942 and became a doctor. My first post was in Dr Steeven's Hospital, where I had been a student, and I then moved on to Newcastle Sanatorium, Co Wicklow. While in Newcastle, it became clear that I was wasting my time working in an Irish sanatorium. The facilities were grossly inadequate. Because of the delays experienced by waiting patients, treatment was almost useless by the time a bed was available; at one time there were almost one thousand sick people on the waiting list.

My first clash with politicians arose over my refusal to give priority over the year-long waiting list to a Dáil deputy, a member of the government party. I was afterwards told that the department official I had refused advised my hospital to get rid of me.

Possibly the busiest room in the average sanatorium was the mortuary. The 'Pigeon House' at Ringsend was kept especially busy in this regard, although it was under the care of an unusually fine physician, Dr. John Duffy, who did his best with little or no help from anyone. The building was a former cholera isolation hospital, and no conversion had been considered necessary by Dublin Corporation because the inmates were all terminal cases of tuberculosis. They were terminal mainly because of lack of diagnostic and treatment facilities.

Most of the sanatoria in the country were in the same bad repair, but the Pigeon House was one of the worst. It was cold and, as at Newcastle, the roof leaked into buckets in the centre of the ward floors. Inevitably there was a continuous line of undecorated, cheap deal coffins, in the simple glass-sided horse-drawn hearses of the poor, leaving the hospital. Because the hospital was at the end of the road these hearses had to pass the windows of the men and women who waited their turn to be put into the ground in the 'Nevin' (Glasnevin cemetery).

As with so much else in the new Irish state, all the old rigid arrogant class attitudes common to the ascendancy doctor were readily assumed by the newly emergent Irish successor. The rigid class-structured pecking order observed in Irish hospitals is shown in a story told by a psychiatric nurse. One morning he had passed the outgoing medical superintendent while walking in through the door of the psychiatric hospital. The nurse muttered a brief 'hello' and went on. Instantly he was called by the medical superintendent, who asked him his name and his work. The nurse gave his name. The RMS then said: 'You had better know that if you are to survive long in this hospital, you'll always address me as "Good Morning, Sir".'

Another incident of this type happened me at Dr Steeven's Hospital. Early one morning I had tumbled out of bed and run down the steep stairs from the 'cock-loft', where doctors and medical students slept, to care for an emergency in the casualty room. Having dealt with the accident I was strolling back to the Mess to have my breakfast. I was shouted at — 'Hey, you!' I turned in some disbelief and saw that the caller was a particularly pompous member of the consultant staff with a considerable opinion of himself. I leaned back against the wall, my arm resting easily on the iron handrail; the consultant was compelled to continue making a fool of himself by shouting at me, or move towards me, and the latter he eventually did. I asked him quietly, 'Who do you think you're shouting at?' Clearly surprised by the reception, he quietened down and settled for giving me a lecture about the propriety of seeing patients in my bedroom slippers and no socks. I did not trouble to explain the emergency nature of the call when, understandably, my first concern was for the patient. The consultant went on his way, yet, vindictively, he reported me to the hospital medical board for having been disrespectful to him. I survived the encounter.

In 1943 I set out for wartime England to gain experience at the best sanatoria, with the intention of returning to Ireland. Hospital work and staff relationships in England were remarkably different from those of my recent Irish experience. In the first of these hospitals, the Cheshire Joint Sanatorium, I was to learn much more than the imaginative, unorthodox, original diagnostic and care procedures devised by a remarkable, infinitely charming, autocratic bully, Dr Peter Edwards. Incredibly, he ran a sanatorium staffed almost entirely with former consumptives; nurses, administrative staff, laboratory staff, doctors and even Peter Edwards himself had all recovered, or were recovering, or indeed, had no hope of ever recovering, from tuberculosis. Yet they were carefully ambulant and mentally active. This was unheard of in tuberculosis practice at that time, but Dr Edwards had original and heterodox ideas on virtually every subject you could think of.

He despised Catholicism as a 'primitive, idolatrous, pagan, yellow-ochre religion', and regarded my education and background as a disqualification when I later applied for a permanent post in his sanatorium. But there were times when he could be completely indifferent to religious convictions, particularly if the person concerned was 'good company'. He formed a lifelong friendship with an Irish colleague, Dr Joe Logan, later head of Peamount Sanatorium, Co. Dublin. Dr Logan, who exercised a valuable restraining effect on Peter Edwards at the Club bar, had that most priceless asset, a fine sense of humour. He was a very entertaining raconteur, could accompany himself singing at the piano and in fact was the quintessential good-humoured Irishman. Peter forgave Joe Logan his Catholicism and they had some great times together. In contrast I was inclined to be a solitary serious fellow in bibulous company, and, alas, still am.

Peter confided in us that he had developed the principle of employing tuberculosis staff in his hospital on the general thesis that the healthy doctor who chooses to go to work at the rather somnolent pace of a TB sanatorium must be either 'a drug addict, an alcoholic, or a lazy bastard'. While it is true that he himself lived a relatively wild and rumbustious existence, the régime imposed on his patients and expected from his staff was one of monastic sobriety and asceticism.

As well as a considerable store of information about the care of tuberculosis, I also learned from Dr Edwards his insistence on the egalitarian values of a good radical Welsh liberal. There was no distinction whatever in his sanatorium between the disparate roles of the hospital staff. We all contributed equally to the struggle to help and to care for our patients. There were no titles; we all used Christian names. Technicians, technocrats, male nurses, doctors, porters, ambulance drivers and administrative staff were all on equal terms, and co-equal members of a fine social and recreational club. It was here that we had the bar, staffed by each of us in turn, Peter excepted. Even the exception of Peter was an exercise in democracy, since it was agreed on by all of us that we could not permit him to enjoy its freedom unsupervised.

This camaraderie and lack of pretension was a refreshing contrast to my experience among the medical staff of the average Irish hospital, and was invariable among the Welsh medical men whom I had the pleasure to work with later in England. There was no cap-tipping deference to the doctor among the Welsh, so many of them distinguished and world-renowned members of the medical profession, particularly in the speciality of chest diseases.

It was the practice when I was in Dr Steevens Hospital for a medical student or a junior doctor to carry the consultant's bag with medical equipment during morning rounds of the hospital, walking a respectful three or four feet behind the consultant. He would like to be left alone when he ducked into a private patient's room or behind the curtain of a cubicle when that sacred ritual of settling or collecting his fee was negotiated.

During the latter part of the war the Atlantic blockade was particularly effective, and there were serious shortages. Hospital food was nearly always 'spam' or an indescribable concoction of dried eggs. There were times when a handful of vitamin C tablets appeared to be the only meal of an evening. Yet this was also a time when a state could and did take those powers needed to establish a system of priorities, so depressingly absent in our free enterprise societies at other times. All young children and babies, irrespective of wealth, were better fed in Britain under the rationing scheme than ever before or since. Just as I found the easy-going but sensitive working democracy of the Cheshire Joint Sanatorium valuably educative, so was I deeply impressed by the possibilities open to a caring society. We watched a society under siege establish Aneurin Bevan's 'gospel of socialism', which is about priorities. In this socialist system,

unlike monopoly capitalism where the strong prevail over the
weak, it was the weak and the helpless who were the privileged
and protected ones.

Later, in a fine new chest hospital at Harefield near London, I
continued my education in a working democracy. Harefield was
run by the Middlesex County Council, and its superintendent
was Dr Kenneth Stokes, yet another utterly charming Welsh
doctor. I could watch the emergent British welfare society in
action. In Dublin, the almoner's role was to collect hospital and
consultant fees. At Harefield, it was the almoner's function to
cater for those in economic or personal distress. The almoner
could provide anything from a new mattress or cradle for a
newly-born infant to advice for a lady in distress whose marriage
had irrevocably broken down, helping her with the details of
getting a divorce. It was at Harefield that I heard a patient tell
an officious ward sister, 'Please don't speak to me like that, sister,
it is I who pay your salary'.

Standing in my white coat in the magnificent front hall of this
enormous modern chest hospital, I was approached by a visitor
who politely asked me if it would be possible for him to see over
'his' hospital some time. Possibly accustomed to being a master
race for centuries, the British had no small opinion of themselves.
Yet I infinitely preferred this easily presumptuous 'arrogance' of
the masses to that of our own small privileged wealthy few who
liked to see around them the suitably obsequious and grovelling
masses. This new experience I found very refreshing.

For security reasons the famous London hospital of St Mary's
at Paddington with its distinguished staff, including Sir Thomas
Dunhill, Dr Tom Holme Sellars and Dr Pickering, was
evacuated to Harefield, which had been expanded enormously
through the use of what seemed to be hundreds of well-equipped
Nissen huts. Because of this, and since battle casualties were sent
directly to Harefield from the Normandy beaches, our surgical
and medical experience was limitless. Simply by signing our
name to a consultation request chit we had access to some of
the finest surgeons and physicians in London. In spite of the
harrowing nature of our work, medical practice was broad,
rich, and rewarding. Meetings, discussions, seminars and con-
sultations went on continuously, in spite of the fact that the
first V-bomb fell a few miles away; we happened to be in the

middle of what was known as 'bomb alley'. The work continued uninterrupted; nursing, domestic, medical or administrative staff casualties from the civilian bombing were simply replaced. The cosmopolitan staff included refugees or volunteers of many nationalities and races. I heard a consultant remark that of the thirty or so men in the mess he was the only Englishman amongst us.

All of these experiences constituted an exciting and attractive new life. My archaic Irish and public school snob values were healthily upended in a consciously liberating way. It is possible that I had recovered the egalitarian instincts and fairminded values of my own home, which had been distorted by my class-orientated school experiences. Whatever the cause, after my English hospital service, I had found my real self, and I was changed irrevocably. In those hospitals in Britain I had met consultants who were among the world's leading physicians and surgeons, and yet worked for state salaries. They worked ceaselessly, conscientiously, and with complete satisfaction at their profession. I have always found the cash nexus between the patient and doctor indefensible. It cannot be a link, and frequently it can be an impediment. It is little wonder that Bernard Shaw could write about it with such satirical accuracy. Being a doctor, with all its connotations of relieving human distress, was to me such a privilege that I could not consider the need to take money from a patient for any help which I might have given to them. Within this heterodox attitude to medicine, I found myself to be very much of a misfit with many of my Irish colleagues. Their approach seemed to be just the same as that of the butcher, the baker and the candlestick maker, that you made the customers pay as much as you could get out of them.

Because of these beliefs, that money should not be made out of the misfortunes of others, I chose throughout nearly half a century in medicine to work for an institution, or for the state, receiving a salary; no matter what the amount of work or how many hours I attended to patients, no money passed between the patient and myself, and every patient, I like to believe, was treated with the same care. My sheer inability to compromise on this principle became very clear on one occasion, when a colleague in private practice developed tuberculosis, and died. I was asked to take on the practice. Since my pay at Newcastle at the time was but £21 monthly, with a lodge, in the interests of my uncomplaining, financially hardpressed wife and family, I agreed to the proposal. Yet it was impossible for me to continue that form of private practice; I simply could not ask for money from men and women who clearly had difficulty in paying. After a time, I compromised with the device of a plate on my table in the hallway, mentioning to the patients that they might put into the plate whatever they thought they could afford. This amounted to far less than the cost of rent of the rooms, the necessary medicines, the drive from Newcastle, and above all, it did not help my patient and long-suffering wife. Yet we decided to discontinue the practice, while continuing to care for the patients at Newcastle. It was an experience of this kind, no doubt, added to what I had known in my early life, which, in the end, helped to turn my mind towards finding a way in which I could change life for the underprivileged sufferers from tuberculosis, and ill-health generally, in Ireland. Had my wife and family not shared these beliefs with me, I could not have taken the adamantine stand on those principles which I did, later on, when Minister for Health.

On 14 January 1944, Phyllis Harrison and I were married at a rather strange ceremony which took place in a small church near Uxbridge. Three people attended. Since none of us knew that a Registrar should have been asked to attend, the marriage could not take place until the following day. No doubt relieved after the disappointment, confusion and delay of the first day, a Highland Scot colleague at Harefield, feeling to some extent responsible, drank the only bottle of Irish whiskey which we had for the celebration. There was no conventional honeymoon; to use the phrase of the time, 'there was a war on'.

Phyllis was the youngest child of a large middle-class North Dublin Church of Ireland family, all intellectually gifted. Like so many children of big families, she suffered the emotionally barren milieu inevitable where a parent is already pre-occupied with considerable family worries and work. From a very early age, she believed that she was the last straw for a mother who had given to the other children the limited capacity for love she possessed. In place of a Christian name, her birth certificate carries the bleak message, 'female child'. When her mother lay dying, some thirty years later, her last words to Phyllis, as if she was being deliberately hurtful, were 'Who is she? Who are you?'

Exceptionally quiet, shy and sensitive, Phyllis lived a home life of uncared-for loneliness. Observant from an early age, sceptical and critical, she noted the squalor and humiliation of the black face and dirty clothes worn by the wretched man draped in a damp canvas sack who delivered the coal down the long passages and steep stairs of her Victorian home. A surprising child in many ways, she favoured what she knew of the old Jim Larkin and his work for trade unionists, and became a republican despite her Anglo-Irish background.

She considers love to be the only civilized dynamic of relationships in an egalitarian society; it was typical of her, rearing our own family, to say, 'you should spare the rod and you should spoil the child'. It was she who supplied the rational structure to back my own instinctive powerful feminist faith. With growing knowledge and experience of practical politics on the left during fifty years in the harsh testing grounds of Irish public life, she reinforced her conviction that the proper path for us to follow was that of social revolutionaries. She accepts the Marxist analysis of society, and what some have described as its mechanistic coldness, as mediated for her by that fine Italian socialist philosopher and political martyr, Antonio Gramsci.

Her socialist attitudes were absorbed from two gentle ladies, Miss Savage and Miss Beck, who taught her at the Church of Ireland Sunday School. Phyllis did not get a conventional academic education at university level, though she did attend both the College of Art and Miss Read's school of Pianoforte in Harcourt Street. This did not prevent her from applying her fine intellect to the unravelling of the complex emotional processes by which we humans are motivated. Because she rarely accepted or judged the act or comment by its superficial meaning, at all times she looked behind the facade of behaviour for a deeper explanation and understanding. She was always moved so much more easily to compassion than to anger. Believing as we both do in the psychodynamic effect of childhood experience in determining later behaviour, forgiveness came more easily and resentment was rare. The arcane world of psychology has in Phyllis lost a creative, original, ruggedly independent and adventurous mind. Happily for me and for our two daughters, Ruth and Susan, psychology's loss has been our inestimable gain.

Her special virtue for me was not alone our loving relationship, but, within this, her inexhaustible patience. She could help me find my way back out of the maze of emotional defence mechanisms with which, after the dissolution of my family life, I had learned to surround myself. Her patience was needed in abundance. While it is true that I have gained most from our relationship, we each complement one another's intellectual and personality needs.

Once the war was over, it was very tempting for us to consider continuing to live and work in what we both felt to be congenial company and surroundings. Yet we believed that now that our responsibility of making a contribution to the allied struggle against fascism was over, we would and should return to Ireland. With the experience I had gained we would try to create similar conditions of care and efficiency for our fellow countrymen.

Unhappily, because I was a 'Trinity Catholic' I was suspect and unwelcome within the state medical services. To admit to a medical training in TCD, irrespective of the quality or extent of one's subsequent training, was an automatic disqualification from posts in any of the local authority sanatoria, the only sanatoria which provided medical care for public patients suffering from pulmonary tuberculosis. There were plenty of doctors ready to treat private patients, but this work did not interest me. Eventually I was offered a post with a salary of £21 monthly, and a lodge, at my former hospital at Newcastle, Co. Wicklow.

While I was glad to return to Ireland, I soon realised that nothing had changed at Newcastle or, indeed, at any of our hospitals. Indifference, apathy and complacency that amounted to sheer neglect prevailed everywhere. Our sanatoria were staffed for the most part with one or other of Peter Edward's categories: drunks, dope addicts, or simply lazy bastards. There was, of course, one exception, the gentle, hard-working and talented Dr John Duffy of Dublin Corporation.

It was impossible to work to any real purpose with the substandard, ill-equipped facilities in our own hospital. I decided to meet the more active of my colleagues in the tuberculosis service. After a number of such meetings, we decided to try to form an association of doctors concerned with the disease. I also lobbied the Red Cross and members of the trade union groups to see if they could help. We hoped to raise enough funds to build a properly-equipped 250-bed sanatorium. People expressed their full support and sympathy for the idea, but nothing was done.

Incredibly, our attempt to form a TB association was sabotaged by religious complications. Those of us who had started the project hoped to include doctors from all hospitals concerned with pulmonary tuberculosis. Invitations were sent to Dr Synge, a distinguished Fitzwilliam Square physician and brother of J. M. Synge, and Dr Rowlette. Both were fine physicians, neither of whom was interested in financial gain. To my surprise the steering committee, of which I was not a member, received an instruction from the Catholic Archbishop of Dublin, Dr John Charles McQuaid, that he would not permit Protestant doctors to sit on our committee. The committee accepted this ruling, the usual practice at the time at all levels in the country. Dr Rowlette and Dr Synge were excluded. The association was established, but did nothing to establish the primary physical needs of tuberculosis services. It was surely naïve of me to expect that collectively they would do much more together than they had done singly over the years.

Thirty or forty years ago doctors enjoyed a popular respect, born of a mixture of gratitude, mystification and fear. Only this could account for the fact that no matter how clearly in virtually any Western country the case has been made for radical change, the money-making part of our health services remained unchanged or even, from the doctors' point of view, simply improved. From the actuarial point of view, as well as in a professional sense, there is no logical or valid reason why a national health scheme should not be based on a salaried system of payment. Such is the successful practice in our limited state health services as they apply to infectious diseases in Ireland. The nearest comparable profession is that of the salaried nurses, than whom there is no finer group of individuals in service to the community. Yet the 'best' general medical practices in Ireland are based on the crude donkey-and-carrot money stimulus. Unlike the salaried postman, who is trusted to deliver every single letter given to him, the doctor cannot be trusted to work conscientiously for a salary like everyone else. Together with his colleagues in the law, the doctor must have a sweetener in the form of a fee every time he serves each individual in the community. Contemplate the success of the postman's union or busman's union were they to demand payment for every letter delivered, or every ticket checked. What about paying every nurse for every bed made and for every post-operative painkiller given when needed?

Time and again through recent history the medical profession has successfully resisted a fair and even distribution of their services all through the community. One of the results of the fee-for-service medical practice system here has been an enormous growth in the cost of the health services without a significant increase in their efficiency.

It was the practice for Dublin consultants of varying specialities to visit our patients at Newcastle in an advisory capacity. There were many conscientious consultants whose conduct was selfless and impeccable, but there were also those who simply used the hospital to unload those patients from whom fees could no longer be extracted. These consultants could be callous and careless about keeping sick men and women, who were not paying, needlessly waiting. They would then stroll into the consulting room as if the delay was of no importance.

One evening, after a considerable wait for the consultant, one such clinic began, attended by Harry Kennedy, a friend of mine. Harry, a journalist of considerable distinction, had written widely from a liberal point of view on many subjects in the *Irish Times*, then a liberal newspaper under the editorship of R. M. Smyllie. However, because he had preferred to help others with whatever money he had, he remained relatively penniless. He had frequently watched the long-suffering patients treated with cavalier indifference, and could no longer tolerate the injustice of it.

It was a hopelessly uneven struggle. On the medical side was the imperious, tall, impeccably-coiffed consultant, who dyed his hair jet black until he was in his mid-seventies. His hands were carefully manicured. He wore a gold seal and pendant watch across his taut, well-stretched waistcoat, and flourished that useless hallmark of his omniscience, the stethoscope. He was clearly a busy man and in a hurry. There was obviously little to be gained in financial terms: anyway he had a social committment, a dinner party.

The journalist was a small tubby unhealthy-looking man,

sandy-haired and pink-faced. His well-worn pyjama trousers had slipped down on his hips. But his powerful thoughtful eyes, of a distinctive brittle blue, told of a mind of power and courage not often encountered. Public patients had been taught to behave submissively but there was no submission here. Too late, the consultant realised that this was not just another bucolic 'grateful patient'. Instead this tousled, half-dressed, terminally ill man slowly looked up and, in his clear musical voice whose origins were in the Glens of Antrim, asked the consultant if he had any understanding of the measure of the mental and physical stress of the father or mother, wife, son or daughter, represented by the huddled weary patients still waiting outside the door. He asked the consultant was it his practice to treat his wealthy consulting room patients in this way; was it money or medicine which most motivated or concerned him? Were his patients divided into the sick rich and the sick poor? Did he believe that the sick poor could suffer and feel pain and separation and even avoidable or inevitable death less than the sick rich? He declined to submit to the cursory examination, took a dignified leave of all of us present, and left the room to the deeply embarrassed consultant. This was a moral victory for my courageous friend, yet there was no doubt who would win in the end.

The consultant made only one comment to my colleague, who was in charge of the hospital: 'I would get rid of him if I were you'. Simply because he had spoken freely and truthfully to one of those responsible for the discrimination between rich and poor in Irish medical care, this sick man was to be denied any treatment whatever. It was a particularly callous decision to send him home to die because it put at risk his wife and small daughter. Fortunately I arranged that he be re-admitted the next day, with the tacit approval, I believe, of my medical colleague, whom I did not consult.

The story has a bleak ending. Because of the inadequacy of the surgical and other facilities at Newcastle, Harry, through the generosity of his fellow journalists, was sent to a London surgeon at Brompton Hospital. Unhappily, his condition was already too advanced, and he died shortly after his operation.

6

Into Politics

AFTER THE war, though a secure, well paid and profess-
ionally rewarding job in the English health service was
open to us, Phyllis and I chose to return to Ireland to work
towards some form of socialised medicine. In pursuance of this
aim, I entered politics in 1947 on the recommendation of two
politically experienced friends, Noel Hartnett and Harry
Kennedy. Through Hartnett, whom I had met when he visited
Harry Kennedy at Newcastle, I was to be introduced to Seán
MacBride, Clann an Poblachta and Irish public life. I felt the
Clann na Poblachta party was the only political option open to
me, as the three main political parties were conservative, and the
Labour Party said that my membership would not be welcome.

MacBride and Hartnett had been involved as defence lawyers
in a number of Republican trials. Their relationship developed
so that in the Law Library, when MacBride appeared, it was
certain that Hartnett would be there, two paces behind him. He
became known as 'The Shadow of a Gunman'.

Their most important republican trial was their appearance
at a coroner's inquest into the death of a young republican
named McCaughey who had died on hunger-strike at Port-
laoise jail. (Later, as Minister for Health, it was one of my first
official acts to inspect McCaughey's cell deep underground, a
truly awful place in which to die, hungry or not). At the
conclusion of the inquest, Seán MacBride asked 'You would not
keep a dog in conditions like that, would you, doctor?' The
doctor declined at first to answer. Following persistent
questioning he finally agreed. Though young McCaughey did
not survive to enjoy it, this was considered to be a victory for the
Republican cause.

Hartnett was the Junior Counsel in the case. He was to suffer because of public revulsion at the disclosures at this inquest of what it was like to live and die in one of de Valera's jails. Shortly after the case he was sacked from his post in Radio Éireann: it appears that, in a moment of vindictive reprisal, de Valera had convinced himself that Hartnett was a security risk. With all his family, Hartnett had been a lifelong de Valera admirer, and was shocked by the pettiness of the act. After all, was he not honouring the universal code of offering a defence which the legal profession must give any client? For this and other reasons, Hartnett decided to resign from Fianna Fáil. He told me that when he saw the first cheque for £1,000 from Denis Guiney, a shopkeeper, on the table at Fianna Fáil headquarters, he realised it was no longer the republican party he had joined.

Hartnett was well skilled in the intrigues and intricacies of fighting and winning elections, learned over the years at the highest level in Fianna Fáil. With widespread social discontent, economic stagnation, high unemployment, the teachers' strike and unprecedented emigration, he realised that the time was ripe for the formation of a new political grouping in Ireland.

As Seán MacEntee was to disclose, Fianna Fáil knew of republican links with the Nazis, and MacBride had been a lawyer and one-time chief of staff of the IRA. It is difficult to believe that neither Hartnett nor MacBride knew of the links between the republican movement and the Nazis. How could these two men have concluded that it would be possible to found a social, democratic political organisation on the powerfully anti-democratic forces of the republican army?

Hartnett had much personal charm. In spite of the episcopal ban, he had as a Catholic chosen to go to Trinity on a Kerry County Council scholarship, in its time a dangerous thing to do. He was to become a distinguished scholar, winning the Berkeley Gold Medal for oratory. He was an Irish language revivalist in the early days but, as with so many others, was later repelled by the opportunism and jobbery associated with the movement. By joining with Seán MacBride to form Clann na Poblachta, he had made sacrifices of his own and his family's treasured personal and political associations with Fianna Fáil. Above all he suffered a personal loss, the friendship of Eamon de Valera. Lemass is reported to have said that looking down the table at the Fianna Fáil executive, of which Hartnett and Erskine

Childers were members, it was Hartnett rather than Childers that he expected would join a Fianna Fáil cabinet.

Hartnett's disenchantment with Fianna Fáil had more complex origins than his sacking from Radio Éireann by de Valera. His loss of enthusiasm for de Valera paralleled the change in the intensity of Fianna Fáil's republicanism. This profound transformation into conservative sectarian nationalism was enshrined in the lamentable provisions of the 1937 Constitution. Hartnett used to give two illustrations of internal conflicts in Fianna Fáil during this period.

In the mid-1930s, it appears, Seán Lemass had made a speech in Cahir shortly after Fianna Fáil's assumption of power, pounding out the simple grating truth — the romantic struggle to liberate Ireland is over; we must forget our old grievances, bind up our wounds, and get on with the work of building a new and a prosperous Ireland. These sentiments dismayed many of the old soldiers, inflamed by memories of their real and imagined heroics in the national struggle.

A call was made to discipline Lemass. Hartnett, who sided with Lemass, noted that de Valera sat through the long and heated executive debate and made no attempt to rescue Lemass from the old soldiers snapping at his heels. Late in the night, de Valera proposed to adjourn the debate. Lemass, who had sat silent, spoke up for the first time and said, 'No, finish the debate. Make your minds up.' In the end, after a close vote, he survived. What was clear to Hartnett was that while de Valera had feared no rival since Collins, he did not disapprove of Lemass's power in the party being visibly curbed.

Hartnett himself was involved in the second incident. During a Dáil debate in the early 1940s, a seemingly placatory speech was made by Seán MacEntee about the Fine Gael party. He seemed to express doubts about the validity of the anti-treaty 'republican' cause and even to sympathise with Kevin O'Higgins. Hartnett was a traditional Irish republican whose family had been burnt out in the civil war, and it appeared to him, and to those who supported him, that MacEntee's speech was a betrayal of the Republic. In addition, the name of O'Higgins had been mentioned, and not in revulsion. Was there not the bloody reality of seventy-seven republican comrades executed on O'Higgins's orders, without trial?

A move was made by Hartnett to have MacEntee disciplined. Once again, de Valera played the non-committal sphinx. The debate went against the republicans. Towards its end Erskine Childers, embarrassed by the anger and hatred expressed, stood up to walk out. Hartnett stopped him, as he attempted to pass, and pleaded, 'Stay for the vote, Erskine, you must know it is your father's name we are vindicating.' Childers passed on, and out of the room. Hartnett noted that de Valera made no attempt to take sides, or to defend the republican position.

Hartnett was probably the only member of the leadership of Clann na Poblachta with a wide academic training. The army sector of Clann na Poblachta, including MacBride, began their orthodox political lives virtually on the same day as the rest of us beginners. Whatever else divided us, we had in common this dependence on Hartnett. Hartnett was a small plump pink-faced figure, under five feet in height, Pickwickian in shape. He had fine thin auburn hair, which normally grew as it would. On formal occasions a quickly wetted comb was briskly produced to induce a transverse Kerry 'quiff'. This lay across the top of his forehead; the rest, untouched, lay in continued chaos behind. He himself frequently but tenderly ridiculed the unquestionable ugliness of his face. Its most notable features were his two small menacing flinty blue eyes, and his disproportionately large nose, which gave him a rich, mellifluous speaking voice. In repose, his mouth went straight across his face, like two razor blades.

Hartnett's smile was used in its strictly primordial social role, 'to reassure a hostile tribe', and was rarely sincere. Like a bullet shattering a plate glass window, his face could splinter into that blazing smile. Its effect was instantaneous, disarming and bewildering.

In spite of his fine mind and academic training, Hartnett showed much of the confused sentimentality and spontaneous romantic nationalism of the Kerry republican. He had a natural gift for moving platform oratory in the old oratorical style of rhetoric and phrasing. He also had his weaknesses, a dangerous one being a petulant intolerance and impatience of dissent with his opinions or prejudices. While this mellowed with time, there was more of the didact and authoritarian than the democrat to Hartnett. I have listened to him harangue a civic guard who quite rightly stopped us for a minor traffic offence. From behind his customary poisonously-smelling Woodbine, drumming an angry tattoo on his quivering knee with pudgy heavily-nicotined fingers, Hartnett complained haughtily, 'Garda, I would have you know that I am a member of the Irish Bar.' Not for the first time puzzled by his contradictions, I wondered how Hartnett could conclude that being a member of the legal profession could qualify him to break the law. Hartnett once criticised McQuillan and myself in the Dáil because we had ridiculed the guards of honour, wigs and gowns of the Law Courts. Neither he nor his fellow republicans have ever chosen to discard these silly trappings of our colonial past. On being challenged at a meeting in Beggar's Bush to socialise the lawyers now that he had decided to socialise medicine, Hartnett instantly sprang to their defence and called out 'hands off the law.'

I recall canvassing with Hartnett in the early 1950s at a city centre block of flats, Oliver Bond House. It was a winter election, the wind cold and gusty off the river. The rain plopped down from the eaves onto the stained frilly edges of his grey trilby hat, onto his face and down the side of his bulbous nose, from which, fascinated, I watched it trickle off, seemingly unnoticed by him into his mouth. I was reminded of one of those unpredictable amusement arcade pinball games. Water soaked his overcoat which, being off the peg and ill-fitting, came down over his shoulders on each side, and trickled down onto his lumpy, uncleaned, good quality 'reverend mother' black leather shoes, soaking his obviously uncared-for, accordion-pleated trousers.

We passed on slowly and mournfully, followed by poorly nourished, ill-clad, thumb-sucking, begging youngsters. They appeared to come out of the hallways, the doors, the liftshafts, under, through and over the balconies to harass and torment him. Dying for a smoke, Hartnett was no child-lover, and did not pretend to be. No votes, so no smiles for them. To me wryly through his teeth he muttered, as he delicately tipped the ash of his Woodbine, held as a lady holds her teacup, finger fanned out, 'Let's make it a part of our party platform, Noel, to employ a fleet of helicopters to fly over all the working class flat areas of Dublin, seven days a week for a year, to start with, and shower them with contraceptives'. He was not smiling. We stumbled on.

Towards the end of his life, Hartnett became disillusioned by the sectarian bigotry of Irish society. For him the classical Greek writers had already spoken for all of us, and for all time. He spoke of 'throwing the baby out with the bath water,' a Trinity intellectual's classic snobbish summary of the communist manifesto and Lenin's socialist revolution. He could ignore the disagreeable features of Plato's republic with its elitist assumptions; no doubt he presumed his own membership of that elite. He told me, 'The day will come, Noel, when we will have to seek refuge from these petty bigots here, and look for justice North of the border.' In disgust, he once protested that we should all 'get out of this inhospitable windswept island, it's only fit for the seagulls.'

Hartnett had many of the characteristics of the leading figure in a story he liked to tell about Kerry republicanism. The scene is a wild isolated village on a dark wet winter's night in south Kerry. The 'republicans' have been excommunicated by the Catholic Church and are on the run. The small church is just about to conclude Benediction. The front door is thrown open. Seven unkempt, weary-looking men, armed with the usual strange assortment of rifles, shotguns, and pistols, stand there deferentially with caps in their hands. The leader halts the service with a shout, and strides up to the altar rails, followed by his guerillas. Then, brave fellow, he calls on the priest and congregation for a decade of the rosary for the soul of the man lying in the coffin in the small side chapel, a republican comrade who had been killed in action. Republicans at that time were denied by the Church their last cherished ritual of prayers for the dead. Armed as he is, he has no difficulty in getting the 'Hail Marys', with the concluding 'May the Lord have mercy on his soul'.

Satisfied, he smartly calls his men to order, 'about turn' and out the door. The last man to leave, he swaggers after his men through the door and, as he does so, turns on his heel, snaps his fingers in the priest's face, and calls out, defiantly, 'Now you can turn me into a canary if you want to, Father.' He was a typical superstitious Irish republican, who sought to ridicule the 'druid', yet, in spite of his braggadacio, he was both respectful and fearful enough to address the priest as 'Father' and ask for his prayers. Hartnett himself was to die with all the rites of the church to help him on his way.

Hartnett and MacBride were complex characters. As a psychologist, it puzzles me beyond belief that these two highly intelligent yet totally disparate personalities should have believed at any time that they could have formed a permanent working relationship. It is difficult to avoid the conclusion that here were two talented experts in different forms of political activity, each determined to make use of the other for his personal ends.

My first close encounter with MacBride was a surprise to me as it has been, no doubt, to many people before and since. Seán MacBride will always excite curiosity and interest on entering a room. Of medium height, round-shouldered, he looked frail, indeed positively consumptive. But when he stayed near us in Connemara during an Attlee-Noel Baker visit in 1949, he was seen when swimming to have a surprisingly powerfully-built body. He appeared always as the 'well dressed lawyer', wearing conservative, dark, well-cut suits. Overall he had a gaunt, cadaverous appearance and his sallow complexion gave him a Mediterranean look. His curved crescent-shaped nose suggested a distinctly Middle Eastern appearance, and left an impression of foreignness. He could have modelled for a powerful Epstein head of a man who had suffered much. The mouth was well-shaped, thin-lipped, and obstinate — a dangerous man to cross! His rare smile was a momentary muscular response, as used by a well-mannered diplomat; it did not infuse a sense of warmth, nor was it ever completely reassuring.

To the Irish electorate, Seán MacBride was the unknown mysterious figure. He had all the personal charisma of the ex-prisoner legendary gunman 'on the run', who was also the son of an executed martyr to the cause of Irish Republicanism, and the notorious Maud Gonne MacBride. What an impeccable list of credentials for a leader in the *Boy's Own* world of Irish public life. Though a forbidding-looking figure, he was a man of much personal charm, and impeccable drawing-room manners, reserved for whomsoever he wished to impress.

As I came to know him better, he seemed to me to be an insecure person, a product, no doubt, of his disturbed and turbulent upbringing in his Paris home. Earlier writings by Fenichel and more recent studies by the psychoanalyst Victor Wolfenstein on men such as MacBride have quoted the 'effects of a long absence of the parent in childhood.'

There were few of us with whom Sean MacBride seemed to make close friendships. I certainly did not. Then, neither do I make lasting friendships easily. I have often wondered if he had ever been a close friend of anyone. The unwary, of whom I was one, looked in vain at him for the swaggering, Sean Keating Prototypical Republican 'broth of a boy' man on the run. I confess to having been finally floored by the broken English but fluent French-speaking, rabid Irish Republican with an aristocratic half-English background.

Maud Gonne MacBride, his English mother, once showed me a photograph of Seán as a child over which, for all to see, she had written 'Man of Destiny.' His later campaign for peace, following her death, is hard to reconcile with his former violent lifestyle. Did he wish to redeem that promise which, over-optimistically, his mother had inscribed on her young child's photograph? To what extent was the powerful and dominating personality of this notorious rebel mother responsible for his earlier career of violence? Was Seán MacBride dominated by her either through fear or through love? Was it that, sub-sequently deprived of all political power — he had lost his Cabinet post, his Dáil seat and his party — he was left with no choice but to play peace-maker? In such matters Seán was a particularly versatile performer.

On the occasion of Mr Attlee's visit, we visited Kylemore Abbey and were greeted by the Abbess. There was a sudden movement beside me from Seán MacBride. For a moment I believed that he had been overcome by some sort of weakness and was about to collapse forward, flat on his face, on the floor. Instead, with the ease and grace of a practised nobleman at the Court of the Sun King at Versailles, he slid forward on one knee and gently, slowly and deferentially, bent his head to kiss the ring of office on the delicate white hand held out to him. With equal grace and timing, she graciously submitted her hand to him for his courtly gesture. Pleasantly surprised, I watched the charming *pas de deux* being performed before my eyes. I simply shook hands with the Abbess in the conventional way, and admired his capacity for the theatricals.

Clann na Poblachta had its remote origins in the 1922 split in the republican movement. Following Eamon de Valera's even-tual entry into the Dáil in 1932, a section of the Republican

Army continued to oppose what they claimed to be his betrayal of true republicanism. Seán MacBride had been a prominent member of that organisation throughout its years of anti-state subversion and violence, at least until the late 1930s. Because of repeated, often farcical, failures, betrayals by informers and the ferocity of de Valera's reprisals, the IRA realised that with the defeat of Hitler, which they regretted, there was no hope of defeating de Valera. this led them to redirect their energies into building a political movement on the strong national network of support they already had in the Prisoners' Aid Committees.

As nearly always in Irish public life, the electorate was disillusioned with its politicians. They had offered nothing but unemployment, much human distress, and mass emigration. Virtually any new political party would have been welcomed. There were also deep divisions among the normally pro-Fianna Fáil teachers, because of de Valera's refusal to give in to their salary claims; they were 'on strike'. There was widespread discontent. As a doctor, I shared that discontent; I was especially unhappy about general medical needs and the virtually non-existent tuberculosis eradication programme. So without knowing very much about Clann na Poblachta, I welcomed it, all else having failed to give results. There were many of my age with a general radical outlook who were weary of the gross incompetence of a succession of civil war generation politicians. If Clann na Poblachta were not quite what we were looking for, then we could work to make it so.

By the creation of a new concept of multi-party government, Clann na Poblachta was to end the sixteen years' long hegemony of Fianna Fáil under de Valera, but its effect on the deeply conservative Fine Gael party was to give it new and vigorous life. This development was gloatingly summed up for me by a Fine Gael cabinet colleague, James Dillon, whom I met one day in 1948 returning from the Mansion House where the Fine Gael Party were holding their annual Árd Fheis, shortly after the formation of the first coalition. 'Last year', he thundered, 'because Fine Gael was on its last legs in the country, it would have been possible for us to have held our Árd Fheis in Powers Hotel. This year, the Mansion House is full to the door with loyal members of the Fine Gael Party.'

Each of us saw Clann na Poblachta as answering our own

special needs. The ex-IRA men simply wanted an end to partition and a united Ireland. I wanted our health services restructured. Jack McQuillan, another radical, hoped for a serious land and agricultural policy.

The first Clann na Poblachta statement in 1949 perpetuated the tradition of an influential leader class in a two-class Catholic state. Hartnett must have had some influence in the acceptance of this statement, if not in its preparation. Since the formation of the state in 1922 a fundamental compromise with Unionist Protestants would have meant a compromise with rigid doctrine Rome-dictated religious and political beliefs. A clearly-stated socialist manifesto from the young party, as with Saor Eire in the 1930s, would have meant its instant condemnation by the church.

The party's Árd Fheis failed to establish a properly structured organisation, with clearly defined radical, social and economic policies. It merely emphasised the party's utopian woolliness and reflected MacBride's tenuous understanding of political, economic and philosophical problems. For instance, under social services the party promised that 'a national monetary authority will be established, whose function will be to create currency and credit for the economic needs of full employment, and full production, and to provide credits, free of interest, for full employment, and national development'. Clearly the printing presses, at least, would be busy.

Section five went on: 'the means of production and distribution of commodities, essential to the life of the people, shall be so organised and controlled as to ensure a fair distribution.' This was a worthy platitude, no more.

Following MacBride's by-election win in Dublin South Central in 1947, de Valera called a snap general election in the following February, 1948.

Hartnett was chosen by MacBride to mastermind strategy; as Director of Elections he was given authority to determine day-to-day tactics for the campaign. Since none of us new radicals had had any previous political experience, we depended on his political judgement. Hartnett's association with Clann na Poblachta dated only from the end of the negotiating period that led to its formation.

Whatever about Sean MacBride's political inexperience,

which was comparable to my own, he knew enough to welcome Hartnett's advice as an experienced political campaigner. They were to be closely associated; until shortly after the formation of the first coalition government, Hartnett even lived in the tiny lodge at the entrance to the drive leading to the MacBride family mansion at Roebuck House.

My first dealings with Seán MacBride had occurred when travelling by boat and train to London in late 1947. Hartnett had sought to honour his promise to our late mutual friend Harry Kennedy to provide an efficient tuberculosis service in the republic. Using the influence which he had at that time with MacBride, Hartnett had this included as a priority issue in the new party's election statement. Because of my special knowledge of the subject, I was chosen to travel with MacBride and Hartnett to Ealing Studios in London, where Liam O'Leary had organised the making of a Clann na Poblachta film by Brendan Stafford showing the need for political change in Ireland. It outlined the broad strategy needed to bring about these changes. I was to speak on the subject of our defective health services, with special reference to tuberculosis. It was an effective and enlightened effort in the political education of an electorate whose politics were of the crudest emotive civil war tribal variety.

The film showed the suffering and poverty in which the mass of our people, especially in city tenements, were living; high unemployment, forced emigration, widespread uncontrolled tuberculosis. In the cities there was a very high death-rate for infants in their first years of life, from infantile gastro-enteritis caused by dirty milk and dirty vessels. There was no efficient health service to cope with all this distress. The inertia of both Fine Gael and Fianna Fáil in providing a service for these mainly preventable diseases was obvious in every aspect of life at that time.

The film is still extant and its merits can be verified. Though its portrayal of life in Ireland at the time was limited in its scope, it was without doubt fair comment. It well justified a wider circulation than it received. Because of censorship we had to be content with showing it on the derelict gable walls of the city's dance halls, tenements, and other centres.

Following de Valera's call for an election, I was immediately nominated as Clann na Poblachta candidate for Dublin South-East. Partially disabled by tuberculosis as I already was, I took a serious risk in standing for election because of the hardship involved in a mid-February election in this challenging three-seat constituency, which had John Costello, the Taoiseach-to-be, and Seán MacEntee, Minister for Finance for Fianna Fáil, as rival candidates. Phyllis with her invariable courage and selflessness, accepted the risks for both of us. (In fact I did relapse and was infected with tuberculosis shortly after taking Ministerial office. This was not generally known.)

Though we did not know this at the time the innocents in Clann na Poblachta were to be used as political mounting blocks for others, to ease the real 'republicans', the ex-IRA, into Leinster House. My function in Dublin South-East was to elect a long-standing member of the IRA, Donal O'Donoghue, who had been Quarter-Master General to MacBride in the 1930s. But he polled a mere five hundred votes. It was O'Donoghue's practice to turn up impeccably dressed at the street corners where our meetings were held, with an expression of resigned acceptance on his face as though he had been beaten into it. Our platform was an unprepossessing coal lorry. O'Donoghue would stand there incongruously in his expensive-looking brown trilby hat and spotlessly clean yellow chamois gloves, gingerly holding at the ready a folded black silk umbrella. He was a diffident apologetic man, and an unlikely member of a guerilla army.

The 'army' policy for us was well summed-up by a tough and ruthless party apparatchik named Michael A. Kelly. Unlike O'Donoghue, Kelly had a lurid record of violent underground military activities in the IRA. As General Secretary of Clann na Poblachta, he stood for election in Roscommon in 1948. He was obsessively ambitious. In one short phrase he summed up our role in Clann na Poblachta: 'with McQuillan's boots, and my brains', Kelly confided to a friend in Galway, 'I'll be elected in Roscommon.' Happily McQuillan, who had been a county footballer and an all-Ireland medal holder, was easily elected instead, and was to become probably the most valuable and talented of all the deputies elected for Clann na Poblachta, or any other party.

I had no experience of public speaking, but fortunately I had five enthusiastic and experienced election workers. Tommy

Moran introduced me to the delicate art of the door-to-door canvass: truly impressive are the manners and patience shown to all politicians equally by the Dublin electorate. George Lawlor, my Director of Elections, had been a fully active member of a Republican Army active service unit. He had become a serious-minded, well-read socialist politician and Marxist, and is still a close friend of mine. It was George who first initiated me in the fearsome ordeal of standing up in public and addressing my fellow citizens. Cait Clancy, who has since died, was an Irish-speaking teacher in her late fifties from Co Waterford. Throughout the atrocious wintry weather, Cait with her folded umbrella sat bravely on our platform. She was well-known and respected among teachers in the Gaelic revival movement, and gave me respectability in that sector of Irish nationalism. 'Pa'Woods was a good-humoured, kindly, somewhat cynical national school teacher, and an experienced political worker. Finally there was a most important supporter, Mick Dowling. Mick's asset was a lorry, which he generously put at our disposal. Mercifully, he spoke very little, since he still hankered after the 'great little equaliser' as a solution to the Northern question. Unlike others of that ilk, Mick was apt to say so publicly.

We were helped by a powerful non-political organisation of absolute amateurs, a group of former TB patients and their relations. They worked diligently for long hours, canvassing from door to door. In the *Irish Times*, after the election, R. M. Smyllie commented, 'Even if Dr Noel Browne had been a Red Indian, they would have had him elected because of their enthusiasm and sincerity.' Most certainly I was not elected as a republican; Donal O'Donoghue got the miniscule republican vote.

We had an election fund of about fifteen pounds. Because of the precarious nature of my own finances, I had to borrow my hundred pounds deposit. (This was always the case throughout my career as a politician, until the late sixties.) The campaign followed a standard pattern; every night we moved from one street corner to the next until people no longer wanted to listen to us. Hundreds of speeches must have been made. As though playing a part in a play which had been written for me, I used the same speech with minor variations for the whole of the campaign. It was the practice for some of my more enthusiastic supporters, former tuberculosis patients, to follow me around to my different meetings. Somewhat embarrassingly they would stand below me in the crowd and preview what I was going to say ('Now he comes to the...,'Next he will say...'), so well did they know my speech. As a comment on my delivery and bearing, one lady was heard to say, 'It's like listening to a Jesuit preaching'.

It would not have been an election in Dublin South-East if there had not also been critical and uncomplimentary reflections on my candidature. One of my Fianna Fáil opponents, Seán MacEntee, was a first class orator, caustic and articulate, one of the Belfast Catholic refugees from the Northern struggle so commonly found in the safety and security of southern republican politics and journalism. Noted for his ruthless electioneering tactics, he fought to win every time, but when he won, all was forgotten. Unschooled and unskilled in politics, unused to criticism or abuse, I was a soft and sensitive target.

Fianna Fáil always did things in style: he would speak from a tricolour — flag-bedecked platform blazoned with slogans, supported by distinguished supporting speakers and local dignitaries, and could rely on an efficient public address system, as opposed to our own whimsical apparatus. Having warmed up with a tirade of 'communists', 'fascists', 'murderers', 'bank-robbers', MacEntee would then 'fill in' the listeners about my own personal history: '...an interloper who dares contest the seat against Fianna Fáil...the strangest piece of flotsam ever to have been thrown up in the history of Irish public life.' Enthused by his own rhetoric, he went on to describe me as 'an out of work doctor, touting for patients.' For a doctor, it could hardly have been more offensive. In fact, I was employed at Newcastle Sanatorium as Assistant Medical Superintendent, and MacEntee well knew it.

Speaking at Rathmines Town Hall in January 1948, MacEntee claimed that the leaders of Clann na Poblachta had led the IRA. Supported by precise dates, stated names, places, types of assault, mostly murder or attempted murder of civilians or state servants, MacEntee went on to accuse Seán MacBride of being, directly or indirectly, responsible for these murders or attempted murders. Altogether MacEntee accused MacBride of twelve serious crimes of violence.

Those of us who had not known of this alleged bloody record of violence were shocked by it. But our hopes that immediate disclaimers would be issued by MacBride were not realised. He made no attempt to defend his name by legal action in the courts.

During the campaign I angered the ex-IRA group by a speech I made. De Valera's speeches were repetitious, dreary monologues on the 'injustice of the gerrymandering of Tyrone, and Fermanagh, south Down, and south Armagh' and the need to 'revive the Irish language.' He offered no solution to the realities of our mean and bankrupt lives, nor to the neglect and suffering of the people. Had he forgotten his own childhood, or did he not know of such suffering? Was it that he knew well, but no longer cared? Speaking, I believed, for my generation, I protested: 'We are sick and tired of hearing about 1916 and 1922 and of the futile wrangling about the past. There are present social and economic evils which need resolution.' Immediately there was a call for my expulsion from the party, led by Finaun Breathnach. MacBride invited me to dinner at the Bailey Restaurant, with Noel Hartnett. He remonstrated with me about my speech and advised that, in future, I 'be more careful.' Somewhat obscurely, but I suspect concurring with MacBride, Hartnett murmured, 'The gods of the Hebrews are jealous gods, Noel.'

It was only after I had stood for election that I fully realised the difficulty of contesting a small three-seater constituency like Dublin South-East in which two sitting members, Costello and MacEntee, were already firmly entrenched. It was an electoral risk breath-taking in its audacity. Now an experienced politician, I would not dare risk trying to win such a seat first time out in a short campaign lasting a fortnight, nor would I advise any young invalid friend of mine to do so.

Yet our innocence paid off. John A. Costello headed the poll with 8,473 first preferences, followed by Sean MacEntee with 7,371. I won the third seat with 4,917. The unsuccessful candidates were E. Butler (Labour) 2,399, J. H. Douglas (Fine Gael) 2,980, D. O'Donoghue (Clann na Poblachta) 559 and Michael B. Yeats (Fianna Fáil) 2,928.

Despite seven years as a medical student, culminating in the stress of 'finals' examinations, nothing I had so far known had prepared me for the ordeal of the counting of the votes. I was lucky to have been befriended by a strong supporter of Mr Costello who subsequently became his aide-de-camp when Taoiseach. He was named 'Steeler' Byrne because he had an artificial arm, shaped as a steel hook. A brilliant 'tally-man', early on in the count he was able to tell me, after counting figures on the back of an envelope, that I would be elected.

MacEntee was one of the first to come over to me after the count. Throughout the previous fortnight he had vilified me from one end of the constituency to the other, but now, hand outstretched, in his soft Belfast accent, he welcomed me to the Dáil and wished me a long life in politics. This was my first lesson in the many faces of a politician. A budding politician myself, I held out my own hand and shook his.

Of the Clann na Poblachta deputies elected in Dublin, Seán MacBride and Con Lehane were from the ex-IRA group. Peadar Cowan, a solicitor, was also elected to a Dublin constituency; he had been a member of the Free State army. All three made excellent deputies. Paddy Kinnane, Mick Fitzpatrick and Sean Tully represented Irish republicanism, *pur sang*. All three were respected old-timers, elected mainly on sentimental grounds. They had little of serious political content to offer. All of the other deputies in their own ways were of a high quality, and made worthwhile contributions during their short stay in the Dáil.

7

In Government

WE WERE to find that Irish republicanism in Clann na Poblachta had many forms. First there was the elite body of republicans, former members of the Republican Army, often with blood-stained active service to prove it. Then there was a lesser breed, such as ourselves, young people with no record of violence. We could have been in the 'movement' and had not joined. Next was the category of young men who to their undying shame, judged by the Republican Army group, had joined the national army; they were despised. Jack McQuillan was one of these. Finally there were those, like Noel Hartnett, who had impeccable old republican credentials. Yet in the opinion of the IRA, and this included Seán MacBride, Hartnett had betrayed the Republic by siding with de Valera who, by entering parliament in the early thirties, had in their opinion also betrayed the Republic. We of these lesser breeds had one thing in common: we were not to be trusted as republicans. Neither were we to be trusted with any power in the management of Clann na Poblachta.

Steps were taken to incorporate the permanent dominant position of the Republican Army group in the party's controlling mechanisms by carefully-drafted provisions in the party constitution. Seán MacBride recently admitted to a student historian at University College, Galway, that 85% of the party's forty-five executive members had had a Republican Army background. This factor was to become of decisive importance during the last days of the party's existence. Significantly, in accordance with the constitution drawn up by MacBride, clause 9 laid down that 'the national executive shall elect a Standing Committee of ten members, and shall have the power to co-opt an additional five members.' Power was thus guaranteed to the Republican Army and to the party leader. In Clause 12 the Standing Committee is empowered 'to make from time to time such additional rules as they may decide,' and this section goes on, 'the Standing Committee may refuse to ratify a candidate.' Such a candidate for the Dáil in a Galway constituency was rejected on the ground that he had held a commission in the national army.

It is possible that the standing committee encouraged MacBride to drop Noel Hartnett as his political adviser. Their influence for a short period prior to the election, and throughout the election, had been mediated by the presence of Noel Hartnett. They suspected Hartnett of having harassed them while he was a member of the higher ranks of Fianna Fáil. It was said that Hartnett was closely associated with Jim Ryan, an influential Fianna Fáil minister, thought to have been connected with the Special Branch and to have used Stephen Hayes, Chief of Staff of the IRA, as a police informer. Hartnett's effective disappearance from the Clann na Poblachta circle of power was inevitable at the end of his usefulness as Director of Elections.

It is generally accepted that a campaign director, following a general election, has some right to recognition by the party leader. Even if this were not so, Hartnett was one of the very few within Clann na Poblachta at that time who had had any experience of representative democracy. Yet MacBride failed to nominate him as his party spokesman in the Senate, a post in his gift; instead he nominated Denis Ireland, from Belfast, who, while a thoroughly worthy person with hardly any republican credentials, was not in any way experienced in parliamentary politics. It was not easy to see how he might make worthwhile contributions to the bread and butter politics of the Oireachtas, let alone further the destinies of Clann na Poblachta. This choice demonstrated clearly MacBride's political priorities. A former Captain in the Royal Irish Fusiliers, Ireland was ostensibly promoted to the Senate post 'as the symbolic union of orange and green'. The true reason later became apparent.

Hartnett was deeply hurt by MacBride's failure to appoint him to the Senate, yet this was not as hurtful as the loss of MacBride's trust in him. In spite of his considerable intellectual and academic talents, Hartnett needed constant reassurance because of dissatisfaction with his own self-image. He had suffered the emotional loss of his relationship with de Valera and with Fianna Fáil; he had been publicly insulted by them. MacBride was now clearly anxious to sever their newly-formed close relationship. What was especially hurtful was the publicity with which this break occurred. Hartnett was shocked that as a shrewd and experienced political figure, he should now be summarily discarded by MacBride, whom he considered to be a political beginner.

There was a spontaneous feeling of incredulity among the Clann na Poblachta former 'republicans' at Seán MacBride's decision to join in coalition with Fine Gael. They were bewildered by the unexpectedness of this decision. I was to hear one of them describe General Mulcahy as a 'bloody murderer.' Following the announcement of the proposed coalition, it was rumoured that there was an 'army'-inspired plot to kidnap myself and Seán MacBride and so prevent the formation of a Fine Gael coalition. As always in the end, MacBride mesmerised them into consent. It was a measure of their confusion that we were subsequently abused and threatened by these same men for having wrecked the coalition.

In the talks leading to the coalition my own Director of Elections, George Lawlor, gave an ultimatum to Sean MacBride that we would not tolerate the leader of Fine Gael, General Mulcahy, as Taoiseach. After an interval, MacBride assured him that should there be a coalition John Costello, whose hands were clean of any blood-letting, would replace Mulcahy as Taoiseach. Another contender, I understand, was Sir John Esmonde, rejected because of his knighthood. Unselfishly, Mulcahy decided to stand down to facilitate the formation of the coalition, which brought together Fine Gael (31 seats), Labour (14), Clann na Poblachta (10), Clann na Talmhan (7) and National Labour (5).

From now on, after sixteen years of unchallenged political power, Fianna Fáil would face a succession of similar multiparty coalitions. Never again were they to enjoy their former sovereign authority as the party 'born to rule.' To some extent de Valera could blame his unaccustomed sojourn on the opposition benches on his decision to sack Hartnett from Radio Éireann.

It was soon obvious that Seán MacBride had fallen in love with the trappings and aura of politics, and, above all, of

Cabinet office. With egocentric optimism, he believed that he could outwit all the other political leaders in that Cabinet. On one occasion he was speaking to Hartnett and myself about the diamond-hard Paddy McGilligan, easily the brightest intellectual in the coalition Cabinet. Airily MacBride claimed that 'with a little work, McGilligan was educable.' Of all the men in the Cabinet, McGilligan was easily the one man who under no circumstances would have gone our way.

From the moment he assumed leadership of the ten deputies after the election, MacBride's policies were hard to rationalise. It has been said that he appointed me to Health instead of Con Lehane, the obvious choice, since in his opinion, I was an unknown nonentity appointed to an unimportant department. Con, a well-known solicitor, a rugged, opinionated republican, and well-liked, might have questioned the doubtful compromises to be made on republican issues in a Fine Gael coalition. There is also the possibility that the promise given by Hartnett to Harry Kennedy that the party would introduce an efficient TB service had had some influence.

Even to a seasoned experienced politician, the problems of coalition government are formidable. A succession of minority party leaders during the last forty years has failed to reconcile their membership of a coalition with their responsibilities to their own electorate. MacBride's problem was that he did not even appreciate the size of the dilemma. The Fine Gael leadership never fully trusted him, even though he believed he had captivated and out-foxed them. It is a grim statistic that of the five parties that formed the first coalition three, Clann na Talmhan, Clann na Poblachta, and National Labour, have not been heard of since and a fourth, Connolly's Labour Party, has declined continuously and no longer matters as a serious political entity.

Throughout the 1948 election, and especially after Seán MacEntee's revealing and unrefuted attack on MacBride, there was a feeling among some of us that we were working with people with whom we had little in common. Those of us who were non-army accepted the proposed coalition with Fine Gael because we had entered public life in hopes that we would see the end of the damaging and meaningless political alignments of the civil war. The proposed coalition would end the monopoly of office of Fianna Fáil. Since there was no precedent from which we could gain experience or warning of the possible insoluble contradictions in a coalition, we welcomed the innovation, with its possibility of breakthrough to conventional European-style left-right politics.

As it later transpired, the ex-IRA group, led by Seán MacBride particularly on the issue of the primacy of the Catholic Church over parliament, had no serious policy differences with Fine Gael. As Mr de Valera was to show later, neither had he nor his party.

I was powerfully motivated by my hope that we might make progress on general health needs in our hospitals, and especially to curb tuberculosis. In a discussion before the formation of the Cabinet about possible ideological conflicts with Fine Gael, as I even then envisaged them, Seán MacBride and I made a pact designed, in effect, to achieve limited objectives. This was certainly my understanding of it. MacBride went on to summarise it succinctly: 'When your health service objectives are fulfilled, tuberculosis controlled, your hospital buildings that high, Noël, we will go to the country, and ask for an increased mandate.'

With a mixture of innocence and naïveté I accepted this assurance. A little thought, and more of the scepticism which I later developed about such promises, would have shown me that whatever about Seán MacBride's good faith and the sincerity with which it was offered, such an assurance would cut no ice with his ex-IRA comrades. Had he indeed gone back to tell them that since I had now achieved our main objectives in the Department of Health, he intended to call an election for a larger mandate, his comrades would have been astounded.

In the negotiations leading to the formation of the coalition, an interesting piece of black propaganda appeared in de Valera's *Irish Press*. The paper issued a list of probable ministerial candidates for office were a Labour-Fine Gael coalition to be formed. The black propaganda element was the inclusion in the list of young Jim Larkin as Minister for Education. Larkin, many years previously, had returned to Dublin following a spell at universities and colleges in Moscow, and had stood for election as a member of the Communist Party. He backed his election campaign by putting out lurid anti-Catholic propaganda and called for the virtual suppression of the power of the church as the influential institution it then was in Irish

public life. Not surprisingly he was defeated. Having become a
respected member of the Labour Party, Larkin was elected to a
Dublin constituency in the 1948 election. What the writer of the
Irish Press article well knew was that the proposal of Larkin as
Minister for Education would almost certainly scupper any possibility of the formation of a coalition government. A Communist
in the Department of Education, even today, is unthinkable.
That fine liberal politician, Owen Sheehy Skeffington, had been
expelled from the Labour Party merely for being a liberal.

To give some idea about the attitudes to Communism at that
time, even in Labour circles, I recall asking Jim Everett, leader
of the National Labour Party, how it was that the very
experienced, widely acknowledged and talented Larkin had not
been nominated by William Norton or elected by the party for a
Cabinet post, even the most innocuous. Everett's reply was brief
and instructive. There was no possibility of Larkin being
brought into Cabinet because of his Communist background: 'If
Larkin politically ever shows the whites of his eyes, we'll blow
the top of his head off.'

With a mixture of bewilderment, unbelief, and delight at my
new access to power and authority from a subordinate medical
post in an obscure small country sanatorium, I took over the
Department of Health determined to revolutionise the quality
of the health service. In a small way we were to show just how
much could be gained through the existing state bureaucracy, in
spite of its inherent inefficiency and defects.

Easily the most important immediate need was the elimination of tuberculosis. We had promised to do this, if given
power by the people. The response to my call for help from the
much maligned 'intransigent' civil servant bureaucrats began
my own re-education about the true potential of our civil
service. There was no need for a Commission of Inquiry into
what needed to be done. Tuberculosis control had been a special
study of mine since I had qualified as a doctor.

The Department of Health was transformed into a battle
headquarters. Since I had considered the need for an efficient
tuberculosis service for many years a clear plan of action was
quickly outlined. The first essential was the limitation of the

disease by the isolation of existing known possible sources of infection. The nearly pandemic nature of the disease stemmed from the failure to establish a disease control organisation in which diagnosis, followed by isolation of the index case, was the most immediate need. Denmark, a small country, had already shown what could be done simply by efficient diagnostic isolation and treatment facilities. They had succeeded in containing the disease as a first step towards its control, long before the introduction of the miracle anti-tuberculosis drugs.

Although we were fully engaged in the anti-tuberculosis drive, we also established a badly-needed diagnostic and cancer hospital treatment service based on an entirely new, superbly equipped hospital, built on a new site on the outskirts of the city. This became known as St Luke's Cancer Hospital. A group of provincial centres was also established. These proposals had been recommended by the Cancer Council which we had established in April 1948, some two months after taking up office. We also set out to build anew or reconstruct some seven thousand hospital beds all over Ireland. We reconstructed and re-quipped our county homes. We launched a new 'clean food' code, backed with a press, radio and film campaign directed to educate the public in methods of hygienic food preparation, sale and usage.

We established new regional hospitals in Cork, Limerick, and Galway in addition to St Vincent's Hospital, Crumlin Childrens' Hospital, St Loman's in Dublin, Ardkeen in Waterford, County Hospital in Manorhamilton, Kilkreene Hospital in Kilkenny, Gurranebraher Hospital in Cork, Foynes Children's Hostel. There were St Mary's Hospital in the Phoenix Park, the James Connolly Memorial Hospital, the St James's Municipal Hospital in Dublin and many more. We established a new National Rehabilitation Organisation in Dublin; it is now a great multi-million pound national institution. There was a BCG inoculation service, a diphtheria vaccination scheme, a mass radiography scheme.

Early in my association with Seán MacBride, he, Noel Hartnett and I were dining in the Bailey Restaurant. Seán was called away urgently to the telephone to hear that his wife Kit had been taken into Jervis Street Hospital, dangerously ill. Kit desperately needed a blood transfusion, yet Ireland did not have a national blood transfusion service.

It was late on a Saturday evening. The speediest and safest way in which we could be sure of getting the needed blood was for each of us to join members of the hospital staff in scouring the streets of Dublin for a member of the defence forces. The pubs were the most obvious starting point and for obvious reasons not the most desirable. Meanwhile the staff had set about calling up the various army barracks for assistance. It was the practice for soldiers to carry a disc on which was stamped their blood group. Eventually we found a hapless soldier, who appeared to be quite sober, and Kit's life was saved, following a transfusion and treatment.

Now I was in a position to set up the National Blood Transfusion Organisation with the job of acquiring premises and mobilising equipment, staff and an administrative organisation throughout the whole country to provide what became one of the finest blood transfusion services in the world. Though I made valiant attempts to establish the headquarters for the blood transfusion service in the centre of Ireland, I was fascinated by the civil service ingenuity with which it was not found possible to find a suitable centre outside Dublin.

Our new young department was faced with truly astonishing demands on its dedication, its ingenuity, its technical and professional skills in coping with this gargantuan step towards a worthwhile high-level health service for our people, and it performed magnificently.

We commandeered Colaiste Mobhi, a joint army barracks-Church of Ireland Teacher Training College in the Phoenix Park. The army was transferred to alternative army accommodation down the country. That was simple to achieve, soldiers being accustomed to being 'ordered around.' Persuading the teachers to vacate their institution was somewhat more difficult. In the end, they accepted alternative accommodation in a former castle, once the Shanganagh Hotel, set in a considerable acreage of land on the Bray Road. Colaiste Mobhi, lavishly reconstructed, became the magnificent St Mary's Hospital.

With the agreement of the local authority, we acquired temporarily a new general hospital in Mallow, Co Cork, as yet unopened. We requisitioned as a TB sanatorium a mental hospital just opened as such in Castlereagh, Co Roscommon. We mobilised a number of small fever hospitals, which because of the decline in infectious fevers were no longer used, as well as a number of underused district hospitals, and reconditioned a number of workhouse ancillary hospital accommodation beds. We erected dozens of surplus army Nissen huts as extensions to existing sanatoria facilities. Anywhere and everywhere that emergency facilities could be mobilised, we sought help. In both local and state authorities, everyone worked to end a great national tragedy.

The immediacy and spontaneity of the response, its versatility, originality, and creativity, make it hard for me to understand the adverse criticisms so frequently made about the rigidity and lack of imaginative planning of the civil service and the state bodies. Would that our politicians, industrialists and farmers had the dynamic qualities of many of our state services as shown at that time, both at local and central level. Is this not simply another example of the civil servant taking the blame for the less than competent politician, businessman and farmer?

Contracts for reconstruction of old buildings were on the risky but speedier 'time and material' basis. Working all through the night builders did not on the whole abuse its possibilities for excessive profits. Trade unionists were happy to help. In answer to our advertisement for a surgeon to organise a new national thoracic surgical service, Mr Maurice Hickey strolled into my rooms in the Department of Health, a truly refreshing and exciting personality, well over six feet tall. All his energies were to be preserved for the job ahead of him; a chauffeured car was put at his disposal. We guaranteed all the help he needed, at local authority level and at central government level. He need only ask. Every facility was given to him to set up his regional operating theatre requirements all over Ireland. Only a man of his total dedication, limitless energy and personal charm could have taken on so successfully the outrageous demands made on him by us. Mr Hickey was to be on the road continuously when not in the operating theatre; his whole-hearted response to the challenge of the time epitomised the behaviour of all involved in our campaign.

Because major construction work had ceased during the war years and with the general inertia of Fianna Fáil in the post-war years, there was an enormous backlog of work. Departmental pigeonholes were full of promises to build hospitals and health clinics, extending as far back as the mid-twenties. Because of the low priority given to health matters by Fianna Fáil and indeed by all our native governments, few had been started by 1948. It was fortunate that while hospital building activity had stopped during the war, the planning of hospitals and clinics through the country had gone ahead. Virtually every local authority in Ireland seemed to be in need of some health facility, and to have its new hospital plan. Our first health estimate showed that 135 proposals for new hospitals, and repair to existing ones, were under review, the cost of which was estimated to be £27 million.

During the laying of the foundation stone for Galway Merlin Park Regional Hospital, a Fianna Fáil deputy, Mark Killilea, a member of the opposition who had been generously helpful to me on a number of occasions, asked me in a guileless way: 'What are you at? We used to make great mileage out of simply promising hospitals coming up to an election, and then forgetting about them. We would keep the hospitals until the next election. What will you do when you have built all these places?'

Deputy Killilea was simply following a pattern set for him by his leaders on all sides in politics and in public life in Ireland. 'We'll drain the Shannon, restore the language and end partition' (Eamon de Valera and Brian Lenihan): 'We'll provide a hundred thousand new jobs' (Seán Lemass); 'We'll throw all the rocks of Connemara into the sea' (James Dillon); 'We'll drown the British in eggs' (James Dillon); 'We'll twist John Bull's tail' (Seán T. O'Kelly); 'We've taken the gun out of politics' (John Costello). Brendan Corish, when Labour leader, promised 'Socialism in the seventies'. There is even Dr FitzGerald's recent liberal 'crusade' for a pluralist Ireland, not to mention his promise of some years ago: 'I've done my sums and the cost of living should not rise by more than five, or at the most six, percent when we join the EEC.'

All the regional sanatoria, the James Connolly in Dublin, Merlin Park in Galway, Sarsfield Court in Cork, were designed in the architectural section of the Department of Health under our imaginative, infinitely patient and talented New Zealand architect Norman White and his staff. These great buildings, still serving the public, stand today as monuments to their high standard of workmanship, design and finish. Who says that a state department cannot be creative, imaginative, and practical? Our massive hospital building programme was to lead to one of the very few occasions in which the Republic of Ireland was paid the highest of accolades. Shortly after the completion of the building programme in the late 1950s an international jury of experts voted Ireland, with Sweden, as 'having the most advanced and finest hospital system in the world.' This rare honour was barely referred to or commented on in the national press or radio. It must be assumed that this collective silence was an act of deliberate censorship, required because the 'discredited' former Minister for Health was now a forgotten man on the backbenches.

Our total programme entailed a proposed expenditure of £30 million. We planned to replace all existing hospital beds, or otherwise upgrade the standard of accommodation in existing hospitals throughout the country. The programme amounted to a total of over 7,000 new hospital beds.

Luckily, the finance needed to build so many new hospitals was available from the Hospital Sweep funds. Unlike the rest of my Cabinet colleagues, as Minister for Health I had absolute personal control over these funds, under the Hospital Sweeps Acts. There was none of what James Dillon, Minister for Agriculture, ruefully complained of as 'treasury control' over spending. I enjoyed the added advantage that all my predecessors had followed the same miserly spending on hospital building work. They spent only the income from the interest on the accumulated capital invested from successive sweeps. This amounted to a mere £100,000, but I needed millions. The £100,000 annually could not possibly build badly-needed hospitals all over Ireland. We decided to alter that policy radically, and proceeded to liquidate all the available assets in the Sweep funds invested. When we costed the various projects, it became obvious that we would still not have sufficient funds to meet our needs, so I decided further to pre-empt the income expected from the fund during the following seven-year period. This permitted us to carry on the building of all the hospitals, sanatoria, and clinics which were needed. They could be paid for as the projects matured from projected incomes of future sweepstakes. The Department of Health quickly established the seriousness of its intent to provide eight to ten thousand beds in eight to ten years, a massive building programme unequalled before or since.

This radical departure from former spending in the Department of Health must have tested the patience of my departmental secretary, Paddy Kennedy. Our early days together were turbulent. I was the youngest minister ever to have been appointed to a new ministry on his first day in parliament. To the apprehensive Mr Kennedy I must have appeared to be a woefully inexperienced person. I had been appointed to the post of Minister for Health, and at the same time I was a doctor, in conflict with the accepted convention of parliamentary politics; it is preferred that the political head of a department should not himself be involved in the speciality controlled by that department.

Further to Mr Kennedy's worries, I had no administrative experience. I had worked as a medical officer in sanatoria in England and in Ireland. A technocrat I might be, but without any serious administrative experience. Not surprisingly, Mr Kennedy, a mature and experienced civil servant who at one time had worked with Mr de Valera, felt apprehensive about working with his new Minister for Health. It is probably true to say that my innocence of all that was involved was in many ways a useful cushion between myself and my intimidating new responsibilities.

I set out with many of the layman's misconceptions about a politician's life, and what it entailed. With the end of the cheers, flashbulbs, photos and congratulations, an early assessment showed that there was a price to be paid.

The serious-minded Cabinet minister must work very hard. He is a departmental head and attends twice-weekly Cabinet meetings. He must meet hundreds of citizens, individually or collectively, who wish to consult him. He undergoes the critical and trying ordeal of parliamentary work, including parliamentary questions. As a working politician, he must keep in touch with his political base in his own constituency. Then there are his family and his children. Because of his frequent absences, they grow up with all the disadvantages of a one-parent family; family life becomes impossible.

It was my custom to leave a chocolate biscuit under the pillow of each of our daughters when I returned late each night. Frequently, because of school on their part, or my early departure, I

My father and mother in their marriage portrait: 'an elegant pair of happy young innocents eager for the years ahead together'.

From left: Martha, Eileen, myself, Kitty, Una and Jody with my father who was to die shortly afterwards, a victim of tuberculosis.

Beaumont First XV Rugby Team 1933-34. I was a Captain of the school and here am seated on the extreme left.

Again seated on the left — now as house physician at Dr Steeven's Hospital in 1942.

As Minister for Health — a
formal portrait taken in 1948.

With Phyllis, three years later in 1951.

The Republic is declared at a formal ceremony outside the GPO in 1949. Lieut General MacNeill salutes. Patrick McGilligan stands to my right, William Norton, John A. Costello and Daniel Morrissey to my left.

The Cabinet proceeds to the declaration ceremony. I never favoured the top hats of my colleagues.

might not see them throughout the whole of that day, or possibly even during that week. The chocolate biscuit was no substitute for a conscientious parent, nor was their mother's reassurance that 'Noelie is out building hospitals for sick people'. With a predictable five-day week at Newcastle, we had forged a timetable within which I could play my role as medical officer, husband and father. That harmonious interplay of a stable two-parent home, so important in the maturation process of our two daughters Ruth (born in 1945) and Susan (born in 1949), came to an abrupt end.

It was considered politically wise, that, as Minister for Health, I should vacate the small lodge in which we lived at the hospital. Thereafter, during my three-year period as Minister, we were to change our rented homes five times. Ruth and Susan's hitherto sheltered life was irreparably shattered. There were enormous mental and physical demands on my wife, forced to organise these periodic moves on her own. For the children, there were no more seaside visits, walks and talks in the woods, picnics, swimming in the Wicklow streams. Overnight, their father had gone, had disappeared. In this aspect of their lives all politicians make considerable unrecognised sacrifices for the sake of the public, frequently at the expense of their own families.

There were also financial implications. At that time, ministerial salaries were absurdly inadequate, based on the old convention of British parliamentary government when politicians were propertied gentlemen with private means. A minister was paid less than his departmental secretary. Added to this was the peculiar dispensation imposed on a Clann na Poblachta minister, because of MacBride's belief that a minister should contribute the ministerial part of his salary to party funds. It was a measure of his ignorance of the even greater financial and social demands on a minister over those of a deputy, heavy though these are. Since I had leave of absence from my hospital work, we were totally dependent on my Dáil salary. Far from being highly paid it was during my period as minister that, as a family, we contracted unavoidable debts from which we were freed only twenty years later, when deputies and ministers were properly paid.

It was believed that there had been widespread abuse of

ministerial cars by our predecessors; Paddy Smith was said to have brought his calves to the fair for sale in his ministerial car. A Clann na Poblachta minister was expected to use his ministerial car exclusively for government business. This entailed greatly increased physical and financial demands on us. It was even further increased because we had the whole country to cover and there were only two of us. I was constantly on the road, driving myself to the four corners of Ireland for party political reasons.

I recall a long, dangerous and stressful drive in the unreliable open car we then owned, all the way from Dublin to the top-most point of Donegal. The phrase used by local party workers, 'over the Gweebarra Bridge' is still engraved on my heart. Our journey was made in order to fight the Neil Blaney by-election, caused by the death of his father. After a hard weekend of chapel gate meetings, we travelled back from Donegal to Dublin. There was snow on the Curlew Mountains. Because I was the only driver who could see at all where we were going, with the windscreen lying flat on the car bonnet, I was chosen to lead the way home during the worst part of the cold, wet, wintry night of wind, rain and fog. Even if I did not suffer the dangerous threat of tuberculosis, how could a minister carry on his difficult job throughout the following week after a weekend of such activity?

Becoming and having been a minister can distort the personality of the man or woman who is unwary. For instance, beware of becoming pompous and vain; it does happen. Ministerial protocol demands, and I never failed to find it embarrassing, that a senior civil servant, such as Mr Kennedy, would feel bound to stand by my side, as I signed important law-enforcing documents which would alter the lives of our fellow citizens. Mr Kennedy's job was merely to blot my signature. This distinguished civil servant, it appears, must address me neither as 'Mr', 'Deputy', 'Doctor,' or even the democratic 'Noël', but only as 'Minister'. The word was hissed out with the kind of reverence which the Chinese reserve for their aged.

Happily for me, there were antidotes to this heady sense of delirious intoxication. Other than the damaged ego that follows return to one's usually commonplace civilian ordinariness, the ill effect rarely survived the experience. Yet, sure that within myself I had not changed in any way, I wondered at the servile transformation of so many, when it was they who had honoured me. Does society unconsciously promote such pomposity and inflated self importance among a chosen few, so that in time, whimsically, humpty-dumpty-like it may destroy it?

There is an incongruous aid to this process of exclusivism, the mean and unimaginative substitute republican 'magic' devised to replace that of the old British raj. It takes the form of a purpose-less, to me at any rate, 'laying on of hands' ritual ar Áras an Uachtarán. In spite of our new republican status, in the absence of a sovereign monarch our seals of office were formally bestowed on us by the President. Having been studied by each of us for a matter of seconds, the seals were then demanded back by the President, Seán T. O'Kelly. Even an all-Ireland finalist gets a permanent memento of his momentary glory!

I had never even been to see parliament in action. A few days before the opening of the Dáil it fell to the Deputy Secretary, Paddy Murray, to bring me over to Leinster House and, in the privacy of the empty Dáil chamber, explain briefly parliamentary procedures. 'This is where the government sits, over here the opposition . . . Here sits the Ceann Comhairle. This is where the journalists sit . . . Your civil servants will sit here, so as to be of help to you.' In a brief half-hour visit, I had to absorb the complex protocol of parliamentary debate that later I came to know so well.

Initially, the most worrying aspect of my job as Minister was Question Time. With the exception of the incorrigible Sean MacEntee, deputies of all parties showed an unusual restraint in deference to my newness to the job. For MacEntee, it was war to the death from the beginning. On one occasion a question was mischievously submitted to me in Irish by a Gaelic-speaking deputy, Gerald Bartley from Connemara. Bartley well knew that because of my mainly English education I had no Irish. (Mr Kennedy had to translate even the two words 'Aire Sláinte' on the first occasion I signed a legal document for him as Minister for Health.) The Fianna Fáil party wished to establish Mr MacEntee's thesis that I was a 'piece of flotsam', and an uncaring anglophile West Briton.

I decided to take a risk. Mr Kennedy, a fluent Gaelic speaker, translated the parliamentary question for me into English and then translated my reply into Irish. He kindly tutored me in the phonetic version of the reply. On the day, miserable with fear, I presented myself in the Dáil Chamber. Having replied to a number of questions in English, difficult enough in themselves, I came to Gerald Bartley's question in Irish. Collecting whatever nerve is conjured up by us on these occasions I spoke my reply in phonetic Irish to a silent and surprised Dáil chamber. I then sat down. To his credit and my intense relief Bartley made no attempt to show up my ignorance. He asked no supplementaries.

In deference to the fact that a good number of our people at that time spoke Irish, and as a courtesy to them should they wish to speak to me in that form, I set out to learn the language. Here I was fortunate to have the willing help of Seosaph O'Cadhain from Connemara. Seosaph attended three days a week at the Department of Health or at any convenient venue to both of us, sometimes at his home in Crumlin. I spent whatever free weekends I had in Connemara with him. There I met another distinguished Gaelic scholar, Seán O'Conghaile of Cnoc. During my many weekends in Connemara, and later on all our family vacations there, we lived with Seán and his hospitable wife Máire. Not alone did I learn to speak the language but, since Seán's father was still living, I was privileged to encounter the unique ambience of our ancient ethos and culture. Lamentably this culture has now become virtually extinguished.

To speak the language became one of my most powerful private ambitions. It was then that with my wife Phyllis and our two daughters I came to know Connemara and its people. We have made it our chosen home before anywhere else we know. It is sad that as a nation we have abandoned hope that our people will now ever speak their own language. The language revival was bound up with national prosperity. An intelligent parent, at least one out of three of whose children must emigrate to England, could not be unduly concerned about learning a language which for them would become an unspoken language in the country of their adoption.

One of my first acts as Minister for Health was to remove the special preference for Irish speakers in medical appointments outside the Gaeltacht areas. However, I believe that we were the first government department invariably to print our advertisements, educational and information literature bilingually. We were the first government department to make bilingual educational films for schools and other interested groups. Our booklets and leaflets were invariably bilingual. Finally, I was proud to be awarded the Fáinne by Seosaph O'Cadhain.

I entered the department convinced that the civil service would set out to control its Minister. To some extent this was true, and for sound reasons. There was at that time a distinct difference between the education level of the permanent civil servant and the average working politician. The civil service head of a government department must have proved himself as a literate and skilled administrator. Since there was little or no industrial outlet, the only significant opportunity for the average citizen in the 'forties who wished to be an influential administrator was the civil service. Admission by examination was competitive. Progress thereafter was dependent on merit. Yet there was at least one of our Cabinet colleagues who could only read English with difficulty. Consider the dangers faced by the civil servant head of a government department whose political superior might have literacy problems. Add to this the fact that there was at least one junior minister who, because of his carefree attitude to government contracts, had his access to outside telephone conversations curtailed.

The civil service dealt with such a minister by giving him a 'free run' where his constituency was concerned. 'Priority' was given for the minister's local political needs, in the hope that thereby his activities could be curtailed.

I did not understand, as I later came to, the importance of the practice whereby the minister ideally should discuss all matters of serious consequence with his departmental secretary, or his deputy. I resented and feared the possibility of being 'managed' and took an early precaution to ensure that my will was to be the final authority. A senior member of my staff had been heard on the telephone advising the Department of Finance that they should ignore a proposal put to them from my department, saying, 'It is one of the minister's hare-brained schemes.' On hearing of this, I called for my departmental secretary and told him what had been said. Giving him the name of the civil servant, I instructed Mr Kennedy that the individual must cease working in my department. He was transferred immediately to another department. This replacement of a senior civil servant made it clear to everyone that, right or not, I knew my own mind, and I was in complete charge of the department from there on.

The public could not do more for its politicians. Every branch of expert specialist knowledge in administration is made available to their chosen minister, if he or she is prepared and competent to use it. Those three years working in the Department of Health, among civil servants led by Mr Kennedy and Mr Murray were the most educative, satisfying, and memorable years of my working life. I came to understand how unjust are charges commonly heard about the civil service, accused of using red tape, delay, prevarication, or making reactionary penny-pinching decisions. Definitive decisions may be taken only in accordance with the law as passed by the people's elected representatives acting with the authority of the Oireachtas and government. The fact is, and I certainly showed it in my own department, as did Lemass, that if it is made clear that all decisions must be made in accordance with clear policy directives set out by the political head of the department, an efficient departmental machine can accomplish much. Within these clear limits, I encouraged the civil servants to use their own judgement and make their own decisions. I told them that I would stand over their decisions, but only in the context of my departmental policies and not otherwise. It is the elected representative who must be the final authority. It is the elected representative whose right it is, on behalf of the public, to make the decisions, even bad ones and wrong ones. All politicians are responsible and, more important, are answerable to the electorate for our decisions. We benefit in repeated re-election. Equally we should be made to pay for the consequences of unjust or incorrect decisions made by us in office. The regrettable fact is that, either through political incompetence or inadequacies, at times there are ministers in charge of government departments who are temperamentally or educationally unfitted for office.

I believed that a minister must maintain close and continual contact with his department's work as it progressed, and for this reason I instituted a practice, which I understand had not hitherto been used, to establish that contact at weekly intervals would be made between myself and my senior civil servants. I instructed my department secretary to mobilise all the professional and technical department heads to prepare a detailed schedule, listing clearly the important component decisions involved from initiation to completion in the implementation of hospital, sanatoria, and clinic building projects — the sketch plans, the outline drawings, the working drawings, the electrical and plumbing quantities, and suchlike matters. It was arranged that a large wall-chart be erected in my office. On this chart was a colourful representation of the position in regard to every stage of every hospital, sanatorium or clinic in our vast nation-wide building project. I could tell at a glance the exact position in relation to every project within the scope of our departmental building programme. Visiting deputies or councillors could also be kept informed about the progress of their own special project.

Further, I instructed my personal secretary that each Monday forenoon be kept free of engagements so that, together with the staff involved, I should examine the precise state each week of our building programme. This procedure was carried through each week, all relevant staff being present to provide in detail and in person explanations for delays, failure to make decisions, or reasons for wrong decisions made on current projects. These delays in progress had to be defended or justified by my staff, from week to week. As their minister, I too was subjected to that same discipline. This procedure had the further advantage that as minister I came to know and have direct access to each one of my staff, which gave me a chance to assess their capabilities and work capacities. In turn, the civil service staff had the advantage of getting to know me and my ideas. Such continuous contact between us, I believe, led to the creation of an understanding rapport of mutual trust and efficiency.

The civil service staff at the Department of Health slowly appeared to gain in self-confidence and efficiency, enjoying a clear vision of their role and their future function. Above all, we had financial resources at our disposal. Indeed our department assumed such a powerful dynamic that we were to find ourselves in trouble with other government departments. During the Korean War in the 1950s, in anticipation of shortages, departments were advised to stock up with essential goods. Shortly after this advice was given Dan Morrissey, Minister for Industry and Commerce, who was woefully unfitted for such a complex department of state, complained bitterly of the fact that when his departmental officials had gone to Britain to lay claim to our national building needs, they were told that Ireland had already received its quota. It transpired that civil servants in the Department of Health had already moved in before any other department and had a lien of all available stocks for the nation's enormous hospital and housing building programme.

Our programme had immediate results. By July 1950, 2,000 beds had been provided for TB patients, bringing the total up to 5,500. The tuberculosis death rate dropped dramatically from 123 per 100,000 in 1947 to 73 per 100,000 in 1951.

8

Gathering Clouds

FOR THE first time in Ireland, Cabinet ministers were having to work within a coalition of differing political viewpoints. There was much hostility between the individual Fine Gael ministers, though it dissolved when faced with outside opposition in the Cabinet. James Dillon, who was notoriously wordy and could run everyone's department except his own, appeared to delight in tormenting the hapless Dan Morrissey over his clear inability to cope with any of the complex problems of the Department of Industry and Commerce. Morrissey did not appear to understand his briefs, and was rarely able to explain them fully to us; I have seen him in tears after a ruthless interrogation, mixed with ridicule, by Dillon. Quite justifiably, Dillon demonstrated Morrissey's incompetence; the insensitive methods used, however, were not justified. The replacement of the clear-minded Lemass, who for so long had run this department, by the blundering and inept Morrissey must have been a shocking experience for the civil servants.

Dick Mulcahy, Minister for Education and one time leader of Fine Gael, who had selflessly yielded his right to become Taoiseach to John Costello, was also treated with a mixture of levity and contempt by his party colleagues. This was not completely surprising because like Morrissey, Mulcahy appeared unable to articulate his simplest ideas or clarify to us his departmental needs. Unlike Morrissey, however, and unhappily for most of us, in Cabinet Mulcahy showed complete aplomb. He had an unlimited capacity to verbalise, as distinct from articulate, his needs. He spoke through the voluminous, resonating sound chamber made by his parrot's beak-shaped nose. Words tumbled out, soft, shapeless, indistinct. He did not trouble to assemble a sequence of ideas.

There was no sense, no intelligible form to his sentences; he did not bother with paragraphs, full stops or commas. Deeply and impenetrably buried in the centre of all this tormented English was whatever happened to be the simple needs of his department. With the non-writing end of his pencil, Mulcahy drew a succession of strange and elaborate hieroglyphics in the air in front of him. These airy movements of a deeply frustrated man were punctuated by incisive stabbing jabs at the air, with the pencil. No doubt he intended to emphasise for us points he wished to make, but was unable to articulate. The invariable effect of the intervention by Mulcahy was to transform the Cabinet into a collection of openly chattering individuals, or small private cabals, completely ignoring him. They joined one another in noisy discussions, sometimes even across the Cabinet table. The more polite would appear to recall some problem for which their personal attention was urgently needed in their department. Apologising to the Taoiseach, and muttering importantly to themselves, they would slink slowly out of the room and away. Quite rapidly, the Cabinet would disintegrate temporarily. Even the ever-attentive and polite mind of Costello would seem to wander. I felt so shamed by the ill-mannered behaviour of his colleagues and their obvious disinclination to try to decipher what Mulcahy was trying to say that, out of embarrassed pity, I recall attempting hopelessly to hold an interested conversation with him.

Early on I was confronted with the cavalier indifference to 'merit' of my Cabinet colleagues when deciding qualifications for appointments. Seán MacEoin had submitted a list of candidates with their qualifications for a post in his jurisdiction in Co Clare. I noted that the man appointed had graduated from his national school at twelve or thirteen years of age; he had no visible qualification, other than his friendship with MacEoin or his probable membership of Fine Gael. I protested that this was a political appointment and 'Fine Gael jobbery' because of the demonstrably superior qualifications of each of the other candidates. My colleagues were shocked by my 'immoderate' language. Unperturbed, MacEoin smilingly replied, 'That's not a bad way to make an appointment Noël!' I continued to protest that despite the principle of collective Cabinet responsibility, I would not justify this Fine Gael 'fix'. Either they must cease to advertise posts as being vacant, or have the courage to make blatantly political appointments and take the consequences. Otherwise, I suggested, we should establish a proper appointment system. The latter proposal was finally agreed.

During Cabinet meetings I was initially overawed, as the youngest Cabinet minister surrounded by a number of men who had helped to make our history. I was treated with patience and courtesy all through my period of office until the very end, during the mother and child crisis, but I was rarely listened to over-seriously. My departmental work appeared to me to be all-important; I begrudged the time I spent away from it, even to attend Cabinet meetings. I had become completely single-minded about the use of my time. At all costs, it must be used to the optimum effect in winning my objective of a better health service. I soon formed the conclusion that the important decisions which we debated in Cabinet had already been determined elsewhere. Quite reasonably, Seán MacBride was accepted by my colleagues as the senior spokesman of the two of us. In my opinion it hardly mattered whether I attended meetings or not. MacBride did not discuss Cabinet business in any detail with me, prior to Cabinet meetings, nor did he ask for my opinions. My sense of not being needed became strong. It was his custom simply to tell me the position which he intended to take up, and, understandably, I supported him. In the end, the rest of the Cabinet came to treat both of us with equal indifference; when they finally got MacBride's 'measure' they ceased to care much about the opinions of either of us.

The Minister for Health was held to be apolitical in the narrow sense of that word. In the early days and right up until the latter end of 1950, Seán MacBride would appoint me to deputise for him. As acting Minister for External Affairs, I received a number of notable statesmen, of whom one was Pandit Nehru, on a visit to Dublin following negotiations in London. India had been liberated relatively bloodlessly by Mahatma Gandhi, Nehru and their comrades, a tribute to the courageous use of peaceful means. I asked Nehru, conscious of our own civil war on much the same issue, if he would not find himself in trouble on his return to India for remaining within the British Commonwealth. Unlike our political leaders, Nehru recognised the virtues of an association of co-equal sovereign nations with common objectives. He expected his colleagues to share his own mature outlook.

Both Seán MacBride and Noel Hartnett were always available to me for advice when I needed to expand my knowledge of public affairs. My great regret was the tragic conflict that was to develop between them. Once it had begun, I found it difficult to believe that Clann na Poblachta could survive.

MacBride wrote lengthy treatises on the many abstruse subjects which attracted him. In his brisk, crisp Northern accent McGilligan, who shared Hartnett's moderate opinions about MacBride as an intellectual and scholar, also dismissed his seeming expertise on economic or financial matters. Nevertheless MacBride worked continuously from early morning until late into the night. He especially enjoyed the diplomatic dinners, tea parties, and soirées which he organised in the Department and which in his absence fell to my lot.

Increasingly during 1950 Seán excluded me as his deputy, as if to ensure that his authentic voice would be heard untrammelled by any 'rehashing' by me. He would scan the cabinet agenda, and on those subjects in which he had a special interest, would submit a treatise to the Taoiseach. In the early days, this memorandum was carefully unfolded and conscientiously read out by the Taoiseach to a politely attentive Cabinet. It was treated with some respect. After a time, they began to notice to my embarrassment that the contents of the memorandum were as novel to me as they were to the rest of them. As the memoranda proliferated, it became obvious that all was not well in Clann na Poblachta; they were now treated with a tolerant amusement, and the epistles filed somewhere.

The most simple illustration of our helplessness in Cabinet was the fact that on a number of occasions both of us argued for clemency for men under sentence of death before the civil courts. The Cabinet was the supreme authority under the President in matters of life and death, and could commute the sentences to life imprisonment. Because of what I had heard about General Mulcahy and the 'seventy-seven', I watched his reaction. In his usual style on such 'simple issues', he was curt, brash and uncomplicated: 'They must hang.' The deeply religious Blowick's comment, in his high-pitched squeak, was, 'Hang them, hang them.' There was no attempt to argue or to rationalise their positions. With their majority they had no need to.

It is important to understand the process by which decisions were arrived at in that coalition government. A Minister who required a Cabinet decision to carry out his ministerial functions would formally submit a written request for permission to act, supported, usually, by documentary justification for such action. Occasionally a request might be agreed to without question, but it was the usual practice for each minister or additional ministers likely to be affected by any decision taken to submit a supporting or a contesting case with documentation.

Such, without doubt, would have been the case were the government to take such an important decision as to decide formally to repeal the External Relations Act, 1936, which maintained the link between Ireland and the Commonwealth. At the time there had been powerful opposition in the Fine Gael party to the repeal of this act, and MacBride and the Clann na Poblachta party had agreed to put the question of repeal 'into abeyance' for the lifetime of the Coalition. Yet to the astonishment of politicians and public alike, on both sides of the Irish Sea, members of the Cabinet read one September morning in 1948 in the *Sunday Independent* that according to the Taoiseach, Mr Costello, speaking at a meeting in Ottawa, we had 'unanimously agreed in Cabinet' to repeal the act. This was not true. This incident and its sequel had serious political and diplomatic consequences for politicians and journalists alike.

The repeal of the External Relations Act had little significance for me. Because of the silly protocol under which 'accreditation' of our foreign diplomats must in the first instance be approved by the British monarch, I was satisfied that it should be repealed. At the same time, I believed in the validity of the case made by de Valera for its retention in part. He claimed that as the last remaining link in common between the North and ourselves, possibly leading to, or facilitating, membership of the Commonwealth, its retention might help reconciliation between both parts of this country. However, it was a subject with which I was not deeply concerned.

With other available ministers, I was called urgently to a

'caucus meeting' of the Cabinet one Sunday afternoon soon after the Taoiseach's return to Dublin following the Ottawa meeting. Costello appeared to be visibly distressed and unhappy. He told us that he had decided to repeal the External Relations Act while attending a formal government dinner in his honour at which the host was Lord Allanbrooke, the Governor General of Canada. Realising that he had no authority from the Cabinet for his decision, he deeply regretted his action and had called this emergency Cabinet meeting to explain and apologise to us for his unconstitutional action. He then went on to offer to resign as Taoiseach.

In the absence of Mr MacBride abroad, and speaking for Clann na Poblachta, I dismissed the suggestion that Costello should resign. We were glad to see the act go. With varying degrees of enthusiasm the members of the Cabinet remaining assured Costello that he must not resign. Seán MacEoin appeared to me to be as pleased as I was that it should go; he was his usual pleasant reassuring self in his attempt to comfort Costello.

When I gave this detailed account on radio in 1976, it was at once dismissed as untrue in a series of letters and statements to the press. I found myself accused by my former ministerial colleagues of lying. All of them shared the same story, that no such meeting had occurred, and that no offer of resignation was submitted by the Taoiseach. The ministers concerned were James Dillon, Dan Morrissey, Seán MacBride and Paddy McGilligan. For a number of years I was compelled to live under the cloud of having told a distasteful lie about Mr Costello. This assault on my integrity was further supported by a letter in the *Sunday Independent*, on 22 January 1984, from Hector Legge, who had been editor of that paper at the time of the repeal of the External Relations Act and had had close associations with the coalition government and MacBride. In an offensive suggestion that I was being consciously dishonest, Hector Legge's letter sought to reinforce the case against me by calling on what he described as a 'distinguished civil servant', now retired, Patrick Lynch. It was my understanding of civil service protocol that senior civil servants do not repeat confidential information for publication in the public press. Mr Lynch had been secretary to the Taoiseach and had travelled with him to Canada, and he now joined the hunt, declaring that no such meeting was ever held.

Labelled as a liar until early in 1984, I was helpless to refute these offensive slanders. My vindication occurred following my review of Ronan Fanning's book *Independent Ireland*, published in 1983. The Cabinet papers for 1948-1951 had become available, and Dr Fanning made puzzled references to the absence of any Cabinet papers relating to the repeal of the External Relations Act, in spite of Costello's claim 'that a unanimous Cabinet decision had been taken.' In the course of my review I reassured Dr Fanning that no Cabinet decision or papers could exist since no formal Cabinet discussions had taken place.

Hector Legge, supported, he claimed, by Paddy Lynch, once again accused me of repeating an untruth. Within days MacBride, who as Minister for External Affairs knew better than most that there could be no such papers and that there had been no 'unanimous decision of the Cabinet', repeated his charge in the *Sunday Independent*, 1 February 1984, that 'there was no such Cabinet meeting and Mr Costello did not offer his resignation.'

Though it took nearly ten years to do so, this sordid episode ended happily for me. Proof of the accuracy of my account of what had happened came from a casual conversation which I had with the political journalist Bruce Arnold. Arnold told me that in the course of his professional work, he had had a long interview with the former head of the Department of External Affairs, Frederick Boland. Fortunately he had taped the interview. Mr Boland, now retired, had been departmental secretary to both Mr de Valera and Mr MacBride, and later Chairman of the United Nations. He was well-known internationally as a distinguished and experienced civil servant.

How deeply relieved and gratified I was to hear Mr Boland say on that tape, in a reply to a question by Bruce Arnold about the unexplained 'out of the blue' repeal of the External Relations Act, that 'Noël Browne's version of the repeal of the External Relations Act was correct'. Further, he confirmed that no Cabinet decision had been taken. The versions of MacBride, Dillon, and Morrissey, according to Mr Boland, were mostly fantasy. He disclosed on further questioning that there had been no consultation with the British. As with the rest of us, the announcement that the Irish government intended to repeal the External Relations Act had taken the British by surprise.

While greatly relieved to hear my version of the facts verified I did not refer to Boland by name, but simply as a 'senior civil servant', in a subsequent letter to the newspapers. In spite of Hector Legge's jeering invitation to me 'to name the civil servant' I believed it improper to mention Boland's name in public in what was blatantly a political matter. When I told Bruce Arnold of my dilemma, he helpfully told me of one other person who knew precisely what had happened. This was Maurice Dockrell, a member of a former Unionist Protestant Fine Gael family and himself a former TD.

It seems that the Taoiseach had doubts about the political effects of his decision on the Unionist sector of the Fine Gael vote in his constituency. He decided to speak to Maurice Dockrell who could be depended upon to help undo the damage by telling his co-religionists in confidence the exact story, as told to him by Costello, about what had happened in Ottawa. Apparently, at the reception for himself and his wife given in Ottawa by the Govenor General, Lord Allanbrooke, Costello got the impression that 'there was a certain coolness' to himself. He was displeased at the placing at the banqueting table and believed that there had been some intended discourtesy to his wife. Later a silver replica of 'Roaring Meg' was placed in front of either Costello or his wife. 'Roaring Meg' was a famous cannon used by the Protestants in their defence of Derry's walls against the Catholics during the Siege of Derry. Costello went on, 'I was so insulted by these things' that 'I lost my temper and declared it' (the repeal of the External Relations Act). Arnold concludes, 'That, dear reader, is how Ireland left the Commonwealth.'

It is most important to note that this story of the repeal of the External Relations Act is also confirmed by Mr Boland. It was Boland who first brought the surprise news of the repeal to both MacBride and Lord Maffey, who were dining together at the Russell Hotel when the news came through from Ottawa. Maffey was later to be reported as saying that 'no conversation had taken place between the two governments on the issue.' Arnold also notes, 'Costello did offer his resignation on his return but it was refused.' Though this story was published in the *Irish Independent* on 4 February 1984, no attempt was made by the surviving former Cabinet ministers, MacBride and Dillon, to apologise for their defamation of my character.

The process of the repeal of the External Relations Act was irresponsible, incredible and ludicrous. Indeed because it was so ridiculous, it was not surprising that my correct version was not believed. It was surely both ill-mannered and ungracious of Fine Gael and Mr Costello to deprive Seán MacBride of his rights, as the relevant Minister, to introduce the Bill repealing the External Relations Act. Mr Costello chose to introduce the Bill himself. MacBride, in a pitiful protest, did not appear at the Easter Sunday march-pasts and volleys from the roof of the GPO trumpeting the celebrations of a 'famous victory.' In his absence, I acted as Minister for External Affairs at the circus.

Annoyed by the cavalier behaviour of the Irish government the British, in a devastating riposte, introduced the Ireland Act, 1949, without MacBride's knowledge. Because of his absence, yet again, I acted as Minister for External Affairs in receiving the copy of the Act in great secrecy en route to the government. This Act shocked the Irish government with its guarantees, which stand to this day, to the Unionist population in the North. The operative phrase ran: 'That in no event will Northern Ireland, or any part thereof cease to be part of His Majesty's dominions, and of the United Kingdom, without the consent of Northern Ireland.' This provoked a solemn protest from the Irish government. In truth, Mr Costello's Canadian capers were to cost us dearly.

De Valera's position on the repeal of the External Relations Act was that this last link with the Commonwealth, if repealed, would have the effect of consolidating the border and so further delay North-South reconciliation. Events were to prove that he was correct in his analysis. The British Prime Minister, Clement Attlee, said in a statement on 12 May 1949: 'It was the act of the Éire Government itself, deciding to leave the Commonwealth, which made inevitable a declaration as to the position of that part of Ireland which was continuing in the Commonwealth. The Ireland Bill merely recognised that fact.' Further, the official reports of the House of Commons Debates for 17 May 1949 showed that no documents had passed between the British and the Irish governments, and 'no conversation had taken place between them' that such a pronouncement was to take place, that the repeal of the External Relations Act had been decided on either by the Irish Government, or Mr Costello. Indeed, they went on to declare that the decision of the Irish government 'came as a painful surprise to the British.'

With hindsight, and access to Irish and US State papers, we may attempt to puzzle over the private workings of Seán MacBride's mind which led to his strange nomination to the Clann na Poblachta Senate seat of a former British Army officer, the Protestant northerner Captain Denis Ireland. Until the announcement of this name MacBride had remained secretive about his plans.

Taken on its own this appointment was surprising. It is true that Ireland had edited a cross-cultural journal in the North, yet what had he ever said or done which fitted him for the position while the hard-working and experienced Noel Hartnett clearly stood in line for the appointment? Republicans, including MacBride, had shown their distaste for Irishmen such as McQuillan who in their opinion had been disloyal to the Republic by joining Ireland's national army. What then about the loyalty of an Irish officer in a British regiment? What did Captain Ireland know about the social, agricultural and economic problems of rural Ireland? The short answer is, not much, but clearly these were not the important issues to Seán MacBride.

In time we were to get an explanation for MacBride's appointment of Denis Ireland. It had been made because of their joint unrestrained enthusiasm for the abandonment of the Republic's neutrality as a prelude to joining NATO.

As soon as Denis Ireland took over his position in the Senate, he proceeded to articulate a policy on NATO which was diametrically opposed to that which we felt should be our party's policy. Ever since 1939 there had been all-party agreement in the Republic on Ireland's neutrality. The new aggressive militarist line put forward by Denis Ireland with increasing frequency could be summed up in a statement made by him in the *Irish Times*, on 10 March 1951: 'What Napoleon saw clearly from St Helena was that Ireland was the key to the subjugation of Europe, and that Eastern adventures were a snare and a disillusion . . . the best answer to all this would be an Ireland united for at least the purpose of defence and transport, with a centralised Irish command, and within the Atlantic pact. All Ireland available, ports for the navies of the Atlantic nations, airports, and airfields. Ireland would then be harnessed to the defence of Ireland, Britain, and Western Europe, in that order of priorities. That is an ideal solution'. Without any reference whatever to his party's executive bodies or annual conference, or, as far as I know, even his closest party colleagues, it became clear that this total reversal of the policy of Irish neutrality was to be the newly-stated policy of Clann na Poblachta, laid down unilaterally by Seán MacBride and Denis Ireland.

Few of us took any notice of what Denis Ireland said or thought about NATO until we realised that these policy statements must have the approval of the party leader. His strange decision to appoint a former British officer as spokesman in the Senate slowly became comprehensible. There were those who said that Denis Ireland had been an undercover supporter of the Republican movement. What if he were, on the contrary, a secret member of British Intelligence whose job it was to bring the Republic into NATO? Who was using whom? However, this sudden explosion of official authorised enthusiasm for membership of NATO, albeit conditional, represented a dramatic policy change in Ireland's defence strategy.

In the *Irish Independent* of 7 June 1950, MacBride is quoted as saying: 'Ireland is the most anti-Communist country in the West. It is the only country in the West in which it is not possible to form a Communist party.' Quickly MacBride's secret strategem to bring the whole of Ireland into the anti-Communist NATO alliance was unfolded, showing a complete indifference to the opinions of his political party or institutions.

Early in 1949, as Minister for External Affairs, he decided to set out on a coast-to-coast speaking tour of the United States in an attempt to drum up Irish-American support and the help of the State Department for Ireland's right to join NATO, having first resolved the problem of partition. This must have been his undisclosed intention as far back as the formation of Clann na Poblachta, but neither MacBride nor any of the rest of us sought support for NATO during the general election, or the authority to abandon neutrality. There is no reference in the party constitution to the party's intention to abandon neutrality or to join NATO. No public reference whatever had been made to what is surely the most important conceivable policy issue for the people of the nation, their neutrality or involvement in NATO. Had MacBride succeeded, Ireland would now be clearly preemptive first-strike nuclear target in a possible Armageddon.

At much the same time as Denis Ireland became party spokes-man in the Senate, we acquired unexpectedly the enthusiastic public support of another distinguished British Army military strategist from the North African desert campaign. This was General Dorman Smyth, renamed O'Gowan. General O'Gowan appears to have conceived a high regard for Mr MacBride, which was reciprocated. He became a member of the party with an equally dedicated single-minded devotion to the promotion of Ireland's membership of NATO. General O'Gowan is reported in the *Irish Independent* on 6 January 1951, as saying: 'Partition will have to be faced as a strategic anomaly. This implies that the unification of Ireland is a politico-strategic sine qua non of NATO'. He went on: 'Spain and Ireland, with France and the United States, are essential to a properly co-ordinated security organisation. It is to be hoped that this will be one of the subjects to be taken up by Mr MacBride when he visits Washington'. We were shortly to find that the one-time republican, MacBride, was the third member of this bizarre British officer-dominated three-man cabal determined to take us into NATO.

MacBride began to beat the NATO alliance drum at every opportunity. On 7 January 1949, before he left for the United States, it appears that the Republic was privately invited by the United States to join NATO. This offer was rejected by the Irish government on the grounds that Article 4 of the NATO agreement guaranteed existing national boundaries. Clearly MacBride had no principled objection to joining NATO. In pursuit of his approach, he circulated an aide-memoire to all twelve government members of the NATO alliance, declaring: 'The Irish government are in agreement with the general aims of NATO'. He then went on to beg that partition would first be solved and then we would join. The State Department rejected his proposal.

MacBride then set out for the United States, where his message was, 'We welcome NATO, and would be grateful if we could find ourselves in a position of being able to give it un- qualified and unreserved support'. He added wistfully, 'We have no steel, and we would need arms for our defence'. On 16 April 1949 he visited the White House, where he was received by Dean Acheson, given a three-quarters-of-an-hour interview, and photographed. Once again MacBride offered Ireland as an all-purpose unsinkable army, navy and air-force base, in exchange for help with the partition problem. The State Department politely told him that 'they were not interested'. It is of interest to note that on 22 March 1949, de Valera also said that 'he too would advocate joining NATO, if Ireland were united'.

The relationship between MacBride and Hartnett at this time was one of growing mistrust. Yet there was a strange interlude in their relationship before the final break, on the Irish republican politician's ritual drum-beating, begging-bowl visit to Ireland's permanent 'wailing wall', the Irish in America. Needing a speech-writer for the kind of nostalgic rhetoric enjoyed by American-Irish republicans, MacBride took Hartnett. Though he had lost his fervent esteem for de Valera, Fianna Fáil and the Irish language, Hartnett still retained all his sentimental Kerry republicanism, and enjoyed that kind of speech-writing. All went well with the two of them for the first half of the tour at least. Hartnett wrote the speeches, and MacBride and himself appear to have used them. Then Hartnett unexpectedly returned to Dublin alone. It appears that there had been a blazing row with MacBride but it is uncertain precisely what happened; Hartnett told me that MacBride had disapproved of the aggressively republican tone of the scripts and had refused to use them. Sometime later, though he never withdrew the first explanation, Hartnett also claimed to have been disturbed to find that, while ostensibly making the ritual tour of the Irish American groups, Seán MacBride had visited Washington, paying a visit to the White House and meeting President Truman. Hartnett said, 'MacBride has been "dickering" with the Americans over neutrality'.

Hartnett became more and more convinced of the seriousness of the blunder which he had made in helping to form Clann na

Poblachta, and putting Seán MacBride into the Department of External Affairs. To make matters worse, as the Fine Gael group came to understand Seán MacBride's anxiety to retain office at any price Hartnett saw the gradual defection of the coalition parties away from the Mother and Child Health Scheme and watched the continual loss of whatever small authority and power the Clann na Poblachta party had exercised in the early days of the coalition.

Relationships between them became progressively more embittered and probably had passed beyond hope of repair. Though I did all in my power to remain detached from their quarrel, I was unsuccessful. Each believed that I was disloyal to the other becaude I declined to take sides in a quarrel of whose origins and causes at that time I was unsure. MacBride had not discussed his meeting with Truman with myself or in Cabinet. On the other hand Hartnett never referred to it as being the specific reason for his having been sent home from the United States, or the cause of his decision to return home, whichever was the truth. The collapse of their relationship contributed to a great degree to the final collapse of Clann na Poblachta and the first coalition government. Without Hartnett's political guidance MacBride was drawn into the mother and child débâcle on the side of the Fine Gael party, the medical profession and the bishops.

It was over the disgraceful Baltinglass affair (see Chapter 12) that Hartnett finally chose to resign from Clann na Poblachta in February 1951. While I agreed with him about the principle involved, McQuillan and I felt that tactically he was mistaken in resigning from the governing bodies of the party, the standing committee and the party executive. Reluctantly I must conclude that this was an essentially self-indulgent, petulant gesture on his part. It was ill-judged, and serious in its consequences for those of us who remained on in the party.

As so often in politics, there was an added personal complication, caused by Hartnett's ill health. To some extent this may have accounted for his irritability and intolerance. When we arranged for him to visit a leading consultant cardiologist in Scotland, there were two results. The first was the consultant's enthusiastic tribute to the enormous charm and personality of his patient. The second, not so pleasant, was that he considered Hartnett very sick. What came as a complete shock to me was that the consultant offered only a brief prognosis for his continued survival.

During the last days of this increasingly troubled relationship MacBride, using a simple phrase, gave all of us an enlightening but shocking summary of his political philosophy. Hartnett and myself pleaded with him to make some public protest against Everett and the Baltinglass incident; we argued that an anti-corruption campaign had been a major plank in our party platform at the election. In defence of his failure to protest, and in exculpation of Everett's decision to sack and evict a widow in order to give a job to a political crony in the Baltinglass post office, MacBride pleaded weakly that 'unsavoury matters are inseparable from politics'. That was the phrase which finally finished Hartnett's relationship with MacBride and the Clann na Poblachta party. Deeply angered, Hartnett sent in a letter of resignation which he withheld from publication. In it he alleged that Clann na Poblachta, and Mr MacBride in particular, 'had become obsessed with power and had abandoned any political or social philosophy'.

In the grim struggle ahead, with all its complex infighting, debates, and decisions to be taken in the key party committees our group was to greatly miss Hartnett's powerful and courageous advocacy, together with his unequalled experience of such intrigues. Hartnett's resignation also had the effect of pushing MacBride back into the arms of his old 'army comrades' and at the same time leaving him little choice but to seek refuge with the Fine Gael bloc within the Cabinet, who knew his problems and were simply waiting to crush him. For a man of his experience in various clandestine movements, MacBride, with extraordinary naïveté, failed to understand that he and all that he stood for in the Republican movement was anathema to Fine Gael. He had told me himself of the occasion during the Civil War on which a dawn knock on the cell door had called his good friend Rory O'Connor out to be shot by order of General Mulcahy. As the shots died away, Seán grimly rolled up Rory O'Connor's blankets. How could MacBride have expected a genuine rapprochement between these two widely different sides?

There were many tributaries which were to form the torrent that finally swept Clann na Poblachta away with its leader, but there is little doubt that the collapse of the MacBride-Hartnett alliance acted as the catalyst which in time liberated the final destructive force. Though the party disintegrated, its transient rise and fall had had the permanent effect of introducing the multi-party pattern of government into the hitherto stagnating political life of the country — a modest gain, coloured by serious disabilities and disadvantages. At the least the electorate, from watching the opposition politicians in power, were to learn that compliant Catholic sectarian conservatism was not a Fianna Fáil monopoly. Fine Gael, Labour and in the end Clann na Poblachta too, were to show that they shared equally in Fianna Fáil's conservatism.

9

The Mother and Child Scheme

I HAD BEEN brought up a committed believer in Catholicism. Both at Beaumont College and at the Cheshire Joint Sanatorium I had defended the Roman Catholic position against criticism. But later experience of life in Ireland was slowly and inexorably to dissolve my final illusions about the desirability of Catholicism and its teachings as guiding principles for the organisation of a concerned and just community.

This distressing disillusion with my religion was accelerated during my work as Minister for Health. I was left with a clear impression that the Church thrived on mass illiteracy and that the welfare and care in the bodily sense of the bulk of our people was a secondary consideration to the need to maintain the religious orders in the health service.

The simple reality of falling religious vocations in the Republic, together with the increasing complexity and cost of modern health care, made such continuing control impossible. The necessity for the replacement of our many run-down hospitals, dispensaries, and clinics was shown up well by the enormous size of our seven-thousand hospital bed building programme. Financially and from the staffing point of view the religious orders alone could not continue their traditional role of caring for the sick, the aged and the indigent; the state had to intervene. Only public finances could provide monies for the rapidly expanding scale of medical and paramedical personnel in our projected health services. Our hospitals were old, run-down, ill-equipped, to the extent that they were more of a danger or hazard to health than they were capable of restoring patients to health.

I had not fully realised the wide measure of control exercised by the Catholic church in the operation of our health services through its nursing orders of brothers and nuns. These were used to staff the senior administrative and management sectors of the voluntary hospitals, the county and district hospitals, many of our sanatoria, some of our psychiatric institutions, many of the workhouses and their hospital extensions in the Republic. There were also religious orders who specialised in domiciliary care of the aged and disabled, such as the Sisters of Charity.

The Archbishop of Dublin, Dr John Charles McQuaid, through his control of the religious orders and in his capacity as Chairman of the Board of Directors of a number of Dublin hospitals, had indirect control of the staffing and the management in the Dublin diocese. His instructions and principles were intended to be observed by the consultants and their patients irrespective of their religious beliefs. I concluded that this was why, surprisingly in a country which so badly needed it, no serious attempt had been made by a native government to establish an independent Department of Health until the late 1940s. None of them dared to interfere with or seek to expand or improve the overall primitive level of care within our hospitals and clinics for fear of political reprisals by the church. It was presumably for this reason also that no attempt had been made to provide a national health service other than that made available at the most crude level under the old British Poor Law national health insurance scheme. It was notable that even Clann na Poblachta, the latest and most radical of the Republican parties, in its first Clár (programme) published in May 1948 made no serious reference whatever to our health services, nor did it refer to the desirability of establishing a comprehensive national health service.

Neither did the coalition government appreciate that in appointing as Minister for Health a Trinity Catholic, educated in a Protestant medical school, they had offered what turned out to be a slight to the Archbishop of Dublin, further compounded by the fact that annually from the pulpit Dr McQuaid forbade Catholics to attend TCD under 'pain of mortal sin'. Nor did the coalition government appreciate that in the person of Dr Noel Browne they had a minister who had very clear views about the proper relationships between church and state in a democratic society.

Little innovation was possible in our health services without the consent and support of the religious orders, and this was rarely forthcoming on my terms. Yet it was clear to all who cared to examine the reality of our society, such as death-rate figures related to social classes, the death rate from tuberculosis and our infant mortality rate due to gastro-enteritis that the standard of care in our hospitals and clinics was quite deplorable.

Major defects had frequently been criticised by the chairman of the National Health Insurance Board, Dr Dignan, the Bishop of Clonfert, as 'reeking of pauperism'. In a plan submitted to the government he called for serious structural rather than mildly innovative changes if we were to end this serious discrimination against the poor. I had every intention of doing all that I could, with or without the approval and support of the Catholic Church, to secure badly needed improvements in the health services. Quite early on in my period as Minister for Health, I was to become involved in a series of fairly minor incidents and disagreements, arising out of the fact that the Church had for so long not been subjected to any serious criticism or examination in her administration of the health services. My most powerful and uncompromising opponent was Dr John Charles McQuaid.

Dr McQuaid suggested that I should release the nurses who were members of religious orders from the obligation of doing night duty in St James's Hospital in Dublin. At that time St James's Hospital was a forbidding run-down emergent workhouse, long established in the city of Dublin. As part of my duties as Minister for Health I made a practice of travelling around to see all the institutions indirectly or directly under my control, and I decided to pay a visit to this sordid work-house hospital. It was surrounded by enormous high prison-like walls. Entrance was gained through a great doorway permanently closed. It was in this doorway, a century or so ago, that a little revolving contraption had been inserted in which mothers placed babies for whom they could no longer care. By turning it around they could send the little child into the awful prospect of almost certain death in the work-house.

The inmates were dressed in shabby ill-fitting clothing and boots without laces, ignored rather than ill-cared for. The most disturbing feature, with my near phobia of high walls, was the fact that there were dozens of walls honeycombed within the great outside wall. Within these spaces the unfortunate inmates walked about, neglected and mostly disowned. Clearly the building was in the last stages of dilapidation. With the help of Mr Seamus Murphy, the Commissioner in charge of the hospital, we took out the plans of the old hospital within days. With my pencil I struck out all those walls, including the main outer wall which I felt should be removed at once, so that the public could see into the hospital. Later following major reconstruction it became possible to convert the grim institution to the modern St James's Hospital.

It was in this old work-house that Dr McQuaid asked me to permit the nuns not to do night duty. I could not accept this request: if the lay nurses could do night duty, so could the nuns. The Archbishop, irritated by my reply, in time removed the nuns altogether from the hospital. We had no trouble in providing lay nurses to do the work.

An inequitable situation commonly existed in hospitals run by the religious orders, ensuring that lay nurses could not be promoted beyond the position of staff nurse. We made a new order which proposed that the highest nursing posts were to be open to all, and further, that in all hospitals promotion was to depend on professional qualifications and general suitability to the post. There was immediate uproar. Overnight, I became a 'Communist who wanted to root the religious orders out of Ireland'. The defence of the nuns became a popular cause for craw-thumping councillors and deputies, including the members of the Labour Party. This was yet another occasion in which a minority of Fianna Fáil deputies took a marginally more mature and independent attitude, notably Martin Corry of Cork and Tommy Walshe of Kilkenny.

The all-party opposition, fanned by the religious orders, suggested that if the nuns were removed from these supervisory positions the standard of care in the hospital and even the moral standards among the nursing staff would collapse. I pointed out to the deputies and councillors that they were being personally offensive in denouncing as incompetent, immoral, undependable and irresponsible their own daughters, their own sisters, and even their own working wives. These were all at present being victimised as lay nurses by this discriminatory system. Depressingly, our enlightened proposals were not supported by the nursing profession for whom I had specifically taken such action. Not one was prepared to stand and fight publicly on the issue or to give me any support. The Irish Nurses Organisation made no attempt to defend the proposals.

Under the enervating influence of their homes and schools, general hospital nurses in Ireland developed the true docile 'slave' mind, in contrast to the members of the psychiatric nursing profession who had created their own independent trade union to defend their interests. The general hospital nurse for years held a snobbish attitude to trade union activity, as had the medical profession. Trade unionism was not 'quite right'. The nurses overlooked the reality of the enormous power of the doctors, through their social, personal and political contacts. *They* did not need trade unions.

Our decision to proceed with the building of St Vincent's Hospital at Elm Park led to another clash. The superior of the Sisters of Mercy, backed by the solicitor Arthur Cox, sought to retain their old hospital buildings in St Stephen's Green. I understand that they hoped to use the building as a private nursing home. A formidable and prestigious deputation, which included the Reverend Mother, Arthur Cox, members of the Board of the National University and the hospital consultant staff, met us at the Department. I had also been lobbied by my Cabinet colleagues. I declined their request to retain the old building in Stephen's Green, pointing to an agreement which a predecessor of mine had already made with the religious order. In recognition of monies granted, St Vincent's Hospital had been conceded to the Department of Health for disposal as it wished. I informed them that the old hospital could readily be converted into an old persons' home, sited as it was in the city centre. Disappointed, no doubt, the deputation departed, but they were successful with another Minister for Health. Some years later I noticed that the old hospital building had been converted into a modern office block called Seán Lemass House. Such are our priorities.

It is also possible that I had been a source of irritation to Dr McQuaid because I had declined to visit Rome during the Holy Year, 1950. Each of my Cabinet colleagues had made the journey. In Rome they were photographed in full white tie and tails with the Pope, and the photographs were 'expressed' back to the national and provincial newspapers. Because it appeared to me that my colleagues were flaunting their religion for political reasons, I did not travel. As part of his duties as Foreign Minister, Seán MacBride was photographed at the formal opening ceremony of the Holy Door.

I next drew Dr McQuaid's attention to the problem of children who had temporarily lost their mothers following their admission to a sanatorium with tuberculosis. This traumatic separation could last up to two years. It was my hope that Dr McQuaid would persuade one of the religious orders to visit the houses of those families. The nuns could prepare breakfast for the children and help those going to school; in the evening they could have their supper cooked, help them with their homework, then put them to bed. The children would benefit from the presence of a mother substitute. Dr McQuaid declined to help. Unbelieving, I listened to his bizarre explanation. He claimed that the sight of nuns going into a home where the wife was known to be absent in a sanatorium with tuberculosis 'would give scandal'.

As with the nurses on night duty, we had no difficulty in getting lay women to do this work. It is surely a strange irony, in the context of Dr McQuaid's peculiar decision, to recall the fine work done through the centuries by the French Sisters of Charity in their domiciliary care of those in need among the poor of many cities of Europe.

Following the decision to proceed with our long-delayed and badly needed Children's Hospital at Crumlin, I tried unsuccessfully to transfer control of that magnificent new hospital to the more democratic supervision of the Dublin Health Authority and the Local Appointments Commission, instead of exclusively Catholic control by the Archbishop of Dublin and his nominees. I was to find that this control had already been designated to the Archbishop by Seán T. O'Kelly, when he had been Minister for Local Government and Public Health, and I had no choice but to honour his signature. The virtue of control by a Health Authority is that the appointment must be made on merit by the Local Appointments Commission. This Commission was one of the few valuable contributions to ensuring that fair and just decisions are taken in the matter of local authority appointments, and was established by the first Cumann na nGaedhael government. On the other hand, medical appointments in the voluntary hospitals are commonly made on hereditary or sectarian religious grounds — the Protestant-dominated hospitals through the Masonic Order, and the Catholic through the reverend mothers, members of the hierarchy or the Knights of Columbanus. Quality of personnel and patient care becomes a secondary consideration.

Some time later, one of my Cabinet colleagues asked me to receive a well-known and popular Capuchin Father, who wanted me to visit the Bon Secours Hospital, then just completed in North Dublin. Since the whole enterprise was sponsored by Dr McQuaid, this was a surprising request. The Reverend Mother kindly offered to show us over the hospital. It was clear that it was an excellent one in every way for its time, and it was to be staffed by a chosen panel of physicians and surgeons, all Catholics, no doubt.

We returned to the Superioress's office for tea, and began discussions about the cost of hospital building at the time. Then we discussed the future use of the hospital. The Reverend Mother referred to her genuinely fine achievement in having built and equipped the hospital; the approximate cost amounted to about six million pounds in present terms. This was a considerable sum, but reasonable for the size of the hospital. To the astonishment of the Reverend Mother and to the delight of the Capuchin present, who had acted as entrepreneur, I made light of the sum, and offered to pay it from Department funds. I informed her that there was only one condition: that the hospital would be administered by Dublin Corporation and would be open for use by the general public.

The Reverend Mother's beaming smile was replaced by a look of mystified pain. Distinctly unsmiling, she dismissed my proposal. The 'lower orders' must be excluded from this hospital; it should be used for middle and upper class patients exclusively. It certainly was hard to credit that for reasons of class alone this Reverend Mother had declined my offer, not only of a cheque for the equivalent of six million pounds, but of the chance to give her life to the care of the sick poor of Dublin.

I then became involved in a unseemly sectarian struggle. It appears that an 'ambush' had been contrived by the Knights of

Columbanus, who were said to be 'close' to the Archbishop at that time, to swamp the Board of Management of the predominantly Protestant Meath Hospital with Catholics, and convert it into a Catholic hospital. The ambush was prepared through a use of membership qualifications, and was to take place at the annual meeting of the hospital. The Meath Hospital at the time was notoriously bigoted and Protestant in its appointment preferences. It was in dire financial difficulties, and sought help from my department. After consideration of all the issues, I agreed to help, on the condition that neither religious sect could have overall control of the hospital. We would introduce the Meath Hospital Bill into the Dáil, and would require a governing board of thirteen members. Of the thirteen, seven must be nominated by Dublin Corporation, thus ensuring that control of the hospital would not be under the control of either of the religions.

There were exceptions to this kind of behaviour by the religious in Ireland. Publicly I have acknowledged the scope of the work done by religious orders for the mentally handicapped. We allocated considerable funds to the St John of God's order both for reconstruction of old hospitals and the building of new ones where required. But it was unfortunate that in Ireland we were taught to believe that religious orders had a monopoly of concern and compassion for the sick, the disabled and the aged.

Health had already been a contentious issue before I entered Leinster House. In 1946 Dr Con Ward, Parliamentary Secretary to the Minister for Health, Mr MacEntee, and later dismissed by Mr de Valera for corrupt practices, had introduced a Health Bill which was opposed by Fine Gael, who tabled so many amendments that the government was compelled to withdraw it.

There was no doubt in my mind that the various compulsory proposals in the Bill — compulsory notification of tuberculosis, inspection of residences and homes, restrictions on the right of tubercular patients to travel on public transport or to attend without notification public gatherings, whether in churches, cinemas, or theatres — were all dangerously unnecessary infringements on civil liberty. They were also impractical. Hotel and guest-house owners would be forced to spy on and notify the authorities if a resident designated in the Bill as a 'possible source of infection' was staying in their hotel. The panic nature of these proposals, with the implied suggestion that tuberculosis had become virtually uncontrollable, was a measure of the government's failure to cope with the epidemic.

From the public health point of view the effect of such compulsory notification would be to drive this very infectious disease underground, which would increase and not diminish the possibility of its spread. The penalty clauses would encourage people to conceal their tuberculosis, and to delay diagnosis if it meant that they would become an outcast in the community. Correspondence about these compulsory proposals took place in the *Irish Medical Journal* between myself, as a medical officer in the tuberculosis services, and Dr James Deeney, Chief Medical Adviser in the Department of Health. It was the first occasion on which I had been involved in controversy in the public press.

Following the withdrawal of the Bill, Fianna Fáil introduced the 1947 Health Bill. It was from this fine piece of legislation that we were to derive our power to introduce both the free no-means-test provisions for the tuberculosis scheme and the controversial mother and child scheme. The main opposition to the 1947 Health Bill was led by James Dillon. He opposed particularly the power given to local authorities to compel children to submit themselves for medical examination in schools. The Bill also sought to limit the present constitutional right of parents to send their children to primary schools at all. On the principle that any interference whatever by the state, in either health or educational matters, was unwelcome, this opposition was supported by the Catholic Hierarchy. It was their opposition to these clauses which led to the confusion later, in 1951, as to whether the church had protested against the mother and child proposals in part three of the 1947 Act.

On becoming Minister for Health I was determined to extend the no-means-test principle of the 1947 Act to the health care of mothers and their children. Knowing what had occurred in Britain, where the British Medical Association had opposed Aneurin Bevan's National Health Scheme, and in the United States where the medical profession had successfully opposed Truman's health proposals, I warned the members of the coalition that the passage of the mother and child scheme would not be easy.

It is important to clear up some of the misconceptions about the mother and child health service. I first entered the Dáil early in 1948, after the 1947 Health Act, which permitted the introduction of the mother and child health scheme, had become law. During the passage of the mother and child health proposals through the Dáil in 1947, the bishops did not contest those issues. It is true that the church did protest during the passage of that Act in 1947, but only about the relatively minor matter of the powers to introduce compulsory school medical inspection. It is also true that the Irish Medical Association had opposed the passage of the 1947 Bill on the grounds that they considered it to represent the 'socialisation of medicine'. The Irish scheme would have been even more advanced in its basic principles than the Bevan national health scheme. The British scheme operates on an insurance principle: everyone must make an insurance contribution. Our scheme would have introduced a genuinely socialist redistribution, paid for out of general taxation. This already existed in primary education, childrens' allowances and the T.B. and infectious fevers health facilities.

There were two main personalities in the conspiracy to subvert my implementation of the free no-means-test mother and child scheme which the 1947 Act had authorised, representing two of the most powerful pressure groups in our society. One was the Minister for Defence, Dr Tom O'Higgins, who represented the Irish Medical Association. The other was Archbishop John Charles McQuaid.

Dr O'Higgins was probably the most experienced and shrewd politician in the Cabinet, and his advice was respected and listened to by the Taoiseach. He was a brother of Kevin O'Higgins, the Cumann na nGaedheal Minister for Justice assassinated on 10 July 1927, and had been Minister for Finance in the same government. A doctor from a rural medical family, he had been a member of the Executive of the IMA. It was this link between the Cabinet and the medical profession which was to be an important relationship leading to the defeat of the mother and child health proposals.

Dr McQuaid ruled his archdiocese with an unbending conviction that his rigid, triumphalist, conservative approach to

Catholicism was the only appropriate stance. He had family associations with the medical profession, and would instinctively sympathise with the doctors in their campaign against the threat of socialised medicine. Of even greater importance was that he considered the health scheme an encroachment by the state on the church's role, which he considered to be, among much else, 'to determine and to control the social attitudes of the family in the Republic, especially in the delicate matters of maternity and sexuality'.

Let an old Clongownian, the then British Ambassador Sir Gilbert Laithwaite, join with me in describing Dr McQuaid. We were at High Mass in the Pro-Cathedral. The Archbishop approached in procession, with all the panoply of the church 'en fête': the demure child acolytes, the robed clerical students, the imposing shining gilt crucifix carried by its tall student bearer. Scented incense rose from the gently moving thurible. Embroidered vestments glowed, bejewelled, ornate and colourful, on the supporting clergy, the distinctive insignia of office of ascending seniority and importance. They contrasted with the stark archaic chalkwhite of the formidable Dominicans and Carmelites, the reassuring benevolent brown of the Franciscan friars. And at its heart walked the Archbishop of Dublin.

A broad white silk shawl covered his frail bent shoulders, falling down on each side to cover his hands, in which he clasped the glinting gold processional monstrance. His dark eyes, glittering in a masklike face, were transfixed on the shimmering white sacred Host. He had a long, straight thin nose and a saturnine appearance, with an awesome fixity of expression, and the strong mouth of an obsessional. One shoulder was slightly raised; it was said that he had had a major surgical operation for tuberculosis (possibly a thorocoplasty). Drowsily fantasising on the imposing and fearful procession in a mixture of dream and nightmare, I was nudged into wakefulness by Laithwaite. 'What an impressive figure, Noël: would he not make a notable addition to the distinguished company of Spanish Inquisitors?'

Some strange happenings during the whole period of the mother and child controversy have never been fully explained. For instance, the proposals under Section 26 of the 1947 Act to which Dr McQuaid and the Catholic hierarchy would later take exception had passed through the Oireachtas uncontested or unquestioned by any member of the hierarchy. Dr O'Higgins made no reference whatever to what he later described as the 'socialisation' of medicine involved. Neither did Dr. O'Higgins contest the mother and child health scheme proposals or refer to any aspect of the scheme whatever as being objectionable during our discussions in Cabinet on the Amending Bill to the 1947 Act, presented by myself in June 1948. My proposals for the amendment of the Fianna Fáil Health Act, as was the practice, had been circulated in advance to each member of the Cabinet.

Seán MacBride would later assert that I had gone ahead 'impetuously' with the free no-means-test scheme without the consent of the Cabinet. This was demonstrably untrue. The book of estimates for 1948 notes the sum of money agreed between my department and Mr McGilligan's Department of Finance. Neither of us could or would have gone ahead with a scheme of that magnitude without the consent of the government.

Neither has it been clarified why the Taoiseach's Department never referred to the fact that de Valera had privately received a protest from the Catholic hierarchy, on 6 September 1947, about the free no-means-test principle of the health scheme sometime *after* the passage of the Act.

It appears that the Catholic hierarchy, on 6 September 1947, had sent a letter privately to the Taoiseach's office in which they belatedly expressed their disapproval of the new 1947 Health Act and its free, no-means-test proposals. This important letter claimed that 'for the State, under the Act, to empower the public authority to provide for the health of all children, and to treat their ailments, and to educate women in regard to health, and to provide them with gynaecological services, was directly and entirely contrary to Catholic social teaching, the rights of the family, the rights of the Church in education, and the rights of the medical profession, and of voluntary institutions'.

The peculiar feature about that letter was that de Valera did not reply to it until 16 February 1948, that is, nearly five months *after* having received it and a mere two days before the general election in which his government was to be defeated. In his brief reply he made no attempt to protest about this clear intrusion by the bishops in a matter already decided on by the Oireachtas, and claimed that the matter was *sub judice*.

Following the change of government, Mr de Valera's department appears to have made no attempt to warn the new Taoiseach, Mr Costello, about this threatening letter. It is true that in 1951, during the debate on my resignation, Mr Costello for the first time made a vague passing reference to having seen it. Why was it that the Department of Health did not appear to have been warned of the receipt of that letter? It is possible that de Valera did not choose to disclose the receipt of the letter to the Department of Health, yet he did write a letter to the Minister for Health, Dr Ryan, now available in the records of the State Paper Office in Dublin Castle. If the civil servants in the Taoiseach's office knew of the letter, why did they not draw Mr Costello's attention to it? If, on the other hand, they did tell Costello of the existence of this protest by the Hierarchy, why did he not refer to it during the Cabinet discussion of my amending Health Bill in June 1948? If Mr Costello knew of the letter of protest, why did he choose to ignore it? Did he fear the possibility of a conflict in Cabinet? Did he fail to read the file carefully? Did he fail to understand its implications? Did he understand its implications, and suppress the letter for later use against a troublesome Minister for Health?

While I always believed that a conflict with the medical profession was nearly inevitable, and I was well prepared for it when it did come, I had no reason to believe that there would be opposition from the hierarchy. Even if I had known I would still have expected the Cabinet to implement the law.

The amending Bill proposed by me to the Cabinet in June 1948 kept the no-means-test principle of the 1947 Fianna Fáil Act as it was. From the centre of the long Cabinet table, beside the Taoiseach, John Costello, and in the proletarian voice which he affected on such occasions, Bill Norton, the Labour Party leader, shouted down to me, 'Yer not goin' to let the doctors walk on ye, Noël?' Before I could answer him, the Taoiseach asked, 'What would you prefer, Doctor?' I replied that I would prefer to keep the existing proposals, free of direct charge, and with no means test, already included in the Fianna Fáil Health Act.

Acting on the unanimous approval received in Cabinet, the Department of Health proceeded with difficult negotiations with the medical profession as well as with various interested departments, including the Department of Finance.

Mr McGilligan was concerned with the immediate and long-term financial charges on the Exchequer. He made provision in the 1950-51 book of estimates for £400,000 for the proposed mother and child scheme. There was a further provision in the book of estimates for 1951-2, for the expenditure of 1.8 million pounds.

At an executive meeting of Clann na Poblachta I explained what was being done to create the essential services infrastructure needed for a comprehensive scheme of this kind. On a scale never attempted before or since, we had set out to replace virtually all the existing dilapidated hospital beds, and upgrade all the existing hospital accommodation by the provision of major hospital and other building projects, supported by radical improvements in medical, nursing and para-medical facilities of all kinds. We wanted to remove the one valid argument which could reasonably be used by the medical profession, i.e. that the diagnostic or treatment facilities did not exist, and so could not bear the imposition of a greatly expanded health scheme. I was able to assure the executive that we were already making good progress with our building programme and the organisation of essential services such as mass radiography, a blood transfusion scheme, BCG and diphtheria inoculations and a national rehabilitation service. There was also a new highly ambitious national cancer diagnostic and treatment service. We established a series of independent limited companies to ensure speedy action in the achievement of these ends.

The party executive was enthusiastic about the proposals. But I reminded them that while we would do all that we could to mobilise the public on the side of the scheme there would be a conflict of interests with the wealthy consultants.

Some weeks after I had been given Cabinet permission to implement the mother and child scheme, I instructed my personal staff to devise a longterm public educational programme, with the help of Aodh de Blacam and Frank Gallagher. The enthusiastic public response in favour of the scheme in the general election that followed the collapse of our coalition showed just how successful this programme had been. Department of Health education and information services hammered home one simple message. Under this scheme there would be no more doctor's bills, no more chemist's bills, no more hospital bills, no more financial fear of ill-health. The message was unanswerable. The people welcomed the prospect of funding a health care service which would be freely available to anyone who needed it.

There is some irony in the fact that our proposals appeared so attractive to the public that everyone was eager to claim political credit for them. Tom O'Higgins was quick to contradict Clann na Poblachta claims to have originated the scheme, and other Fine Gael speakers pointed out that 'the mother and child scheme is not just a Clann na Poblachta scheme, it is a government scheme'. The irony lies in the fact that just as soon as the hierarchy intervened, it ceased to be a Fianna Fáil, Fine Gael, Labour Party, or even Clann na Poblachta scheme; it became the Dr Noël Browne mother and child health scheme.

10

Crisis

IN July 1950 we submitted a formal scheme for a mother and child health service to the Medical Association. It aimed to provide full free medical care before, during, and after child-birth. There was to be an entirely free family doctor medical-consultant service and, if need be, free G.P. and hospital care for all children up to the age of sixteen years. Visits to the home by a midwife were also to be free. Compared to the delay and sordid inefficiency of the dispensary service, it was not surprising that the public gladly welcomed the new scheme. There was no doubt about the well-merited unpopularity of the dispensary services. The Chairman of the National Health Insurance Council, Bishop Dignan, had said about it, 'The poor law system is tainted at its roots now, as it was when introduced, of destitution, pauperism, and degradation'. Bishop Dignan was the only member of the hierarchy to write to me approvingly of the scheme.

It must not be thought that I believed doctors should be exploited by the state in their valuable humanitarian service to the community. On the contrary, as a doctor myself, I well knew the rigorous discipline needed in the long and costly seven-year primary training, with the subsequent further training practice needed as a consultant. A distinction should be drawn between the two types of doctors in practice. The consultant specialises in a narrow range of medical defects and illnesses over a number of years after his already long years in training to become a doctor in the first place. For this special knowledge he expects to be paid higher fees.

Looked at from the practical point of view of the consumer, it is the consumer who will suffer should the medical profession be dissatisfied with its working conditions in a national health scheme. As a practical act of consumer protection, it pays a government to make sure that the medical profession is happy. It is a notable feature of the British national health service that not only did it become the best health service in the world, but repeated surveys showed the medical participants to be satisfied with their working conditions.

With the increasing pressure on the politicians by the medical consultants and the bishops, it became clear that Cabinet enthusiasm for the scheme was waning. This growing coolness froze on 10 October 1950, when I was peremptorily ordered to Archbishop McQuaid's palace by a telephone call from his secretary. I was told to attend a meeting, to be held on the following day, concerned with the proposed mother and child health service and the bishops' position in regard to it.

I could not understand why any bishop should not be prepared to meet a government minister in his department. This was the practice where other citizens of whatever rank or religious persuasion were concerned. It appeared to me to be an affront to my Cabinet office, and to the public who had elected me, that a government minister should be ordered by any private citizen in this way. Yet my Cabinet colleagues informed me that it was in fact the practice, under Irish government protocol, for a minister to be expected to attend, when told to do so, at a bishop's palace. They could not understand my point of view. Neither was I told the conditions under which I would be received; that there would be three bishops present while I, though requesting permission to do so, was bluntly told that I might not bring my Departmental Secretary.

The following afternoon I set out for the Archbishop's Palace. Dr. McQuaid brought me into a small anteroom, and courteously invited me to sit down. Contrary to what I expected, he had a particularly warm smile.

In opening the conversation Dr McQuaid chose, of all subjects, to discuss child prostitution, informing me: 'the little child prostitutes charge sixpence a time'. Concluding this strange interlude, he invited me into a larger and more imposing room, where two bishops were introduced to me as Dr Staunton, the Bishop of Ferns, and Dr Michael Browne, the Bishop of Galway. As soon as we were settled, a letter from the hierarchy was read to me by Dr McQuaid.

10 October 1950

Dear Taoiseach,

The Archbishops and Bishops of Ireland at their meeting on October 10th had under consideration the proposals for a Mother and Child health service and other kindred medical services. They recognise that these proposals are motivated by a sincere desire to improve public health, but they feel bound by their office to consider whether the proposals are in accordance with Catholic moral teaching.

In their opinion the powers taken by the State in the proposed Mother and Child Health Service are in direct opposition to the rights of the family and of the individual and are liable to very great abuse. Their character is such that no assurance that they would be used in moderation could justify their enactment. If adopted in law they would constitute a readymade instrument for future totalitarian aggression.

The right to provide for the health of children belongs to parents, not to the State. The State has the right to intervene only in a subsidiary capacity, to supplement, not to supplant.

It may help indigent or neglectful parents; it may not deprive 90% of parents of their rights because of 10% necessitous or negligent parents.

It is not sound social policy to impose a state medical service on the whole community on the pretext of relieving the necessitous 10% from the so-called indignity of the means test.

The right to provide for the physical education of children belongs to the family and not to the State. Experience has shown that physical or health education is closely interwoven with important moral questions on which the Catholic Church has definite teaching.

Education in regard to motherhood includes instruction in regard to sex relations, chastity and marriage. The State has no competence to give instruction in such matters. We regard with the greatest apprehension the proposal to give to local medical officers the right to tell Catholic girls and women how they should behave in regard to this sphere of conduct at once so delicate and sacred.

Gynaecological care may be, and in some other countries is, interpreted to include provision for birth limitation and abortion. We have no guarantee that State officials will respect Catholic principles in regard to these matters. Doctors trained in institutions in which we have no confidence may be appointed as medical officers under the proposed services, and may give gynaecological care not in accordance with Catholic principles.

The proposed service also destroys the confidential relations between doctor and patient and regards all cases of illnesses as matter for public records and research without regard to the individual's right to privacy.

The elimination of private medical practitioners by a State-paid service has not been shown to be necessary or even advantageous to the patient, the public in general or the medical profession.

The Bishops are most favourable to measures which would benefit public health, but they consider that instead of imposing a costly bureaucratic scheme of nationalised medical service the State might well consider the advisability of providing the maternity hospitals and other institutional facilities which are at present lacking and should give adequate maternity benefits and taxation relief for large families.

The Bishops desire that your Government should give careful consideration to the dangers inherent in the present proposals before they are adopted by the Government for legislative enactment and therefore, they feel it their duty to submit their views on this subject to you privately and at the earliest opportunity, since they regard the issues involved as of the gravest moral and religious importance.
I remain, dear Taoiseach,
Yours very sincerely,
(Sgd) James Staunton,
Bishop of Ferns,
Secretary to the Hierarchy.

Having read the letter to me, the bishops appeared to assume that the interview was over. In spite of this I chose to tell them that there were a number of mistaken assumptions and assertions on which they had based their memorandum, arriving at false conclusions which appeared to me to invalidate many of their claims. For example, there was no question of compulsion for either patient or doctor.

Dr. McQuaid asked why it was necessary to go to so much trouble and expense simply to provide a free health service for the 10% necessitous poor. This comment was not only wrong, since the percentage involved was thirty and not ten, but surely represented a strange attitude from a powerful prelate of a Christian church towards the life and death of the 'necessitous poor' and their children. I replied that if I were an ordinary member of the public, then such a position was possible through ignorance. As a doctor, I believed that a free health service was an essential pre-requisite to an effective and a just health service.

As Minister for Health the necessitous poor, a considerable sector of our society, were my special responsibility. I was implementing a Cabinet decision, in accordance with the law passed by the Oireachtas.

Bishop Browne then took up a question dear to his heart, that of the burden of rates and taxation. He claimed that it was unfair to tax the rest of the community in order to give the poor a free health service. I pointed out that taxation was surely not a matter of morality; as far as I was concerned, it was a problem for the government, the Minister for Finance and myself.

So far their concern had been strictly with temporal issues. There was a distinct cooling in the previously warm manner of the Archbishop. He questioned the right of the state to assume the responsibility of 'the education of mothers in motherhood', or to provide a maternity and gynaecological service for women, and claimed that these were dangerous powers for the state to arrogate to itself. He mentioned possibilities which in those days were quite unthinkable, even in many of the advanced western European countries. He postulated the inevitability of contraception and abortion.

During the subsequent general election in 1951, these two forbidden subjects were to become examples of clerically-inspired 'black propaganda' and were frequently claimed to be part of my health proposals. So also was euthanasia for the aged and sterilisation for the unit. Quickly forgotten was the fact that I was the first Cabinet minister seriously to concern myself with doing something for the sick and aged. At An Cnoc parish church in Connemara, where I spent weekends learning Irish, I was referred to during a sermon in Irish as being one of those people who 'come amongst us disguised as friends, when meanwhile their real work is to poison the wells, and so kill off our stock'. This was clever and damaging imagery. How I valued the courage of my good friends Seosaph O Cadhain, Seán O Conghaile and others who, under such pressure, refused to disown or repudiate me.

I reminded Dr McQuaid that 95% of our doctors, nurses and patients were Catholic. Could he not depend on his flock to obey the teachings of their church? Seemingly not. Listening to this kind of insidious and damaging innuendo, I began to realise the possibilities for misrepresentation by the hierarchy at any subsequent election. I quickly decided that with a Cabinet which was already frightened of the hierarchy and anxious to scrap the scheme, damage could be done to the no-means-test ideal if I were simply to ignore all the fears, real or imagined, of the hierarchy.

Contrary to the image widely fostered about me as an obstinate, doctrinaire and uncompromising person, I compromised on the offending clauses. In respect of 'the education of mothers', I would reconsider these clauses and submit them to the hierarchy. Alternatively the heirarchy could consider the offending clauses and submit them to the Department of Health for improvement. Finally, since these provisions were not the most important section of the scheme, we would agree, regretfully, to withdraw the section completely if it were found impossible to agree.

The Archbishop of Dublin is said to have described this meeting as having been 'incredible' during his later discussions with John Costello. He claimed that I had brushed aside all suggestions about the means test: 'the Minister himself terminated the meeting, and walked out'. What a dilemma faces the student of history, deciding which of two bishops was lying about this meeting. According to Dr. Michael Browne, while he agreed that the meeting was contentious, his phrase was that I was truculent, and he concludes his recollection of the meeting with the words, 'the interview ended amicably'.

As far as I was concerned the meeting was open and frank. While having no wish to make concessions, I knew of my weak position in a wavering Cabinet, and felt that I must at least save the no-means-test principle. It was clear that the bishops would support the wealthy consultants. I felt not anger but simply astonishment that men of their profession should so blatantly side with the rich against the poor. A reasoned discussion had taken place and I had made important concessions.

As to the charge that I left the room and slammed the door, the driver of my car could verify this to be untrue. A courteous host, Dr McQuaid left the room with me. He walked the length of the hall to the front door, enquiring for the welfare of my wife and family. Finally he bade farewell at the door of the palace. By order of the bishops I had been deprived of a witness on my side, but having met their proposals where possible, I was convinced that I had satisfied them. As far as I was concerned the matter was at an end.

I am convinced that such would have been the case if only my Cabinet colleagues, and in particular my party leader Seán MacBride, had not wilted under the medical propaganda hostile to the health scheme. Above all, the subsequent misrepresentation from beginning to end of this whole affair emphasised the wisdom of the advice given to me by my departmental secretary, Mr. Kennedy. Long experienced in these matters, he had advised me to insist on bringing a witness on my side to any negotiations.

I outlined the events of the afternoon to Mr. Kennedy, the concessions we should make, the reaction of the bishops and my clarification of their confused misunderstanding of the scheme. We decided that we would prepare a memorandum for submission to the hierarchy, which would be of paramount importance in the struggle to come, and include a full resumé of that meeting.

Within days of the meeting, the memorandum was sent to the Taoiseach as a matter of courtesy, for his information. Protocol insisted that a mere Cabinet minister had no direct access to an Archbishop's office; it was my intention that with its compromise proposals, the memorandum should and would be transmitted to the hierarchy for their detailed study. For some unexplained reason the Taoiseach did not send this document, either as a courtesy or for their information, to the hierarchy. Cabinet records show that we in the Department of Health had no difficulty either in refuting the bishops' arguments or in correcting the errors of fact in their understanding of the scheme. The memorandum also included the significant concessions reluctantly made by my department to the objections made by the hierarchy.

The memorandum went on: 'The Minister respectfully desires to draw attention to the fact that, in introducing the Mother and Child scheme, the government was simply implementing the law . . . the government is merely giving effect to an act of the Oireachtas passed in 1947. To remove any possible misunderstanding about the basis of the scheme, the Minister desires to emphasise that part three of the Health Act of 1947, which became law on 13 August 1947, provided for the introduction of a mother and child health service, and determines the broad outline of such a service. Our draft scheme has been prepared to conform with, and in fact does conform with, the provisions of that 1947 Health Act.' In order to clarify the doubts about the voluntary nature of the health service, the memorandum went on, 'in view of the fact that the mother and child health scheme is in no sense compulsory, and that whatever guarantees the hierarchy wish in the matter of "instruction of mothers" would be unreservedly given, the Minister respectfully asks whether the Hierarchy consider the Mother and Child scheme to be contrary to Catholic moral teaching'.

Our memorandum, sent to the Taoiseach within days of the meeting at the Archbishop's palace, did not reach the hierarchy until after a delay of several months, on 28 March 1951. Yet it is clear from statements made by him in the Dáil that Mr. Costello was in constant verbal contact with the Archbishop during that time.

Significance must attach to one word in my concluding request for clarification to the hierarchy. Despite the fact that I was the product of four Catholic schools, my knowledge of Catholic theology was vague and unreliable. For this reason I sought the advice of a theologian who had been recommended to me by a lawyer, Brian Walsh, who lectured at Maynooth briefly and subsequently became a member of the Supreme Court. Aware of the implications and dangers for the theologian, we took special precautions to safeguard his identity at all times. Meetings were held under the most stringent security precautions, not in the Department of Health but in Brian Walsh's home.

Surprisingly, still fearful of the consequences though in retirement, and having only fulfilled his duty to offer moral advice to a member of his own church, my theological adviser requested that secrecy be maintained and he continues to request anonymity to this day.

As Bevan's socialist national health service was freely used by Catholics in the North of Ireland without either public or private protest by the teaching authority of the church, I asked the theologian why our much less extensive mother and child health scheme was condemned by the same hierarchy in the Republic, but he could not answer my question. He was as puzzled as we were. However, he pointed out that there was an important distinction between Catholic 'social' and Catholic 'moral' teaching. The conscientious Catholic sins if he transgresses against Catholic moral teaching. There is no such sanction attached to Catholic social teaching, which varies from one period in history to another. The theologian noted that the hierarchy had carefully declined to claim that the scheme was contrary to Catholic moral teaching; there seemed to be no reason why our politicians could not, as Catholics, conscientiously agree to implement it.

The theologian was disturbed by the position taken by certain members of the hierarchy. He was compelled to assume either that the hierarchy were uninformed on this relatively simple matter of Catholic moral teaching or, alternatively, that they were deliberately taking sides against the new health scheme. Since the hierarchy dared not publicly claim that the scheme was contrary to Catholic *moral* teaching, we had removed the one valid objection on religious grounds which could be held against it.

It is now widely acknowledged that the condemnation by the bishops of the health scheme was crudely political. Unashamedly the church was 'playing politics' even to the point of bringing down a properly elected representative government on the issue.

Having considered the theologian's advice, my final memorandum was drawn up. It made significant concessions on a number of points so as to remove all possible sources for deliberate mistakes or calculated misrepresentation by the hierarchy. It then went on to challenge the hierarchy about the morality of the scheme.

Finally, I asked the theologian a question concerning my personal position. Since I wished to survive in the years ahead in order to continue the struggle for a socially just order in the Republic, I asked what my position would be if I were to tell the bishops bluntly that I rejected their objections, as being politically motivated. Having thought carefully, he replied: 'The Roman Catholic hierarchy must denounce you as a Catholic who no longer accepts the teaching authority of the Roman Catholic church'. I was grateful for that advice.

I also discussed my problems with my political colleagues. Having given me their best advice, they told me that any future decisions about my personal religious or political beliefs and actions were decisions that only I could take. Undoubtedly the episcopal opposition and my condemnation by them would be exploited by my political opponents before the 95% Catholic electorate. I decided that for the present, I would try to survive.

John Whyte, in his *Church and State in Modern Ireland 1923-1979*, has suggested that I seriously limited my scope for action by agreeing in advance to the bishops' ruling. This is not true, and for this reason. The bishops are the teaching authority of the Catholic Church. The teachers or leaders of any religious group must decide on matters where their religion is concerned. Because of this, 'I accept your ruling without question' became an inevitable part of my letter to the hierarchy.

Next, my question was 'Is the scheme contrary to Catholic moral teaching?' Inevitably the bishops' reply was that the scheme was contrary not to Catholic 'moral' teaching, but to Catholic 'social' teaching. As already explained by my theological advisor such a decision is not binding on a conscientious Catholic under pain of sin. On the authority of the bishops I could now claim that the scheme was not immoral and that the ruling of the bishops against the scheme could be ignored by the Cabinet. My theologian had assured me that the health scheme could not be publicly condemned by even the most obscurantist bishops as contrary to Catholic moral teaching. The question was put by me so as to make that clear to both public and politicians.

The Bishops were conceded the right to come to any conclusion they chose, but denied the right to dictate to an elected government the kind of health service that it must implement. The theologian's advice to me was fully vindicated by subsequent events when the hierarchy would not dare put in writing whatever they might say individually and privately in order to frighten politicians in both government and opposition at all levels. The very existence of the existing free no-means-test schemes within our own social, education and health services, as well as the British national health scheme in the North, patently gave the lie to the bishops' condemnation of the scheme.

There are those who would say that my behaviour throughout was mildly Jesuitical. In all the circumstances of the powerful forces arraigned against me and of the grave issues of an important health service, as well as the fundamental question of 'Who Rules?', I felt justified.

Many years later, at a public lecture, I questioned Dr Enda McDonagh of Maynooth on the contradictions in the history of the Catholic Church. There is a long litany of important issues about which individuals have been condemned as heretics by Rome, at times at the cost of their lives, with such condemnations later rescinded. Dr McDonagh explained these blunders by the Church as 'the changing word in the changing world'. Dr Hans Küng explains these discrepancies as the 'differing paradigms of Christianity adopted and up-dated to man's intellectual and physical progress, through time'. This facility to change a fundamental truth must make the doctrine of papal infallibility a difficult one to sustain.

In Cabinet I decided to make a stand on two issues: the fundamental rights of the electorate, with power coming from the people to the elected government, and the right of the public to a proper health service. Under no circumstances could we concede to the bishops the right to set aside a law already passed by the Oireachtas.

Archbishop Kinane of Cashel objected to my statement of 'acceptance' of the episcopal ruling on the mother and child health scheme and my refusal to implement their command about the inclusion of the 'means test'. He is quoted in the *Irish Independent* of 2 June 1951 as saying: 'I have recently emphasised that certain graduates of TCD, while openly parading their Catholicity, have, at the same time, publicly set themselves up in opposition to a fundamental part of Catholic religion, namely the teaching authority and the bishops. These people are now claiming the right to determine the boundaries of their jurisdiction. They should not oppose their bishop's teaching by word or act, or by any other way, but carry out whatever is demanded by him. They must carry out political, social and economic theories which are in harmony with God's laws'.

I was the only impediment to the joint plans of the hierarchy and the medical consultants to deprive the public of a fine health service; the hierarchy had become the factual instrument of government on all important social and economic policies in the Republic. Our prospects for the preservation of an effective Cabinet and a badly needed health scheme were now changed utterly.

Of the two issues involved, the more important was no longer

the mother and child scheme. The real challenge being
mounted by the hierarchy was their implicit claim to be the
effective government. Jack McQuillan shared my belief about
this. There was no doubt that we could no longer save the health
service, but it was still important to document, for the sake of the
electorate, the reality of the Dáil's subsidary role. As Seán
O'Faoláin was to observe so acutely about the power of the hierarchy: 'The lightest word from this quarter is tantamount to the
raising of the sword'.

The medical profession heard from Dr Tom O'Higgins of the
dramatic dissolution of my support on all sides in the Cabinet. In
turn, the hierarchy was informed by Mr Costello.

Because I had heard nothing further from the bishops since my
meeting with Dr McQuaid in October 1950, and had not been
told that the bishops had not accepted my magnanimous concessions to their objections, I was genuinely surprised to receive a
letter from them on 9 March 1951, in which I was bluntly told that
they were still intent on preventing the implementation of the
health scheme. They made it clear that their terms for settlement were 'unconditional surrender'.

Mr MacBride insisted that I should call on Dr Michael
Browne, a member of the Episcopal Committee. Dr Browne was
a big man, well over six foot tall, his height enhancing the long
black soutane with its thousand and one split pea-size scarlet
buttons. Meeting him, I wondered how on earth he'd have the
patience to do and undo all those buttons. A concealed zip,
perhaps?

The bishop had a round soft baby face with shimmering clear
cornflower-blue eyes, but his mouth was small and mean.
Around his great neck was an elegant glinting gold episcopal
chain with a simple pectoral gold cross. He wore a ruby
ring on his plump finger and wore a slightly ridiculous tiny
skull-cap on his noble head. The well-filled semi-circular
scarlet silk cummerbund and sash neatly divided the lordly
prince into two.

He handed me a silver casket in which lay his impeccable
hand-made cigarettes. 'These cigarettes', he intoned, 'I had to
have made in Bond Street'. Then he offered me a glass of
champagne. 'I always like champagne in the afternoon', he
informed me in his rich round voice. He appeared ignorant of

the social solecism of mixing cigarettes and champagne. My feeling of awe was mixed with a sense of astonishment that this worldly sybarite considered himself to be a follower of the humble Nazarene.

Our discussion on the mother and child health scheme was cursory. He showed no sign of having any serious interest in or objection to the scheme other than its cost, though later he would thunder that this was not so. Our discussion was mainly concerned with what he feared must be the increase in the 'burden of the rates and taxes' needed to pay for the scheme.

It is reasonable to assume that between October 1950 and March 1951 our opponents had intrigued against us 'secretly and behind closed doors'. These meetings were designed to undermine my position in the Dáil and in the country. Incidentally, the phrase, 'secretly and behind closed doors' was used by Mr Costello during his speech in the Dáil at my resignation, protesting at my publication in the national press of the correspondence containing the details of the intricate process whereby the hierarchy and the medical profession had undermined the proper authority of the Cabinet. There was no difference on this issue between Fine Gael and Fianna Fáil. In the sole comment which he was to make to me about the whole mother and child controversy some years later, de Valera admonished me, 'You should not have published the correspondence with the hierarchy'. This distinction about what the public should and should not know was yet another difference between myself and the rest of the Dáil.

As I slowly progressed through the saga of my disagreements with the members of the hierarchy and heard their readily adjustable versions of what occurred at our various interviews, I valued yet again the wisdom of my departmental secretary's shrewd advice, that in any negotiations it would be advisable to bring a reliable witness. Brian Walsh, who had had some experience of the ecclesiastic courts, told me that when these courts were first established some worldly wise lawyer priest had had inscribed within the precincts of the court the words, 'Nemine Crede' (believe no-one).

Later I was told, by impeccable sources, two strange stories about the mother and child scheme as seen from the side of the church authorities. The first claimed that Archbishop McQuaid

was harshly misjudged; a deeply committed churchman, utterly
dedicated to his faith and its essential soul-saving mission to
mankind, he was a simple and good man who had been mani-
pulated with much skill by Dr Michael Browne, who, it was
claimed, had been in fact responsible for the preparation of the
ten-point document sent to the first Coalition government in
condemnation of the health scheme. It is true that there were
important factual errors in the memorandum which would
invalidate its conclusions. Yet the case argued from these facts
was a powerful plea from the church against encroachment in
matters of health by the 'State bureauracy'. The second story
was more remarkable. It claimed that Dr Browne 'was afraid of me
as a dangerous, Goebbels type of man, deep and sinister'. For this
reason, he did not discuss the scheme with me on my visit to him.

Demonstrably my episcopal visits were fool's errands. My
Cabinet colleagues, and especially Seán MacBride, well knew
that the hierarchy had no intention whatever of supporting me
or our scheme. Possibly they believed I would be worn down by
boredom, demoralised, or exhausted by the tedium and futility
of the struggle. They may have believed that I might even be
intimidated into submission by the sight of all those croziers.
Obedient to the last, my next call was to the diocese of Ferns,
where I had an uneventful meeting with Dr Staunton. Politely
we exchanged pleasantries, and parted.

Finally, on 31 March I set out to meet Cardinal Dalton, of
Armagh. He was a pleasant, withdrawn, scholarly-looking man.
Our conversation was stilted, formal, and with the exception of
one brief period, banal and inconsequential. The Cardinal gave
the impression that he was politely wondering what on earth he
was doing sharing his luncheon table with this odd, earnest
young man who was clearly preoccupied with an abstruse and
awkward health problem. The sole gain for me was the pleasant
hock with the fish at luncheon, which I had arrived just in time
to share with the Cardinal. I suspect that he accepted the ordeal
and decided to 'offer it up', as did I. There was but one reference
by me, and none by him, to the mother and child service. It is
important to note, however, that the Cardinal made no attempt
to answer the one crucial and pertinent question that I did put to
him, about the use of Aneurin Bevan's National Health Service
by Catholics in Northern Ireland. His disdainful reply smacked

of royalty standing on its dignity: 'We are prepared neither to apologise, nor to explain'.

My visits to the bishops were a wanton squandering of valuable time, both mine and theirs. I was merely a mendicant government minister uselessly pleading for the underprivileged of the Republic with the princes of their church. The truth was that neither they nor I had anything of value to say to one another. A final decision dictated by Rome had already been taken in Maynooth, and readily accepted by all members of the Cabinet, that they should rid themselves of this tiresome colleague who continued to believe in the principle of representative parliamentary democracy.

The procedure adopted by my opponents in Cabinet was for each of them either to ask me to their office to plead their point of view about the health scheme, or to come to my room in Leinster House and discuss it there. Using every conceivable argument, they pleaded with me to change my mind about the scheme and to accept the bishops' ruling as they had done. The Taoiseach, the Tanaiste and Mr. Dillon were the main apologists for the Cabinet. All their arguments could be summarised by the refrain of Seán MacBride, later to be publicly recorded by him and by the members of the Cabinet: 'You cannot afford to fight the church'. My reply to all this was clear, simple, and consistent.

Repeatedly I pointed out to them that I had not made the law and that I alone could not make a new one. In 1947 the Oireachtas had passed into law the free no-means-test Section 23, under which the scheme was to be implemented, following a full public debate in both Houses. The decision was later ratified in Cabinet in June 1949. I invited each of them formally to move in Cabinet that it be dropped. Should they do this I would then be glad to re-consider my position as Minister for Health in the coalition Cabinet. None of them would take up that clear challenge. The Cabinet response to my proposal showed that they were still afraid to change the no-means-test principle. The whole matter with them remained a political issue and not one of conscience.

The intention in Cabinet was, no doubt, that I would 'bell the cat' for them, and plead with the electorate on their behalf that medical or episcopal opposition made it impossible for *me* to implement the free principle. The rest of the Cabinet and indeed the hierarchy could then avoid the opprobrium of such a shoddy political compromise. Politically they would exculpate themselves in advance of any charge by Northern Unionists that Rome in fact ruled in the Republic. I had no intention of facilitating this escape from their dilemma.

So began what a civil servant friend of mine, Michael Mulvihill, called 'the retreat from Maynooth'. We continued to work in the Department on the assumption that the scheme would go ahead. I had expected that the Labour Party would be compelled to support such a socially desirable and badly-needed health scheme, but Norton was one of the first to defect. Because of Clann na Poblachta's repeatedly declared enthusiasm for the scheme, and their 'revolutionary' background, I did not expect that under MacBride's leadership they also would desert such a fine cause under pressure.

In dropping the scheme, the Cabinet was to have the full support of the medical profession and the media, with the honourable exception of the *Irish Times*. Of even greater importance, they were to be supported by the power and authority of the church. Throughout the controversy, Bishop Dignan of Clonfert remained a firm friend and supporter of mine, and warned, 'You cannot win against the Catholic hierarchy. A few months, a year at the most, and you and your scheme will be forgotten. Look what happened to Parnell'. My helpless reply was, 'Surely we have progressed even minimally since that time. The Mother and Child scheme will surely not be forgotten with the same finality as has been Parnell'.

On 17 March 1951, back in my department after my visit to Armagh, I reported the details of that meeting to Mr Kennedy. Immediately I was told that a special meeting of the party executive had been called by Mr MacBride. The meeting was already in session. Would I go across at once? This executive meeting, and the way in which each of us handled it, would be crucial to the survival of Clann na Poblachta.

On arrival at the meeting I quickly gathered that MacBride was denouncing me, listing my deficiencies as a Cabinet colleague and my failures as a minister and as a member of the party; I was incompetent, disloyal to the party, disloyal to my comrades, disloyal to Mr MacBride, and anti-Republican.

Most inexplicable of all, for reasons of personal advancement, I had deliberately chosen to pick a row with the Roman Catholic Church over the health service.

While it was true that MacBride had recently become distant in his manner with me, he had never spoken about me to my face in such offensive terms. Understandably I was dazed by the assault. In the jargon of the republican movement, I eventually realised that I had walked into a cleverly prepared ambush. There had been no prior warning of the executive meeting. Unprepared as I was, there was no hope that I could convincingly refute the wild charges being made about me. There was the further reality that on Sean MacBride's own admission at least 85% of that executive had been former members of the IRA; inevitably they were much more likely to side with their old chief of staff than with myself. There was little doubt that, much in the style of the old court-martial, the 'trial' would conclude with all charges 'proved against me'. Following a formal vote, passed by the 'democratically elected' party executive, I would be found guilty on all counts. The executive of the party would then pass a vote of 'no confidence' in their Minister of Health. I could not allow this to happen, although I believed that it would inevitably happen at a later executive meeting, for which I hoped to be better prepared.

It was imperative that I leave at once to fight another day. I called on the chairman for the formal agenda for the meeting. Glancing down the list of items for discussion, on a point of order I claimed that the agenda did not refer to my present indictment by Mr MacBride. This being so, and since I had important work to do in my department, I left the meeting, offering my apologies to the executive. Jack McQuillan came after me, saying that I was under personal attack by Mr MacBride and should return to defend myself. I assured Jack that as soon as I was as well prepared as possible for the inevitably hopeless battle, at the end of which I knew MacBride would gain my 'final conviction', I would call for an executive meeting. There could then be a fight to the finish.

11

Resignation

I RETURNED to my department convinced that MacBride's capitulation had removed the remaining impediment to the Cabinet's acceptance of the end of the health scheme. At the same time, MacBride had seriously underestimated the extent of the opposition the Cabinet would face from the public because of their humiliating capitulation. I did my best thereafter to make sure that every public statement or declaration, every letter to or from the principals in the struggle now taking place, be recorded in writing.

It is unlikely that the majority of bishops intended to pursue the matter so as to bring down the government. I had made it clear to the Medical Association and publicly in the Dáil that I was adamant on the no-means-test position. Within days of my eventual resignation we were given to believe that even Dr McQuaid had been prepared to compromise on a peace formula put by a representative trade union group, which included members from the North of Ireland. This was a suggestion that in order to meet the bishops' principle that the service be paid for, we would allow for the introduction of a single nominal payment of ten shillings by the pregnant mother. This would immediately put her into full benefit for all the provisions of the scheme. I indicated my consent to this proposal and considered it to be well short of a principled compromise, on the no-means-test scheme. If it were possible to preserve the main provisions of the scheme, that nominal charge did not invalidate my no-means-test principle.

In spite of the opposition of the bishops, many members of the Catholic clergy warmly welcomed the main proposals of the scheme. Bishop Dignan, of the National Health Insurance Board, had expressed his disgust with the 'pauper' nature of the dispensary service. Indeed the then Minister for Health, Mr MacEntee, had sacked him for his outspokenness in protesting against the quality of poor law medicine. A parish priest friend of mine confided miserably to me, 'It is people like myself who will have to spend the rest of our lives apologising for the behaviour of the hierarchy in destroying a good health scheme, and bringing down a government'.

With Mr MacBride finally deserting to Fine Gael, the doctors and the hierarchy, I was isolated in Cabinet; the bishops could now safely call for my final submission. It was made clear to me that the phrase used by both the Taoiseach and Mr MacBride, 'I must satisfy the Bishops', brooked no compromise. Their demand was for unconditional surrender on the bishops' terms. I was equally adamant in my determination not to concede the no-means-test principle.

It is important to recall that as this complex crisis developed, an increasingly acrimonious debate between the medical profession and the Department of Health was also in progress. In the beginning memoranda were conciliatory on both sides, but fortified by the knowledge that my Cabinet colleagues had lost their nerve and their enthusiasm for the scheme, the consultants became intransigent. Yet another factor was the continuing disruptive effect of the increasingly angry Hartnett-MacBride quarrel within Clann na Poblachta.

Meanwhile it was imperative that I should maintain the pressure of work in the Department of Health to complete the vast hospital and clinic building programmes. We had to continue with the national plan to eliminate tuberculosis. There was also my role within our overall departmental programme designed to educate public opinion about the real issues involved. I instructed my personal secretary to arrange that at regular intervals of about a fortnight, in different parts of the country, and on the radio, I should outline in detail the benefits of the proposed mother and child health scheme. This I did on occasions such as the laying of foundation stones and similar non-political events. Our educational literature aimed at parents and children was distributed to all suitable outlets, schools, post offices, hospitals or garda stations. It is a measure of how little was known in the Department of Health about the opposition of the hierarchy that quite innocently, and to the intense annoyance certainly of Dr McQuaid, we had sent on 6 March copies of our literature on the mother and child health scheme to each member of the hierarchy. In the circumstances our action was considered to be a deliberate provocation.

There were cleverly-illustrated half-page advertisements in the national and provincial newspapers, packed with information and, as with the booklets and leaflets, bilingual. A deluge of education and information poured from the Department of Health in increasing intensity over a period of months. Systematically we set out to win wide support among the public for the scheme. I recall Fidel Castro's remark, shortly after he came to power in Cuba, 'Everyone is against me but the public'. The coalition government to their cost failed to recognise this.

To off-set the effect of this public campaign the medical consultants issued statements saying that the absence of the money relationship between the doctor and the patient would cause a deterioration in the quality of the health services. The magnificent success of the free fever and TB hospital schemes readily gave the lie to this.

A Jesuit priest, Fr Edward Coyne, wrote to the newspapers, complaining that if there were a free medical scheme 'the standard of medical care for all would be reduced to that standard at present available to the dispensary patient'. What an implicit condemnation of the dispensary services! He went on to criticise the mother and child scheme in the authoritative Jesuit publication, *Studies*.

While I was having tea in the Dáil restaurant on the afternoon of 6 April 1951, a reply from the hierarchy to my memorandum on the October meeting at the Archbishop's palace — the terms of which had been finally and belatedly transmitted to them by Mr Costello on 27 March — was handed to me by my personal secretary Dick Whyte. It was breath-taking in its assumption that the hierarchy of one religion could dictate to a sovereign government on matters of national policy. The letter went on, 'The Hierarchy must regard the scheme proposed by the Minister for Health as opposed to Catholic social teaching'. Just as my theologian had assured me, the reply from the hierarchy made no attempt to support the deliberately misleading claim made by Archbishop McQuaid that the scheme was contrary to Catholic moral teaching.

I went straight across to the General Post Office, at that time the headquarters of Radio Eireann. It had been previously arranged that I should go on radio at peak listening time with a detailed clarification of the health scheme and its full implications. The fact that an explanatory letter to the newspapers about the health scheme had already been suppressed by the Taoiseach was an ominous indicator that our time was running out. If Costello had known of my intention to speak on the radio, he would have prevented me from doing so. Speaking in both Irish and English, my purpose was to mobilise maximum public support for the health scheme in the coming struggle.

Shortly after the broadcast, I was not surprised to be called to an emergency Cabinet meeting later that evening. From the absence of ministerial papers in front of each minister, it was clear that there was only one item for discussion, the letter from the hierarchy. All was tense, quiet and awkward. John Costello told us that the meeting had been called so that we could hear the latest about the mother and child health scheme. Sitting down, Costello took up the letter. Clearly, for him, it was holy writ. No doubt he had already discussed his tactics with his Cabinet colleagues: I had had no information or contact with MacBride about the subject. Slowly and solemnly Costello read out the Archbishop's letter to us all.

He then looked at me and said, 'This must mean the end of the mother and child scheme'. All heads around the table began to nod, like those strange toy Buddhas. They agreed, oh how fervently they agreed, with the Archbishop and the Taoiseach. Costello appeared to expect their agreement and my equally enthusiastic nodding acceptance, followed by my agreement to withdraw and amend the scheme. The new scheme must be in accordance with the demands of the hierarchy. I was unable to oblige; my response was to plead with them for patience. I pointed out that the letter from the hierarchy had referred only to social teaching. Because of this, there was no reason why a conscientious Catholic could not carry on and implement the health scheme as had been agreed upon between us in Cabinet. They would not transgress against their religion as they would do were the scheme contrary to Catholic *moral* teaching. I sought to explain the difference between Catholic social and

The full 1948 Cabinet with President Seán T. O'Kelly. Again I stand on the extreme left beside Seán MacBride.

John A. Costello and Seán MacBride being interviewed for *Picture Post* in November 1948 and explaining the repeal of the External Relations Act.

'In a cabinet room full of dull, earnest and dutiful plodders, Paddy McGilligan was an intriguing and polished anachronism. When he entered that room, always late, with five or six three-inch-thick briefs under his arm, we all had to curb an inclination to stand to attention; the headmaster had arrived.'

October 1962. 'There was the sudden realisation that a large and angry animal with sharp teeth was furiously tearing at your clothes, your body, your head, your face and arms. My first reaction was one of incredulity.'

With Sean Dunne TD and Jack McQuillan TD at Leinster House in 1961.

At home in Connemara 1985.

moral teaching, as earlier clarified to me by my theologian, but they were not interested. Fleetingly and irreverently I reflected that one Judas was bad enough but twelve of them must be some kind of record, even in Ireland.

Grudgingly the Taoiseach allowed my request that I ask every one of the Cabinet the question 'Do you accept?' Boldly Mulcahy agreed, 'He certainly deserves that right'. First I asked the Labour leader Everett, then the patrician McGilligan. Difficult to believe, there was no difference between the landlord and the peasant. Then from Norton, prostrate obeisance. Michael Keyes, a Labour minister who had succeeded T. J. Murphy, was the only one to demur meekly, 'They shouldn't be allowed to do this'. But he too nooded his head. Seán MacEoin was outraged that I had even dared to question him. Angrily he blustered, 'How dare you invite me to disobey my church?' The hierarchy had spoken, in no uncertain terms. He asked, 'Who would oppose the positive teaching of those entitled to teach?' Then he went on ingenuously, and with a welcome edge of blacksmith's humour, 'I don't want to get a belt of a crozier'. The lawyer, MacBride, was concerned with evidence, and no doubt with history. He begged the Taoiseach that his tortuous argumentation, already prepared in writing, be included in the Cabinet papers. Contrary to precedent it was, and is there now for all to see in recently-released state papers. Re-reading it now, it would have been wiser for MacBride to have left his documentation of unconditional surrender to a convenient wastepaper basket, and simply grunted his approval with the rest.

Later Costello was to say, 'As a Catholic, I obey my authorities'. MacBride was quoted as saying, 'Those in the government who are Catholics are bound to accept the views of their church'. Mr. Costello shrugged off any claim he might have had to being Taoiseach in a sovereign government by the letter he sent to the Archbishop saying that the government would readily and immediately acquiesce in a decision of the hierarchy.

I made a remark about considering my future action and left the Cabinet room. Two days later I was summoned to a meeting of the executive of Clann na Poblachta, called by Seán MacBride. All that I had done as Minister for Health had been implemented under authority vested in me. My conscience was clear. I was now to be put in the pillory on a series of grave charges; my actions as Minister and party member were to be subject to systematic distortion. Throughout that afternoon, into the night and until dawn the following morning, my good faith, motives, administrative ability and political judgement were to be ridiculed and belittled.

From all over Ireland my party comrades filed into the room, most of them unaware of what lay ahead. With few exceptions, they expressed good will and their appreciation of the work we had done. There were altogether about forty members in that executive. Anxious to wound and destroy, with the black eyes in his gaunt face suddenly hard and unfeeling, Seán MacBride set out to demolish my respected position in the party. He recited a series of charges that were all directed to one end, first to discredit and then to eliminate me.

The charges dealt with all aspects of my political life. But no matter how forceful the advocate, and no one has ever questioned MacBride's singular forensic skills, even this group of ex-IRA sympathisers needed some kind of proof, if only to contradict the clear evidence of their own eyes. All over Ireland, new hospitals, clinics and sanatoria were being built. Nor could they overlook the fine new health services provided by us during our three brief years. To manufacture this 'proof', MacBride resorted to a series of devious lawyers' tricks. Showing no shame at the breach of trust implicit in the action, he produced what he claimed to be a verbatim account of what I had said to him during the course of a private dinner to which he had invited me at the Russell Hotel the previous November. Though for the most part the account was untrue, it was cleverly seeded with truths that I could not deny, such as my calm demeanour and my ready admission that I had at one time described Norton as 'a fake Labour leader'. He went on to compound this breach of trust by reading from a document within which he claimed was recorded a detailed dossier of my movements, day and night, in the weeks prior to this executive meeting. Clearly he must have arranged to have had me shadowed by a member of the Special Branch or some such accomplice; the shoddiness of such a breach of behaviour between two party and Cabinet colleagues seemingly had not occurred to him.

In line with the anti-Communist McCarthyite smear tactics common then, he set out to 'prove' either that I was a Communist, or had Communist sympathies; that I had vilified fellow party members; that I had challenged his leadership; and that I had deliberately sought a fight with the Catholic church. All these were politically lethal charges. It was the function of his specially-briefed claque of republican supporters to volunteer false verification of the many charges made against me by MacBride. It was clear from early on that the only possible verdict had already been arranged beforehand — I was to be proven guilty.

Having defected on the mother and child issue, I had anticipated that MacBride must now fight to exculpate himself. But the cold venom of his verbal assault on me still came as a shock. With the exception of the unexpected meeting some days earlier, our relationship had at all times been pleasantly uncontentious and even amicable. His near-schizoid transformation from friendliness to cold hostility was truly daunting to experience, especially since I knew myself to be innocent of the many vile charges in his assault. Suddenly my friend and Cabinet colleague, the leader of our party, had become my prosecutor. For the first time I was to confront that other disturbing MacBride of MacEntee's fearsome indictment made during the course of the general election campaign in 1948.

Shocked by the revelation that MacBride had had me followed by Special Branch or other investigators, Jack McQuillan asked: 'For how long have you had Dr Noël Browne followed? On how many of us have you got similar dossiers?' The Kafkaesque-like trial process, were I not the victim of it, was distractingly fascinating. Its tortuous complexity reflected the paranoia, tormented reasonings and unwarranted fears of its begetter. Each time I denied a charge there was an immediate refutation of my denial by a false witness who claimed to have heard and seen everything.

To substantiate his accusation about my alleged Communist sympathies, MacBride read out from his 'Special Branch' file a list of the meetings I was said to have had with young Jim Larkin and Owen Sheehy Skeffington. It is true that Larkin had stood for election as a Communist on his return from Moscow. He had been utterly defeated. Having 'learnt his lesson', he had long since become a respected trade union leader and deeply conservative member of the Labour Party. My good friend John Byrne, a socialist in the Labour Party, had been told by Larkin, 'If it's socialism you want, join some other party'. The truth was that I had met Larkin only once, when he had been part of a big trade union delegation which had unsuccessfully attempted to mediate in the mother and child row. Owen Sheehy Skeffington was in fact a most vehement anti-Stalinist, like his martyred father before him, and the epitome of a greatly respected liberal Irish socialist. Indeed, it was for this reason that the Labour Party had expelled him.

This was to be the pattern of future charges. One of the ex-IRA group, for instance, would say that I had confided in him that I would bring down Seán MacBride as leader of the party or that I would pick a row with the church of Rome, so as to further my political career, palpably absurd suggestions. It was claimed that I had made offensively critical remarks about the republican army and their political immaturity. When I denied these and other damaging charges, the individual making the charge would turn to an accomplice, and ask for corroboration: 'You were there on Saturday the 15th, you heard — ' and then he would repeat whatever the charge happened to be. There would be immediate confirmation of the charge from the second planted witness.

MacBride read out what purported to be a verbatim account of our conversation at the Russell Hotel. It has been suggested that MacBride, during his visits to the toilet, took copious notes of our conversation. To my knowledge he took no notes at the dinner table and I cannot recollect that he left the table more than once. He was not a competent shorthand writer. The purpose of the alleged verbatim account was to assert my intention to usurp the leadership of the party. The suggestion that the aspirant to a leadership 'coup' would calmly forewarn the party leader over dinner in a hotel is palpably absurd.

What did we really discuss at that dinner? Speaking to MacBride very quietly and with great seriousness, I had made the point that he and his family had suffered much for his beliefs; it was obvious that he was seriously committed to a united Ireland. I went on to say that if Clann na Poblachta and the government submitted to the demands of the Roman Catholic church it would be seriously damaging to that cause. I warned him that I intended to publicise to the full any such interference by the church, should it occur, in Cabinet affairs.

I warned that if he and I could not agree to preserve the health scheme the split between us would be obvious to all. In these circumstances the party must suffer, divided as it would be between those who admired him for his work as Minister for External Affairs, and those few, probably belonging to my generation, who believed that I had succeeded in improving the health service. In reply, Seán turned to me and said, 'Noël, what have you done in the Department of Health?'

MacBride then mischievously accused me of having ridiculed the republicans of the party during that conversation. Especially malicious was his claim that I had named Jim Killeen as a particularly useless party member. Killeen had been a sincere, committed member of the republican army, and had been imprisoned for a number of years. He was a man of the highest ideals, respected and deservedly well liked by all of us in the party. Much as I disagreed with Jim's belief in violence, I greatly admired his single-minded integrity, and had every reason to believe that he was a good friend of mine. Whatever I might have said about any member of the party, under no circumstances would I denigrate, ridicule, or criticise Jim Killeen, one of the few of them whom I whole-heartedly respected. The charge had been made with the obvious purpose of alienating me from the executive. Not alone did I lose Jim's support; his old comrades were angered as well. Of the many charges made against me that night, I will always recall this particular charge of having belittled Killeen as possibly the most hurtful of all.

There was only one charge made by MacBride to which I pleaded guilty unrepentantly. This was that once, in a state of exasperation, I had described Bill Norton as a 'fake Labour leader'. Close personal experience of Norton in Cabinet had made this clear. The charge was a measure of the deviousness of MacBride's mind; by quoting this criticism, he sought to discredit me with those who were in sympathy with the Labour Party.

Then came what was surely the strangest charge of all. MacBride's alleged intention had been to implement Tone's plea that 'there should be neither Catholic, Protestant or

Dissenter, but the common name of Irishman'. He had claimed that appointing the ex-British army officer and Belfast Protestant, Denis Ireland, to the Senate seat would unite orange and green, Protestant and Catholic, peacefully in a united Ireland. He now set out to show the executive that I was not sufficiently hostile to the Protestant minority in the republic. He accused me of having been politically foolish in allowing myself 'to be photographed in public shaking hands with a Protestant Archbishop'. He claimed that this act of mine 'had done great damage to the party, and to the coalition government'. The reason he gave for this petty-minded charge was 'that the photograph of myself and the Protestant archbishop shaking hands, had been widely published in the national press'.

What had happened was this. As Minister for Health I had laid the foundation stone for a badly-needed infants' unit at the Rotunda Hospital, which would act as a highly-skilled emergency flying squad of trained nursing and medical personnel for Dublin mothers. In providing the unit, the department was filling a serious gap in the maternity and child welfare service. The Protestant Archbishop, Dr Barton, was the Chairman of the Rotunda Hospital Board, a kindly and gentle man, completely apolitical. However, that I had fraternised with the Protestant Archbishop was one more black mark against me in the eyes of Seán MacBride, and of that executive of grotesquely miscalled 'republicans'.

Recently released Cabinet papers reveal a pitiful attempt by Seán MacBride subsequently to ingratiate himself with Archbishop Barton. It appears that MacBride wrote a letter to the Archbishop in an attempted 'explanation' for his bigoted remark. He protests that he made his remark because I had confided in him my intention, 'by using the Protestant against the Catholic doctors, to split the medical profession on religious lines'. Leaving aside the fact that the majority of Protestant consultants were as bitterly opposed to the new health scheme as their Catholic colleagues, MacBride made no attempt to clarify the way in which my alleged strategy was to work. Because of de Valera's policy against employing Protestant doctors in the public service, it is very likely that among the 800 dispensary doctors on whom the scheme was to be based there were probably no Protestants at all.

Slowly my onetime respected position with the executive was undermined at this trial. Wild charges, no matter how improbable, eroded my support. I marvelled at the systematic disintegration of the Noël Browne that I knew, happening through my ears and before my eyes, and I impotent to halt it. One after the other, genuinely embarrassed friends who had been well disposed towards me adopted a new attitude of mild suspicion and incredulity, turning to active hostility. It was hard to blame them, listening to the arguments offered to them and the 'proof' of those arguments. They heard a cleverly pieced-together picture of an arrogant, personally offensive, disloyal, egocentric power-mad individual. This grotesque caricature was a distortion of the Noël Browne they knew. They knew that I had always been accessible to them; the visible effects of our work in the Department of Health could be seen all over Ireland. As John Whyte had written in *Church and State in Modern Ireland:* 'Dr Browne's energetic efforts paid off. By July 1950, he was able to announce that his emergency bed programme was almost complete. Two thousand extra beds had been provided in a little over two years for TB patients. The TB death rate came tumbling down. These were spectacular achievements.' Professor Whyte concluded: 'Of all the members of the inter-party government, Dr Browne seemed to produce the most in the way of definite results.'

Desperate attempts to save the party came from all over the room, to avoid the inevitable split. MacBride's main charge had been disloyalty to the leader. I had denied this charge. There was an appeal for a vote of loyalty to the leader. In reply, I repeatedly asked both the genuinely concerned and those with mischievous intent whether this vote of loyalty meant that I would be compelled to accept the Church of Rome's right to tell our government to drop the health scheme. Did this motion, if passed, mean that as their Minister for Health I must then introduce the means test into the mother and child health scheme? If their answer to this question was yes, my answer was 'I won't support the motion'.

As the night wore on, I adopted my own formula for survival. I would not promise uncritical, unquestioned loyalty to any man. Men change, principles are constant. This became the final fixed theme on my answers to the many questions, motions, and resolutions put to me. Until the Oireachtas changed the law which empowered me, as their Minister for Health, to introduce a free no-means-test mother and child health scheme, I would and must implement that law.

Martin O'Cadhain, who at one time had been an active member of the republican army council and had also been one of de Valera's internees in the Curragh, told me later that on reading about the trial in the newspapers, he was reminded of his time in the republican movement. When a member of the republican army was courtmartialed on a capital charge because of his disloyalty to the army or to the leader, or because of alleged informer activities, there was an eerie substitute for the ritual black cap of the civil courts. The president of the court would deliberately tap out his cigarette into the ashtray in front of him, while steadily eyeing the unfortunate wretch before the court. This Neroesque gesture signalled to the executioners present that the victim had been found guilty of the stated charge. The man was then taken out, allowed to make his peace with God, and summarily shot. Martin consoled me: 'If that trial had taken place, and you a member of the republican army, you would have lost the back of your skull on the top of the Feather Bed mountains'.

The vote was taken by the Clann na Poblachta executive. With three honourable exceptions, i.e. Jack McQuillan, Con Lucey and Dermot Cochran, the executive voted to support MacBride's condemnation of their Minister for Health. There was no need for MacBride publicly to act as personal political executioner on his former colleague. The executive meeting had taken the matter conveniently out of his hands. He could now play the role of democratic party leader, reluctantly enforcing the wishes of his executive to sack his Cabinet colleague.

Meanwhile there was a surprise intervention by a trade union delegation. There was a possibility that the 'nominal charge' peace proposal might be acceptable to the hierarchy. This formula represented a compromise: in order to put herself in benefit, the mother simply paid a ten-shilling fee. I was satisfied with such a settlement. I did not wish to bring down a government, but I did want to save a fine health scheme. I made it clear that if we could come to a reasonable compromise, we would do so, but the no-means-test principle would have to be left intact.

MacBride, impatient to be rid of me, called for my resignation before any further action could be taken. It is a significant indication of the class origins of the Cabinet that while willing to accept the dictat of the bishops, they were indignant that they should be asked seriously to consider this attempt at mediation by the trade union movement.

On 10 April 1951, MacBride delivered to me personally a letter demanding that I resign my post as Minister for Health forthwith. He had thus ensured the collapse of the Coalition government, his own political death warrant and the disappearance of Clann na Poblachta.

The motion of loyalty had read 'If the leader of the party deems it necessary to call for the resignation or removal of Dr Browne from the government, he will have the loyal support of the National Executive.' It was in accordance with this authority that he now requested my resignation. I complied with that request. Mr Costello later asserted, 'If MacBride had not done so, I would have.'

My resignation as Minister for Health was the first time in the history of the state that a Cabinet minister had chosen to sacrifice office in order to show publicly that the Irish government process was an elaborate sham.

In spite of their best efforts to conceal this fraudulent reality of mock power, the Cabinet's influence and submission to Rome was proven without doubt by Cabinet ministers themselves in their own correspondence, behaviour and speeches. It was my decision to publish such confidential state correspondence, to end the fiction of representative democracy in Ireland. That decision, I well knew, ended any prospect I might have had of ever again serving as a Cabinet minister in an Irish government. I was pilloried for my failure to respect cabinet and church confidentiality. But the pretence of a Cabinet to be the supreme instrument and authority in the state, when in fact it was subject to an outside non-elected pressure group, was to me the supreme deception. Mine, easily, was the lesser breach of trust. In fact, had I suppressed that revelation about the reality of government in the Republic I would have become a guilty partner in the deceit.

My final ministerial memory is of my office in the Department of Health. The last ministerial pronouncements had been issued; the last trade union delegation received; my fine civil servant staff had taken leave of me and I most regretfully of them. Our always dependable and resourceful Michael Mulvihill had delivered the important correspondence about the mother and child service to R. M. Smyllie, editor of the *Irish Times*. This correspondence consisted of sixteen letters from myself, Seán MacBride, John Costello and members of the hierarchy. We had been warned that the government might attempt to place an embargo on their publication, but Smyllie, an editor with genuine liberal beliefs, had promised me that should such an embargo be attempted, then, at the risk of going to prison, he 'would publish and be damned'.

On his return from the *Irish Times*, Mulvihill and Dick Whyte took care that all documents in our files likely to be used or misused against us were destroyed. (I was later told that John Costello's first demand on taking over the department was that he be given all available documents, private or otherwise.) The floor of our office was littered with rolled-up snowballs of paper. Wastepaper baskets were full. As with a front-line soldier who had been in continuous action for a long time, my senses and perceptions were dulled by the continuous bombardment from so many fronts. Bone weary, I sat down for the last time at my ministerial desk. Opposite me sat a dishevelled and as always unkempt Noel Hartnett.

Hartnett had a disconcerting habit under stress of reaching into his tobacco-stained waistcoat pocket, and producing a cigarette butt, by choice a Woodbine (commonly known as 'coffin nails') already half-smoked. He would carefully smooth out the singed ends of the butt before putting it into his mouth and lighting it. In a clear ecstasy of enjoyment, he would inhale as if it were life-saving oxygen, closing his eyes. On this occasion he did not produce the dreaded cigarette butt. Instead, equally characteristically, he dug from that same waistcoat pocket something just as unpleasant-looking, a two-inch stump of heavily-chewed yellow pencil. He turned then, as if to all the world, and defiantly declared 'we have our pens'.

It was agreed that my resignation as Minister for Health should be debated in the Dáil. As I rose to speak, on 12 April 1951, there were, I believed, individuals in all parties who were shocked by the suddenness of it, and shamed by the shoddiness of the behaviour of my Cabinet colleagues. Politically it was the end of what most of them privately agreed was a career which would have served the public well had I been allowed to continue.

I spoke briefly. My heart was heavy that so much work still remained to be done for the health of our people. Here was I yielding up voluntarily, on a point of principle, all the power and authority as Minister for Health in which I had placed so much hope and expectation when I had assumed office a mere three years earlier. In spite of a succession of disappointments where his behaviour did not measure up to the potential and stature claimed for it, there remained for me a slight hope that this was the occasion on which de Valera could redeem himself. The issue was the supremacy of 'his' republic, of the Dáil, and above all, of the people's will. How much glorification had I listened to about the brave self-sacrifice and dedication, even to death, of this quintessential Irish republican! Inevitably, with the coalition a discredited rabble, once more de Valera must be crowned King of Ireland and reassume his own significantly chosen messianic title of Taoiseach, or leader. My hope was for a rally to democracy, the equal of Abraham Lincoln's declaration of the rights and freedoms of a genuinely independent and free people. Would de Valera rise to the challenge?

Not surprisingly each leader of the four coalition parties joined the chorus of denigration and abuse about my personal, political, and administrative defects and failings. Seán MacBride used his one remaining accusation, that I was 'mad' not to obey the hierarchy. He told an astounded Dáil, within the privilege of parliament, 'In my opinion, the Minister for Health has not been normal for the last year'. This insulting clause, by order of the House, was withdrawn. The Dáil had just listened to my well-reasoned opening statement, and it included men who, during the whole period of my ministry, had been in daily contact with me.

The intervention by Con Lehane of Clann na Poblachta was valuable. Anxious to help MacBride, he sought to rationalise the petty sectarian remark that I had been foolish enough to have been photographed shaking hands with the Protestant Archbishop of Dublin. Lehane's intervention corroborated the fact that MacBride had in fact made this charge, and it could no longer be denied by him. There was a notable contribution in my support by Oliver Flanagan, surprisingly, in the light of his noted loyalty to the church. Peadar Cowan also spoke in my favour.

There was a sense of occasion as Mr de Valera slowly rose to his feet. There had been no other occasion on which a native government had so diminished us all by its pitiful submissiveness and failure to realise the supreme privilege of cabinet office. To the disappointment of many in all parties, instead of a resounding declaration of faith in the democratic republican ethic, de Valera muttered almost inaudibly one sentence only, 'We have heard enough'. He then sat down. With these words de Valera and his party joined the political pygmies on the government benches.

Dan Breen sat close to me on the opposition benches. He had not intervened so far. With de Valera safely out of the chamber Breen, the fearless one, as he headed for the bar, leaned over to me where I sat in a mixture of disgust and contempt for my colleagues. In a hushed whisper, lest he be overheard and reported to de Valera, Breen muttered an approving, 'Well done, Noël'.

12

Cabinet Portraits

WITH THE formation of the first coalition government, William A. Norton, leader of the Irish Labour Party, had become Tanaiste (deputy Prime Minister). Although he had been general secretary of the Post Office Workers' Union during the 1940s, it was a measure of his indifference to the welfare of his members that the conditions of work in the Dublin sorting offices were generally atrocious. Even following his appointment as Tanaiste and minister in Cabinet they did not improve significantly.

Norton was a man of many talents, all dedicated exclusively to his own betterment in society. He was persuasively articulate, and could simulate sincerity and pretended concern with impressive and misleading conviction. He could feel deeply only about his own special needs. He was well read on political matters, something of an exception in that Cabinet. As a devout practising Catholic he was an immutably commited conservative in political outlook.

Norton became a wealthy man, with a large house in an exclusive Dublin suburb. He had wide business interests, most of them in the drink trade. He distinguished himself in Cabinet by a complete absence of ethical standards on fundamental issues affecting his own class. He willingly allowed himself to be used by the conservative Fine Gael Cabinet, while neglecting and undermining the welfare or best interests of the working people. Shortly after the formation of the coalition, when I queried the qualifications of a man submitted by Norton for the post of District Justice, the reply was classic Norton: 'He's well able for it, wasn't he Roddy Connolly's election agent?' In reply to a demand for an increase in flour prices by the millers, it was Norton who craftily proposed the device of keeping the price of the loaf the same while minimally reducing its size. He commented, 'Women won't notice the difference.' This device gave the millers their profit at the expense of the hard-pressed women and children whom Norton, as Labour Party leader, claimed to represent. During a bank strike in 1950, in the absence of the Taoiseach, he acted as chairman to a Cabinet meeting. Using the legitimate plea that I would not be party to a lockout, I caused consternation among my Cabinet colleagues, by refusing to sign the government order needed before the banks could close their doors. I quoted back at them their rule about collective responsibility. All, including Norton, had signified their intention of voting for the closure.

Throughout the lifetime of that Cabinet Norton played an invaluable role for his conservative Fine Gael colleagues. Whenever I chose to contest some issue which merited a radical solution, the Taoiseach would turn aside my criticism with the unanswerable, 'But the Labour leader, Mr Norton, agrees; what's your difficulty, Dr Browne?'

It was Norton who devised the escape hatch for his Cabinet colleagues, which justified their eventual U-turn on the health services: the casuist apologia, 'We don't want to have to provide a free health service for the fur-coated ladies of Foxrock.' In this way he parodied the whole rationale against means-test medicine. It was Norton also who devised the dismissive and dishonest charge, later used against me by MacBride, that in making an issue of principle out of the elimination of the means-test from Irish medicine, I had made a 'fetish out of a phrase.'

It was of interest to watch how the Fine Gael group outwitted Norton in Cabinet. Under pressure from the rank and file of the Labour Party Norton was encouraged to press for an entirely new social welfare code. Nothing could have been more unwelcome for Fine Gael. Like the rest of us, Norton was bound by Cabinet protocol, which laid down the Minister's responsibility to make his submissions, giving reasons for any stated proposal. Norton did this. The financial demands on the Exchequer needed to fund his social welfare proposals were considerable, even though on an insurance rather than a seriously socialist redistributive policy; each minister had some 'special' needs which must be curtailed if Norton's scheme were to be implemented.

I noticed a number of queries, counterqueries, objections, tendering of memoranda on ideological grounds, which accumulated around Norton's proposals with each successive Cabinet meeting. One of the last memories of Cabinet meetings I have is of seeing the quarter-inch thick brief with which Norton had earlier introduced his proposals become inches thicker until the final brief was nearly nine inches high. His proposal for a social welfare scheme appeared to be little nearer a final solution and in fact never was realised. This is one of the not-so-subtle ways in which the conservative majority party in a coalition can 'legitimately' frustrate radical proposals submitted by the 'minority' parties. One wonders to what extent Norton had collaborated in the delay.

It is difficult to believe now that on one occasion in the 1950s our annual Budget was under £100 million. The Taoiseach had virtually no understanding of problems of fiscal policy, and was shocked to notice that taken together all our departments' financial submissions required more than £100 million. His response was characteristically simple-minded, and of doubtful morality. He issued an appeal to all of us to send in falsified figures for our departmental needs on the assurance that, after the Budget was passed, we would be permitted 'all the money we needed to run our departments.' This money would be made available in subsequent supplementary estimates. To my surprise, all my Cabinet colleagues appeared to have agreed to these proposals. I refused to accede to their request. Appeals were made to me to change my mind repeatedly, but I declined to do so. What was particularly disturbing to me was the apparent failure of my party and Cabinet colleague, Mr MacBride, to share my attitude.

In a succession of telephone conversations, one of the most persistent of those who appealed to me to change my mind was Norton. 'I'm prepared to do it, Noël, I'll see you get all you want after the Budget. Why not agree, and so help us to keep the figures in the Book of Estimates under a hundred million pounds?' This had been Costello's appeal to his colleagues. Even if there was no moral issue involved, the fact that they had all joined in such a conspiracy to mislead the public, and inevitably Fianna Fáil, would or could be used later by the Fine Gael ministers against Clann na Poblachta and the Labour ministers.

Since difficulties had already arisen about the mother and child scheme, I could become subject to blackmail by all or any one of them. Should the Cabinet decide to renege on it, the fact that I had been party to the conspiracy could be used to compel me to agree to their proposals about a watered-down health service.

Norton was a notorious hedonist. He enjoyed the good life. He was a small, grossly overweight figure, with a great square bullock-shaped head. Though his eyes were buried behind inch-thick horn spectacles, they were, without doubt, his crowning glory. There was never a merrier, more sparkling, sherry-cream brown pair of eyes on any man or woman; they could effect a dangerously disarming influence on a critic. His irreverent and ribald sense of humour was heard only in safe privacy. The clergy and his fellow trade unionists were his favourite targets. He was master of the art of mock indignation. In the Dáil, when angrily replying to MacEntee, his main tormentor on the opposition benches, he had no difficulty in forgetting his rage smilingly to ridicule his opponent for some personal weaknesses. His anger was skin deep, as superficial as his radicalism.

It was said that while in opposition Sean Lemass was responsible for a political column in the *Irish Press*. Understandably he concentrated on the members of our Cabinet, and all of us came under scrutiny. The Lemass column about Norton was one day referred to in Cabinet by Cecil Lavery, our Attorney General, at the conclusion of our usual business. Lavery remarked that he believed Norton had a reasonable cause for legal action against the columnist, who had dismissed Norton as a minister who was only minimally concerned with his Department of Social Welfare and, in effect, bone lazy. Whether acting on Lavery's advice or not, Norton duly took an action in the High Court. A Dublin jury of his peers had little doubt about the validity of the comment, and awarded the Labour leader contempt damages of one pound. Following the humiliating verdict, MacEntee liked to rouse Norton in the Dáil by calling him 'Billy the Quid.'

Norton wallowed in the sumptuous banquets arranged for visiting foreign dignitaries. His childish enjoyment at table evoked feelings of amusement and revulsion. My wife and I would watch increduously as he would call for a second helping of his favourite sweet, a spun sugar confection which stood about

four inches high and was shaped as a bird's nest. With his table
napkin tucked firmly into his straining white collar, his
flickering brown monkey's eyes would lovingly follow the waiter
and his spoon as he loaded the plate down for the second time.
Spoon and fork filled the sugary syrup into his mouth until there
remained only the melted warm honey mixture on his plate.
This too was greedily scooped into his now slobbering mouth.
Like a hungry sucking piglet, frantically probing the fat sow's
belly, spoon and fork were followed by his chubby fingers and
last of all his thumb, each of them lovingly and lingeringly
sucked dry. Fingers licked clean, he would hold a lighted scarlet
and gold-labelled Havana in one sticky hand and caress his well-
filled brandy glass in the other. Norton, the workers' leader,
lived Larkin's 'Nothing is too good for the working classes.' But
for the Irish worker the good things of life stopped at Norton.

The rank and file of the Labour Party were sympathetic to the
social advances proposed in the health scheme, and widely
welcomed them. But the Labour leadership, with the help of the
Stalinist group in the party then, had no great difficulty in mani-
pulating a complete reversal of policy whenever it was needed.
So it was on this occasion. It was Norton, indeed, who devised
the clever arguments — 'I won't go against my bishops,'; 'those
who need it most,' 'fur-coated ladies' — against the health
scheme. They had the advantage of appearing to radicalise the
argument against the means-test. They were gladly accepted
and subsequently used by Fine Gael and other conservative
members of the party and the Cabinet, including MacBride. Mr
Norton's ingenious argument was 'I don't see why I should pay
taxes so as to provide a free health service for those who can
afford one.' So did he coat the pill for the retention of the dis-
criminating medical system for his working-class electorate.

Jim Everett, the second Labour leader in the coalition government, was safely tucked away in the peaceful Department of
Posts and Telegraphs, which was normally reserved either for
nonentities or for potential trouble-makers. Everett was one of
those whom our political commentators knowingly describe as a
'shrewd' politician. In pursuit of his own self-interest he was,
overnight, to launch us on a substantial national wage agree-

ment. It was Everett who was to introduce a new word into our political folklore of jobbery which, in its own small way, had echoes of Tammany Hall. The word was 'Baltinglass.'

As with Norton, Everett was a 'Bishop's man' on the health issue. He had already succeeded in splitting the Irish Labour Party; he led an anti-Communist breakaway called the National Labour Party. His handful of seats qualified him to become a member of the coalition cabinet jigsaw. One other National Labour deputy, a well-known footballer with little else to offer, was given a parliamentary secretaryship; his name was Spring.

Jim Everett was a nondescript, undersized man, of swarthy complexion, with watchful ferret's brown eyes. On a visit to Wicklow town, where he lived, I have a fleeting memory of him sitting beside his driver in the front of his ostentatious American state car. He affected a broadbrimmed, Jim Larkin-style, grey trilby hat whose edge seemed to tip his long nose as he looked down to study his notes on his lap. Everett sat in his car as it swept down into the dark steep narrow laneway to the harbour, a fixed menacing figure, evoking visions of gunmen, speak-easies and Chicago. But he was simply doing his vote-catching rounds, on his way to an old age pensioner or a widow with six children or simply another job to fix.

Everett was an active member of Wicklow County Council. His sole interest in life was to remain a Dáil deputy and a member of the county council, which he did until he died. Through no fault of his own, as with so many others, he had had only a minimal education and a hard upbringing. Yet he was certainly to leave his mark on Irish public life. He attended Cabinet meetings assiduously, taking no part in discussions except when an item came up concerning Wicklow in any shape or form. His contributions were then brief, to the point, invariably self-interested, and usually acted on.

Having carefully 'clocked' into the Cabinet meetings on those days on which the county council sat in Wicklow, Everett would gather his largely unread sack full of briefs, mutter his apologies, and slip away. He had little time for Cabinet meetings compared to the supreme importance of meetings of Wicklow County Council. For Jim Everett it was not in Government Buildings in Merrion Street but in Wicklow town hall that the real business of the state was transacted. Yet being a minister had its uses. Early on in the course of a brief curt speech to the faithful in Wicklow which the Cabinet was to read about for the first time in the morning papers next day, Everett awarded what was then a hefty pay rise to his departmental employees, the Post Office workers. Inevitably this generous award became a mandatory pay rise for the whole of the public service. With minimal effort from Everett, overnight he had become the darling of the workers. The following day in the Cabinet room he was mildly chastised by his colleagues, most of whom envied him his easily won nationwide popularity.

For a time, all went well. Meanwhile his civil servants were to notice that Everett had what, for them, was a disturbing practice of reading out every item of confidential supplementary information in his parliamentary brief, meant only to be used 'with discretion' at question time. It was as if he was attempting to signal to his opposition questioner that he disowned this kind of talk. 'What could you expect from these civil servants?'

One evening, towards the end of our day in the Dáil, there came that cry ringing through the corridors of Leinster House that haunts the waking hours of any Cabinet minister, 'The government has been defeated.' In spite of Fianna Fáil's understandable disappointment at losing office, they had fought back doggedly and noisily in the House, drawing on all their parliamentary experience and skill. This night they had mounted a cleverly-timed ambush; it was Everett who marched us all behind him into it. He introduced an increased postal charge against which there had been a revolt by a number of coalition supporters who now, together with Fianna Fáil, brought down the government. It was a fine parliamentary achievement for Fianna Fáil.

An emergency Cabinet meeting was called at once in the Taoiseach's office in Leinster House. All of us were in differing states of shock at the unexpectedness of the defeat. We felt that there was too much work still waiting to be done in our departments. None of us was anxious for a general election yet. One of the more experienced members of the Cabinet, probably Tom O'Higgins, called in Dr Michael Hayes who was Professor of Irish at UCD and had been Ceann Comhairle at one time. He was at one time an active member of Cumann na nGaedhael, a man of considerable political experience, and an authority on parliamentary procedure, well disposed towards the government. His advice was childishly simple, based on the notorious formula for survival in Irish public life — 'Those are my principles, and if you don't like them, I'll change them.'

Everett had no difficulty in following this advice. He returned to his department and reversed the postal increases. First thing the following morning Mr McGilligan submitted the estimate to the Dáil. It passed without difficulty; we were not the only ones who did not want a general election just then. The disgruntled coalition deputies absent on the previous day had been whipped into line.

All of us hoped that Everett, now out of trouble, would stay there. He did not. He had learned nothing. Early rumblings rolled towards us once again from Everett's constituency in late 1950; it was a really sordid mess this time. It is hard to credit in a Labour minister but Everett had evicted a middle-aged postmistress from a post office in Co Wicklow and appointed a supporter of his own in her place. The name of that Wicklow village, Baltinglass, has since entered into Irish political folklore; a book was even written about it. All this ensured immortality of a sordid kind for Everett.

Throughout their sixteen years in office Fianna Fáil had had no scruples about behaving much as Everett had done, but all that was now irrelevant. They organised marches on the Dáil; there were widespread protests with leaflets and public meetings held all over Co Wicklow. Telegraph poles were cut down. Not only Everett but the government as well were in real trouble. Should they call on Everett to resign? It really didn't matter; Everett had no intention of doing so. The behaviour of the Cabinet during this crisis was in sharp distinction to their treatment of me over the mother and child scheme. (The Baltinglass situation was finally resolved in January 1951, when the postmistress got her job back).

It is probably a valuable yardstick of the standard of politicians who may form a Cabinet in the Republic that in spite of his inept and dubious behaviour when in office, Everett was again chosen to serve as a Cabinet minister in a subsequent coalition Cabinet in 1954.

In a Cabinet room full of dull, earnest and dutiful plodders, Paddy McGilligan was an intriguing and polished anachronism. When he entered that room, always late, with five or six three-inch thick briefs under his arm, we all had to curb an inclination to stand to attention; the 'headmaster' had arrived.

McGilligan impressed people with his sharp-edged Derry accent and the seemingly limitless range of his dialectical and intellectual skills. To Fine Gael he was the progenitor of the great Shannon Scheme, a courageous idea at the time. For radicals such as myself he was the minister who in Cabinet had offered the widows of Ireland the bleak prospect that 'when there were only limited funds at the Government's disposal, people might have to die in the country, and die of starvation.' This speech was delivered at a time when a widow with five children had been found dead of starvation. It was from just such an Ireland that so many of us had fled.

Only Everett separated me from McGilligan at the Cabinet table, yet after three years I knew little about him. He was a graceful, slight figure, with spindle-shaped arms and legs, a Lowry matchstick man. The care with which he chose and matched his suits, shirts, ties, socks, shoes and cufflinks reflected what an elegant Elizabethan grandee he would have made. He had a small, well-shaped angular head with carefully brushed grey hair; even the comb lines could still be seen. He had a broad forehead and a jutting nose and chin; smile lines radiated from his grey eyes and around his mouth, which was strong and tight-lipped. He had all the darting, clearcut, precise movements of a cheeky eaglet, and graceful well-shaped prehensile claws for hands. Watch them unstrap the curious traditional red and bronze tweed strap which is supplied to all ministers to tie up their briefs, carefully unpicking the fine needlelike teeth of the shining steel buckle. He could undo the bow of the narrow pink ribbon used to contain an individual memorandum: no resort to the quick slice of a sharp penknife for him. Infinite patience, always in control, even over a tight knot. Alone of all the members of the Cabinet, with the exception of Tim Murphy, I retained an obstinate respect for the panache, brilliance, and intellect of Paddy McGilligan. This did not prevent my regretting his gross misuse of these talents.

McGilligan was a truly absorbing speaker in the Dáil. The

Chamber rapidly filled when he took the floor. Unlike his carefully dark-suited front bench colleagues, he wore what appeared to be a fine handwoven Donegal tweed jacket of faded brown, with fawn trousers, and suede shoes. When he stood up to speak, unlike the rest of us with our shambles of sheets of paper, McGilligan would produce his single piece of paper, four inches by three in size, open it out and carefully smooth it over, using the knuckles of his closed fist on the desk in front of him. With that piece of paper, or possibly one or two more for a speech of two or three hours, he could tease, torment, ridicule, and humiliate the unhappy opposition speakers, bringing out a protective fellow-feeling of compassion among the rest of us.

McGilligan welcomed interruptions. It was his practice to stop completely in the middle of a speech and obligingly lean over towards his interrupter, his hand crooked behind his ear. He would then invite the opposition speaker to repeat out loud, so that all of us could hear, whatever incautious criticism he wished to make. McGilligan would then take that phrase and, as with his tiny piece of paper, spend up to half an hour scrutinising its grammar, its syntax, its plain facts. The overall effect was to make the interrupter plead for an end to it, and ensured silence for the rest of his speech. He pilloried and ridiculed easily and fluently and at times hilariously, with pithy accuracy, wild wit, and venom. He enjoyed our enjoyment. For me his greatest performance was when he spoke about a 'megalomaniacal' series of Fianna Fáil building proposals. It appears that these were designed to bulldoze most of Merrion Street, followed by Kildare Street, a school, a convent, a hospital, part of the university, University College Church and much of St Stephen's Green on all sides — or so it seemed, by the time McGilligan was finished. The house had filled to listen to McGilligan. It was one of the few occasions on which I felt sorry for Seán Lemass. As far as I recollect, it was he who got the blame for the proposals. I need not have worried since even Lemass smiled too in admiration at the virtuoso performance by a master. Strangely, it was said that McGilligan was not a successful lawyer in court (his forte was Constitutional Law).

He was fortunate in having a striking-looking wife, bright, witty, and intelligent, who was temperamentally suited to him. They were lighthearted and carefree at External Affairs dinners, and would descend as if from another world from whatever pre-dinner gathering was on, drawing to themselves the eyes of everyone in the room. She always dressed in an exotic model dress, unlike my own wife, whose dress was stitched together at the last moment and, if there was time, ironed before leaving home; he wore a finely-cut tailcoat, with a white butterfly tie at his throat. The McGilligans had come to enjoy themselves, and nothing would stop them. They loved life and clearly enjoyed one another's company.

McGilligan's attendance at Cabinet meetings was erratic. He rarely appeared until we had already completed an hour or two's work. I believe that we all feared an inquisition by McGilligan; I certainly did, but my finances were to a great extent under my personal control, because of the peculiar arrangements surrounding the spending of the Hospital Sweep Funds. My main encounter with McGilligan concerned my appeal for money to do something to improve the appalling conditions in which many of our old people ended their days in our workhouses. In spite of his reputation for meanness, he was sympathetic to my understandably special interest in these institutions.

I had had no idea of the truly shameful conditions under which aged people, orphans and the destitute were compelled to exist. As minister, touring the hospitals, mental institutions and workhouses then called 'county homes' I saw for myself the Dickensian state of the buildings and the distress of their inmates.

Children in workhouses, like old-style criminals, carried numbers on their backs to distinguish one from another. Each destitute family was broken up — the father going this way, the mothers that way and the children, according to sex, yet a third and fourth way. In a workhouse which I visited in Longford, an open sewer ran through the recreation grounds. The food was cooked, as it was in most of the workhouses, in a large vat which had a block and tackle to open and close the vast lids in the open air kitchens. Whatever was to be stewed for the inmates was poured into these enormous stew pans. The wards were long, the walls had no pictures, the floors were bare and the sky was frequently visible through the broken slates on the roof. The beds were on raised platforms to accommodate straw-filled paliasses, long lines of them on either side of the room, occupied by pale, mummylike human beings lying semi-comatose, apathetic and completely uninterested in their surroundings.

On my return to the Dáil, deeply moved and shocked by what I had seen, I called on de Valera to resign for his neglect while in government for sixteen years. There was uproar, as always, when there was the slightest hint of criticism of that great panjandrum of Irish life, but privately many on the opposition benches felt shamed by my disclosures. An enquiry into the state of the workhouses was later set up in my department, and my findings supported. We submitted proposals to McGilligan from the Department of Health for funds to remedy the great scandal, and without any serious resistance he agreed to the introduction of a financial aid scheme for local authorities. This was to lead to a considerable improvement, many of the workhouses properly coming to merit the name of 'county homes.' I was grateful to McGilligan for his sympathy and help with this problem, so close to my heart.

McGilligan had one strange weakness. As we came to the end of the financial year, and the budget approached, he appeared to melt into an orgy of inaction and self-pity, skipping Cabinet meetings or arriving late. He clearly dreaded the 'loaves and fishes' job of trying to reconcile our many conflicting claims in such a multi-party government. In financial terms, he was a conventional traditionalist. Balance the books, pay your way, cut capital expenditure, prime the private enterprise pump, and all will be well. Because of his clear panic on these occasions, the Cabinet decided to establish a sub-committee of members of the Cabinet who would help formulate his budget.

There was the surprising fact that this paragon could be erratic and at times a pitiful victim of swinging moods, from a euphoric, bubbling, story-telling, Bar Library raconteur to a face 'as long as a wet week' with long, gloomy silences.

T. J. Murphy, Minister for Local Government, was probably the most dedicated and hard-working member of the Inter-Party Cabinet, but his achievements have either been ignored, minimised, or blatantly filched from him. Murphy was a Labour deputy from Cork in his late fifties, a quiet self-effacing man with a detailed knowledge of local government laws and institutions. He seemed to have much the same sense of awed disbelief as I in finding himself at the centre of real power; he could now do the work he most enjoyed, improving the living conditions of ordinary people. He was an unhealthily pale, spectacled, slightly hunch-backed, frail figure. Possibly he was chosen by Norton because of his quiet, unspectacular manner, and his capacity to listen.

Murphy's contributions at Cabinet were brief and for the most part sensible items of fact, nearly always about his favourite subject, local government affairs. He shared the Custom House building with the Department of Health, working just across the corridor from me. His department had controlled health affairs for the whole community until the Department of Health had been created in the late 1940s.

Early on I realised that Mr Murphy had been allocated enough money to build a hundred thousand local authority houses. I had also discovered that with the important restructuring of the use of the Hospital Sweep funds, I would have some thirty million pounds to spend over a seven-year period. I proposed that our two departments should pool resources, because our joint building programme would provide for an enormous expenditure for those times. Our idea was to try to attract home some of our recently-emigrated craftsmen and professional people. There would be a demand for all kinds of architects, engineers, constructional and building operatives. In his heart, I suspect Tim would have been just as pleased if I would go away so that he could get on with his own work, but in the end he was moved to agree with my proposal in the hope that possibly we would encourage some of our emigrants back. I reassured him that the Department of Health would do all the work, mainly because we were fortunate to have in our department two journalists of outstanding originality and talent: Press Officer Aodh de Blacam, and Frank Gallagher.

Aodh de Blacam was an ardent admirer of de Valera, and wrote under the pen name 'Roddy the Rover' in *The Irish Press*. A large, gentle and charming man, he was a convert to Catholicism. As my speech writer on non-political matters it was his job to research the history of a person, a site, a building, or institution, and work up a speech for me. On a journey across Ireland to lay the foundation stone at Ballinasloe Portiuncula

Hospital, I had had no time to glance through my speech until just before I stood up to speak. Incredulously I heard myself orating, 'Nisi dominus domum aedificat frustu laborant qui aedificant' (Unless the Lord build the house, the builders labour in vain). The audience was astounded. Were they by any chance at High Mass by mistake? The hospital was to be run by the Franciscan nuns and the whole speech was in a similar devout and reverential style. Bravely I waded through to its thoughtful concluding benediction on the enterprise; my audience visibly resisted the temptation to bless themselves and say Amen. A shame-faced Bishop, Dr Dignan, followed me with a few unspectacular mundane words of welcome. A good friend, he smilingly complained to me, 'Dr Browne, I should have made your speech, and you mine.'

Aodh, a feverent Gaelic speaker, told me that in the early days of the formation of Fianna Fáil he had pleaded with de Valera to name the *Irish Press* newspaper in Irish, *Scéal Eireann* or something similar, but de Valera, the hard business man, never permitted romantic Irish proclivities to interfere with financial or political reality.

The second journalist, Frank Gallagher, was an entirely different personality. He was a fanatical supporter of Fianna Fáil and worshipped de Valera, who had the highest regard for him, using him as head of censorship all during the precarious war years. It was a job which needed a particularly able journalist, and Gallagher, if somewhat over-zealous, did it well. He was sent to Health because it was a harmless, non-controversial department under an innocuous uncontroversial minister. We were lucky to be blessed with de Blacam; to have Frank Gallagher as well gave us great scope to do something about the dowdy, unimaginative departmental information services.

The Government Information Service had always been dull, even in its propaganda. Our journalists on the other hand thought of everything: multi-coloured posters, leaflets illustrated with Rowel Friers drawings or photographs by Adolf Morath, catchy phrases and slogans. Competitions were held for imaginative wall posters, one of which, a 'Wanted for Murder' hygiene poster picturing the common house fly, was borrowed for use in a similar campaign in Britain because of its excellence. A particularly striking booklet highlighted our building programme, putting across the messages 'Ireland is Building' and 'Come Home and Help.' Inside were models and architectural drawings of projected sanatoria, hospitals, houses, clinics. The whole programme, with its objective of the repatriation of emigrants, was an exhilarating microcosm of the possibilities if only all government departments could do likewise. We employed Eamonn Andrews to broadcast at peak listening hours. Indirectly the message was conveyed to emigrants through sisters, mothers and wives listening at home. Many emigrants did return but, as always, only for a time. Cynical stagnation recurred on Fianna Fáil's resumption of office.

On the cover of our booklet we had shown a picture of Cashel Hospital, one of the very few which had been built during the Fianna Fáil period of office. With some justification, although we had in fact included it in good faith as an illustration of what we hoped to do, Lemass (surprisingly, since he was never a petty man), exploded in a protest at our 'misrepresentation of the facts.' As it happened, his protest and the heated debate on the issue which ensued helped to publicise further the optimistic overall message of 'Ireland is Building'. On that occasion I was grateful to John Costello who, on the night of the debate, took on the reply to Mr Lemass — I was certainly not up to that level of competition yet. Good lawyer that he was, he had no trouble with his brief.

A sceptical Fianna Fáil deputy, Bob Briscoe, a well-known betting man, dismissed as impossible our challenging hospital building programme. Presuming that it was a safe bet, he promised across the Dáil chamber, 'I'll be the first to raise my hat to you, if you carry through these claims.' Some seven or eight years later, both of us still in the Dáil, I had the pleasure of inviting Bob to 'take off his hat to the Department of Health, for work done and seen to be done.' Our hospitals all over the Republic were there to prove it.

I was interested to watch John Garvin, a Joyce scholar and Tim Murphy's departmental secretary, as I lobbied and gently bullied his Minister with bizarre proposals to publicise our joint programme — recall that we were the junior ministry. He hovered apprehensively behind his minister, as if to save him from doing something silly. I would like to have known his private beliefs about our programme.

Sadly, one summer evening in Cork in 1949, Tim Murphy in full spate (which was still mild enough) was asking for continued support for his programme for 'housing homeless people.' He was overcome by a severe heart attack, and died shortly afterwards. He was a good man, and largely unnoticed and unremembered, except no doubt by his own.

James Dillon was a notable personality in the first Coalition Cabinet. For one thing, right or not, he was the only Irish politician who had taken a principled stand against our neutrality in the Second World War when it had been the unanimous decision of all our other politicians. His lonely and courageous opposition had forced his resignation from the Fine Gael party. Though I, as a doctor, volunteered for war service, I shared the general belief that the nation as a whole, if at all possible, should stay neutral. Other than Nazi Germany, no nation gladly leads its civilian population into a modern war. Yet, as a loner myself, I admired Dillon for that show of independence.

Expensively educated, at first glance Dillon seemed endowed with rich natural talent. He was a wealthy shopkeeper and a member of a distinguished Irish political family. He was at all times courteous and humane, and had a delightfully rich, well-rounded speaking voice. He favoured an old-fashioned declamatory speaking style, giving the impression that he was more concerned about how he sounded than what he said. He was a strong Anglophile and fancied himself as the Dáil's answer to Winston Churchill. A well-read and scholarly man, he admired Edmund Burke, whose regret for the fall of the French monarchy and the ensuing popular revolution he seemed to share.

On closer study it was apparent that, although a clear, reasoned and lucid speaker, he had nothing to say which had not already been said. He was a shallow person, with an unoriginal and uncreative mind. For the most part he refashioned other people's ideas for use in support of his consistently mean, conservative, small-town prejudices. In terms of British House of Commons politics, he would probably have liked to be considered as a Liberal, but in present terms would most likely be considered as a conventional Thatcherite. On one occasion, with the kindliest of intentions, fearful of my reforming zeal, he warned me against the dangers of making too many political sacrifices in defence of the welfare of the masses.

A middle-sized, impressive figure of a man, who wore well-tailored dark greys and blues, he carried a pince-nez on the end of a black ribbon. His great black artist-style hat was a modification of what in those days was known as a 'county manager's hat'. He smoked heavily, using a Noël Coward-style long black cigarette holder: a histrionic personality, anxious to impress. The ephemeral nature of his mind in contrast to his impressive presence was later illustrated by his disastrous brief leadership of Fine Gael for which at first sight he would appear to have been the ideal choice.

On the formation of the coalition, Dillon was already a well-seasoned experienced politician. In spite of his temporary wartime defection, he was once again a respected member of Fine Gael. During my early days I was quite overwhelmed by what I believed to be his breadth of knowledge on virtually all subjects discussed in Cabinet. So stark and clear-headed did these opinions appear that on occasions I wondered if he subscribed to the *Reader's Digest*. For most of the early months in Cabinet, his reasonant booming voice would drown out all but the most determined.

My introduction to him was spectacular and memorable. It was my first day in the Dáil; the shattering reality that 'they' were no longer the government, that de Valera was no longer Taoiseach, irresistibly percolated into the minds of all of us. There is little doubt now that de Valera was overcome with the shock of it; for the first time in his loquacious life, he appeared to be at a loss for words. His deputy, Lemass, was chosen to defend Fianna Fáil's defeat; I was greatly impressed by his resilience and courage. Jack McQuillan called it arrogance, and he was probably right. Lemass in his peroration called on the new young government to have no doubt that their days as a government would be short — 'Government affairs had been handed over in financially sound order.' Exultantly and prophetically he concluded, 'See that you hand it back that way.' James Dillon was picked to speak on our behalf. Bubbling with indignation and the sense of occasion, he rose to reply. His speech too was exultant. It was a celebration of the victory and the meeting of minds in the multi-party coalition. Within it, I felt, lay the seeds of Dillon's hoped-for one-party state. 'Doomed be damned to you', rang out the challenge from our Demosthenes. 'This government will last.'

It was during his intervention on the proposed spending by the Department of Local Government on local authority housing that I came to understand the hostility of men of property towards such capital spending. With considerable detail Dillon itemised each overt or hidden subsidy provided by the state to working-class householders. His grievance was that these subsidies originated in the taxes paid by him as a property owner. This speech first alerted me to the 'them' and 'us' nature of the forces in the coalition cabinet. Wholesome aspirations are commonplace; a will to pay for them rare. I remembered that individual intervention by Dillon as a kind of declaration of war on the beliefs which I held about an egalitarian society.

As with Costello, Dillon shared my hopes for improving the health service. He had led the campaign against the authoritarian 1946 Fianna Fáil Health Bill and knew that improvements were badly needed. Costello had been immediately intimidated by the opposition of the medical profession, as conveyed to him through his advisor on such matters, Dr Tom O'Higgins. To Costello, the medical profession were the unselfish workers who gave their lives in the service of the poor. More of a sceptic, Dillon supported my stand against the resistance of the Medical Association to the mother and child health proposals. Dillon went so far as to send a personal letter to me, in his bold one-inch high lettering: 'I am 100% behind you, Noël.' He went on to dismiss a ballot of members by the IMA as a 'most tendentious document.' I was indeed grateful for what was my sole support at that time, but beneath all the outward trappings of education, wealth and culture, and in spite of his commitment to stand with me against 'the four corners of the earth', as soon as the bishops called the tune Dillon obediently danced to it. He argued long and passionately with me, and voted against the health scheme.

13

Independent

PROTEST meetings followed my resignation; the public was more shocked and indignant about the bishops' interference in parliament than were the politicians. The Dublin Trades Council expressed their disappointment at the loss of the health services. Letters of support flowed in from all over the country, with money with which to fight the election. Within a few weeks, in fear of an inevitable defeat on a Department of Agriculture vote, the government was dissolved, and a general election followed on 30 May 1951. The public believed that the government had been weak and had treated me unfairly, so from all parties they rallied to my support. Yet this is not the stuff of political change. With the exception of Jack McQuillan and Peadar Cowan, none of the working politicians dared support us. De Valera and Fianna Fáil were concerned only with regaining office. Fine Gael and Clann na Poblachta, under Seán MacBride, were committed to defending their position. The rank and file of the Labour Party were drilled into line behind Norton and Everett on the side of the consultants and the bishops and against a people's health scheme. Among the Labour leadership at the time were Donal Nevin, Jim Larkin, Michael Mullen and Chris Ferguson.

So we faced into the general election. The formidable power of the Church was used unscrupulously against us. Noel Hartnett, my director of elections, was forced to threaten legal action against priests whose sermons were particularly dishonest. Bishop Browne of Galway attributed my political beliefs to those of Nazi Germany. Our health scheme was wrongly portrayed as advocating euthanasia for the unfit and the aged, as well as abortion and contraception. In *The Lantern* magazine the Dominican Order circulated a question-and-answer series which portrayed the scheme as being immoral and a form of Communism, e.g. 'Question: Is it a mortal sin to introduce a mother and child health service? Answer: It is a sin to introduce a mother and child no-means-test service'. 'Question: Is it true that the Communist Party believes in free health services? Answer: It is true that the Communist Party has a free health service'. There was a direct attack on the credibility of departmental staff. We had published an English translation of a document in which the head of the pontifical academy of sciences, the Rev Professor Gammeli, had written, 'the British national health scheme was not immoral'. A priest at Westland Row accused us of having 'cooked' the Gammeli document to 'suit our case'. The suggestion was as outrageous as it was false; Aodh de Blacham had had the document authenticiated at the Papal Nunciature. We had no difficulty in disposing of the lie, and my solicitors were instructed to make the priest pay an agreed sum for defamation to the Little Sisters of the Poor, whose work I admired.

As to the media, we were supported by the then liberal *Irish Times*, which had a relatively small circulation. The mass circulation Independent Newspapers suppressed our side of the story, and de Valera's Irish Press Newspapers did the same. There was as yet no television service, and the state radio service favoured the consultants and the church. I was not asked to give fully my side of the controversy, nor have I ever been since, even though I have had to listen to contrary views.

We decided that we should not directly confront the bishops during the campaign. We chose instead to confront the medical consultants. As a final precaution we decided that although distinguished speakers were available to us there should be only two campaign speakers in Dublin South-East, myself and Noel Hartnett. In this way we retained control of our campaign.

We were happy with the final results. Standing as an independent, I nearly doubled my first preferences in Dublin South-East, just failing to oust John Costello from the head of the poll. The first preferences were: John A. Costello (Fine Gael), 9,222; Noel Browne (Independent), 8,473; Sean MacEntee (Fianna Fáil), 8,334; J. H. Douglas (Fine Gael), 710; P. McCarten (Clann na Poblachta), 569; Michael B. Yeats (Fianna Fáil), 2,034. Michael ffrench O'Carroll, a young and politically inexperienced doctor, humiliated Seán MacBride, who scraped home by only a few first preference votes. Jack McQuillan was returned in Roscommon, a remarkable personal triumph for a deputy in rural Ireland. Peadar Cowan, another critic of the church's actions, was easily returned in Dublin.

Only two Clann na Poblachta deputies were returned compared with ten deputies in 1948. The total Clann vote dropped from 274,000 to a mere 54,260. With 69 seats to Fine Gael's 40, Labour's 16 and the Clann's 2, Fianna Fáil were in a position to form a government.

Even under less than ideal conditions the voting process had shown itself capable of reacting sensitively to the behaviour of its elected representatives.

We were now faced with a new pattern of politics in Ireland, the multi-party or coalition concept of government. Henceforward, the Republic was to lose stability of the kind produced by the repeated election and re-election of a Fianna Fáil government. This stability had had its advantages, but these were outweighed by a succession of increasingly inept Fianna Fáil administrations.

Unhappily the introduction of the new coalition factor did nothing to improve the quality of government. Because of the dominance of a deeply reactionary educational system, backed by a rigid censorship of ideas imposed on the adolescent and adult population, public life proved itself incapable of rising above the conformity of a conservative consensus. Emigration dealt efficiently with both the intellectual dissident and the dissatisfied unemployed. The evolution of a serious radical, liberal or left-wing political movement became impossible. The Communist party, though minuscule, was continually harassed. Little or no serious dissent was tolerated; there was no serious debate on ideological issues. The débâcle of the mother and child scheme had not permanently disturbed the electorate; the out-going government was only narrowly defeated.

It was my misfortune to find that my vote was to be the determining one in the formation of the next government. In spite of the superficial attractions of playing kingmaker, an individual deputy placed in this position can rarely survive the experience. In helping to deprive one group of politicians of the power and privilege of becoming the government, the deputy immediately antagonises up to half the membership of the Dáil, which in turn represents about half of the electorate. Any benefits to the electorate from policy decisions taken by the new government inevitably redound to that government because of its superior public relations facilities. The independent deputy is forgotten, unless the government carries through unpopular decisions; then all attention is turned on the voting behaviour of the unfortunate deputy. He is blamed for keeping an inept government in power when it would have been 'so easy' for him to vote against its policies. On finally deciding to vote against the new government which up to then he has consistently supported, he antagonises the other half of the Dáil, together with their supporters in the electorate. He must then himself go to the country with precious little electoral support.

To precipitate a general election is a particularly hazardous decision to take. He must assume this power with considerable trepidation, and his justification for this action must be clearly seen and understood by the electorate. What hope has he of achieving this objective when virtually all his political colleagues are, or have at some stage been, antagonistic to him, and he has lost the support of both halves of the electorate?   I had become bitterly disillusioned with the social policies of the coalition; I could not justify supporting them once again and restoring them to power. Although no pre-election agreement was made, in a conversation with Sean Lemass I was given to believe that Fianna Fáil would try to give the people a worth-while health scheme. Brian Walsh, my legal friend, was very close to Lemass, and through him we had a secret meeting in a car outside the Harcourt Street laundry. Lemass was very honest with me; he said'there's no bargain, no deal, but we'll try to give you a good health service'. Since health was the subject with which I had become most clearly associated, and in which I was most interested, I decided to support Fianna Fáil, with de Valera as Taoiseach. On hearing of my decision Brendan Corish, the young Labour leader-to-be, hoping and believing that this would be the end of my political career, commented, 'At last we've got him in the net'.

Since Fianna Fáil had enacted the valuable 1947 Health Act, with its unique mother and child health service proposals, I felt they would be determined to insist on its implementation. De

Valera had the added advantage that he had a single united party behind him, under a notably rigid discipline. He did not have the disadvantage of Mr Costello's coalition of five differing points of view with which to cope. Nevertheless it proved to be a matter of 'Hobson's choice', and I was to suffer for it politically. But there was no practical alternative.

My misfortune was that this particular Fianna Fáil government, dominated by MacEntee's conservative economic policies, was one of the worst the Republic has ever known. As if in retribution for the defeat of his idolised hero, de Valera, in 1948, one of MacEntee's first acts as Minister for Finance in 1951 was to turn on the working-class sector of the population and abolish food subsidies. As I had during the coalition government, I again chose to ignore those policies disagreeable to me in order to concentrate on the issue of the health services, but in my speech supporting Fianna Fáil I pleaded that the unions should use their influence to redress the balance of the lost food subsidies during their wage negotiations.

Because the state papers of 1951 to 1954 have recently been made available, we now know the precise stance taken by de Valera and Fianna Fáil when faced with hierarchical opposition to their new mother and child health service. The case made by the bishops against Fianna Fáil was the same as that made against the coalition government. There is no doubt that the general belief fostered by historians that de Valera sturdily resisted the pressure of the episcopal committee on health matters is not true. Contrary to common mythology, his attitude and policy in response to the hierarchy was one of unquestioning, unconditional surrender on every point and every demand.

Within the whole spectrum of Irish public life, Eamon de Valera's position was unique. He enjoyed the support of a united and loyal party. He was the only Irish politician whose national and international prestige and standing could have survived a confrontation with the bishops. He failed to rise to the occasion. Far from being the highminded statesman which he was believed to be, under pressure de Valera showed himself to be a commonplace politician intent on retaining Cabinet office in the Republic. He was no more or less of a statesman than his coalition predecessors.

It has been de Valera's main contribution to Irish society that he devised our unique form of conservative, sectarian Irish republicanism. It bears even less resemblance to Tone's liberal, secular, French republicanism than does the American Republican Party; the US is at least secular and pluralist.

Eamon de Valera had all the credentials. He had been to jail and condemned to death, but had managed to save his life when it was found that he was a Spanish American. Thereafter he became the quintessential doctrinaire Irish nationalist, as has been the way with so many foreigners in Ireland. He had opposed the Treaty not because it was a compromise, but because 'it was not *his* compromise'. Marked emotionally by the early loss of both his parents, de Valera had an unconscious contempt for the opinions of others. Significantly he later admitted that he had 'cried all the way across to Ireland from America' as a child. There is little doubt that this early suffering marked him for life.

Of those members of de Valera's cabinet involved in the new negotiations, the sole member who demurred to any extent from playing puppet was the Tánaiste, Sean Lemass.

The story of the controversy between the bishops and Fianna Fáil over the health scheme went back to the 1947 Health Act. This Act had been fully and openly debated in the Dáil before becoming law. A letter was sent privately to Mr de Valera, on 17 October 1947, in which the bishops condemned the health scheme, claiming that it was 'an invasion of parental rights to pay for his own and his children's health services'. In addition, they claimed, 'there was interference in the rights of voluntary institutions, and in the medical profession'. They also accused the state of wrongly taking powers 'to educate mothers in respect of motherhood'. De Valera did not reply to this letter until 16 February 1948, two days before the dissolution of his own government. He pleaded with the bishops that he was unable to deal with the matter, since the law in question was *sub judice* as to its constitutionality. However, on receipt of the letter in October, he had written immediately to Dr Ryan, who was to become Minister for Health. This correspondence was not later made available to me. De Valera enclosed the letter which he had received from the hierarchy, and included the crucially important words, 'You will note that their Lordships consider that certain fundamental rights are threatened by the provisions to which they refer. Will you please look into this, and if it should appear that fundamental rights are endangered by any provision of the Act, take the necessary steps to ensure that, in its administration, this should be kept constantly in mind, and the rights in question respected. I should be glad to have your comments'. The letter from the hierarchy, and the accompanying memorandum, were read at a government meeting. There is very little of de Valera's sturdy 'Republican independence' discernible in that memorandum; in it he laid down a policy of submission to the hierarchy. By reading the correspondence to his Cabinet, he notified his colleagues of the decision which he had already taken. There is no record of any member of the Cabinet dissenting from this.

On their resumption of office in 1951, Fianna Fáil were faced with the dilemma of placating the bishops and at the same time attempting to honour the assurance I had received from Mr Lemass that they would 'do their best' to keep as much of the mother and child health scheme as was possible. The question of simply implementing the mother and child provisions of their own Act did not appear to arise.

In June 1952 the government faced the problem by emasculating the radical proposals of their 1947 Health Act. They decided drastically to reduce the age of eligibility of the child from sixteen years to a mere six weeks. At the same time they made the scheme free to all economic groups, so that there was no means test within this narrow category. There was a considerable scaling down on other aspects of the health service in order to conform to 'the wishes of the bishops'. Yet even this scheme was rejected by the medical consultants, and later by the bishops. This change and others went unnoticed by John Whyte, when he claimed in his *Church and State in Modern Ireland* that de Valera had 'resolved the issues' of the health service without great difficulty.

On 16 September 1952 the Minister for Health, Dr Ryan, met Dr McQuaid. The Archbishop demanded the elimination of the clause empowering health authorities to 'educate mothers in respect of motherhood'. Ryan agreed to meet the Archbishop's wishes. Dr McQuaid then queried, 'Why is the mother and infant scheme without a means test?' He went on to suggest that the scheme should include a means test, and be restricted to the lower and middle income groups alone. From state papers it appears that 'His Grace concluded the discussion by telling me [Dr Ryan] that I would run into trouble over the free mother and infant proposals'.

On 6 October 1952 a further meeting was held; government representatives met Bishop Lucey of Cork, Archbishop Kinane of Cashel, Bishop Michael Browne of Galway and Dr McQuaid. 'A detailed discussion, section by section' took place. The amendments proposed by the bishops were all accepted by Dr Ryan for implementation in the new scheme. The meeting concluded with the triumphant comment by the bishops 'that if the Government would meet their Lordships on the mother and infant proposals, then the scheme would have their approval and blessing'. That is, even this shadow of the original health service *must* include a means test.

Yet another meeting took place, between Seán Lemass, Dr Ryan, the bishops of Cork and Galway and the Archbishops of Cashel and Dublin. The Tanaiste was reprimanded by Bishop Browne for referring to a crucial inconsistency in the hierarchy's position, which had also been referred to by me during my interview with Cardinal Dalton. Lemass asked the members of the episcopal committee why was it that neither Dr Dalton nor any of the Northern Catholic bishops had condemned Bevan's health scheme. He also begged, 'We would like if at all possible to avoid a means test'. Lemass's protest was contemptuously dismissed by Dr McQuaid, who said that a free scheme should not be made available to those who could afford to pay. He went on to claim that Catholic teaching taught that it was morally wrong to deprive the head of the family of his responsibility to pay for a health service and he emphasised that Catholic principles would require a means test. As my theological advisor had earlier made clear, this claim as to the morality of the health service was a travesty of the truth.

It is interesting to note that the bishops had now abandoned any pretence of making the important distinction between what was and is Catholic social and Catholic moral teaching. Nearly invariably they referred to 'Catholic teaching', and appeared to make this up as they went along to suit their case.

There followed a concerted campaign in the national newspapers against the health service. A succession of writers

wrongly condemned as immoral the free no-means-test health
scheme. Their arguments were backed by a series of equally
tendentious and misleading articles by a succession of medical
consultants. It was a measure of the resourcefulness of our
opponents that they were able to mobilise a wealthy Jewish
specialist named Abrahamson and a Protestant paediatrician
named Colles in support of the bishops' opposition to the mother
and infant health service.

It is possible that individual ministers in de Valera's Cabinet
would have preferred to act differently. But Cabinet papers
show that whatever their personal beliefs, they at all times toed
the line.

There was now a strange development which involved a series
of misunderstandings. The Medical Association were unaware
of the secret negotiations with the hierarchy since Dr Tom
O'Higgins was no longer a member of the Cabinet. Prematurely
and wrongly they concluded that Fianna Fáil were intent on
introducing a free no-means-test mother and infant health
scheme, and decided to protest publicly against this. Alarmed
by the consultants' protests, Dr McQuaid and the hierarchy
wrongly concluded that, in spite of their representations to the
government and the assurances given to them, de Valera did not
intend to carry out their instructions, and decided to issue a
letter to the national press (restricted to the two Catholic
papers, the *Irish Press* and the *Irish Independent*). Dr McQuaid's
rationalisation for the decision to issue this denunciation of the
scheme was that 'the faithful were waiting for guidance from the
hierarchy about the health scheme'. The bishops decided to issue
a letter to the 'faithful', protesting strongly and denouncing the
health scheme and Mr de Valera's government. Dr Dalton also
explained that the hierarchy had felt that 'some announcement
was expected by the people, and silence would be assumed to
imply their approval of the Bill'. De Valera's concern, as always,
was to remove the causes of contention, and not to assert his
prime ministerial rights of sovereignty on behalf of his
government. He was deeply shocked at the prospect of being
publicly denounced by the hierarchy.

As soon as he received the statement, on the morning of
Friday 17 April 1953, he immediately telephoned the President,
Seán T. O'Kelly, and asked him to try to arrange a meeting

between himself and Cardinal Dalton. This proved impossible, but the President instead arranged for Mr de Valera to meet the Cardinal that afternoon in Drogheda, where he was attending a Confirmation ceremony. Archbishop McQuaid was out of the country, at the Eucharistic Congress in Australia.

The meeting between Mr de Valera and Dr Dalton took place in the Presbytery of St Peter's in Drogheda, in the presence of the parish priest, Monsignor John Stokes. De Valera was accompanied by Dr Ryan. De Valera appears to have planned for a possible confrontation, for on that same Friday he had ordered that a selection of the relevant documents be immediately despatched via diplomatic bag on the next flight to Rome to the Irish Ambassador to the Holy See, J. B. Walsh. For years Walsh had served as secretary to the Department of External Affairs; Sean T. O'Kelly was said to have singled him out to head the Irish diplomatic service as far back as the days of the first Dáil. Walsh was told to study the documents so that 'he would be in a position to interpret rapidly and accurately any further instructions he might be sent'. This was, presumably, so that as a last resort there could be a final appeal to the Pope.

However, de Valera first sought a peaceful solution to the problem, stating that 'the terms of the statement have caused me no little concern, and surprise, since I was aware that the proposals for health legislation had, on a number of occasions, been discussed by representatives of the Hierarchy, with the Tánaiste, and with the Minister for Health, and since I understood that at no stage in these discussions did it appear that any fundamental or irreconcilable difference of opinion existed'. He urged 'the desirability, in the general interest, of the Hierarchy deferring the publication of their statement, at least until the matter had been fully clarified by further discussions between representatives of the Hierarchy and of the Government'. Recalling how I had been pilloried in the Dáil for having claimed that the episcopal committee 'had been satisfied' following our own negotiations in 1951, I was comforted somewhat to read de Valera's statement that he had been 'astonished' by the contents, as he had understood that the earlier meetings between the bishops' committee and the government ministers 'had not encountered any insuperable difficulties'.

De Valera opened his discussions with Cardinal Dalton, the Chairman of the Bishops' Conference, by asking him to suppress the letter. Dr Dalton pointed out that he was merely the Chairman, and had no power to do so. However, de Valera then disclosed that he had arranged for an immediate meeting to take place on the following day between the bishops' episcopal committee, himself, and Dr Ryan which could take place, if need be, in Áras an Uachtaráin. This arrangement appears to have satisfied Dr Dalton, who agreed to withhold the letter pending the new consultation. The impropriety of so using the President's office does not appear to have occurred to de Valera.

In accordance with these arrangements the episcopal and cabinet representatives once again met on 18 April 1953. They discussed their differences over what remained of the proposals for the mother and infant health services. It transpired that the hierarchy need not have feared that Mr de Valera's government would bring in a health scheme which would contravene in any way those principles considered by the Irish bishops to be in conflict with Catholic teaching.

When I had visited the Palace and met Dr McQuaid and his colleagues I had been forbidden to bring a civil servant adviser with me. Happily for our historical studies, this did not happen on the occasion of this truly momentous meeting at Árus an Uachtaráin. The state papers include a long note made at that meeting by a conscientious civil servant, possibly unnoticed by de Valera. It is disturbing and enlightening. It appears that de Valera opened the meeting with a statement in which he defined categorically his fundamental beliefs for the governmental process between church and state, and the extent and scope of the teaching authority of the Roman Catholic church in the Irish Republic. 'The Taoiseach stated his personal position in regard to the teaching authority and the social philosophy of the Church, with regard to the position of the Bishops, as authorised teachers of faith and morals. The Taoiseach said that the view which he had already held had been confirmed by the relevant portions of an address delivered by the Archbishop of Cashel, Dr Kinane, at Rockwell College, in 1951, reported in the *Irish Independent* of 2 June, 1951'. This statement had dealt with the bounden duty of Catholics to obey their bishops in matters of faith and morals, and the strict prohibition on Catholics from attending Trinity College, Dublin; 'the prohibition is not a mere arbitrary one; it is based on the natural divine law itself'. In a clear reference to myself, Bishop Kinane had gone on to say:

> The need for, and the wisdom of, the prohibition against attendance at Trinity College has recently been strongly emphasised. Certain Catholic graduates of Trinity College, while openly parading their Catholicity, at the same time have publicly set themselves up in opposition to a fundamental part of the Catholic religion, namely the teaching authority of the Bishops, and in addition to other serious scandal, by their action, they have induced confusion in the minds of many Catholics, regarding the binding force of Episcopal teaching. Subject to the supreme magisterial authority of the Holy See, Bishops are the authentic teachers of faith and morals, in their own Diocese, and their authority includes the right to determine the boundaries of their jurisdiction, in other words to determine, in case of doubt, whether faith and morals are involved, so that one cannot evade their authority by the pretext that they have gone outside their proper sphere.
>
> Accordingly, amongst other consequences of this position, subjects should not oppose their Bishops' teaching by word, by act, or in any other way, and positively they should carry out what is demanded by it...
>
> God is the author of organised civil society, as well as of the individuals who compose it, and hence, political and social activities quite as much as those which are purely personal and private, are subject to God's moral law of which the Church is the divinely constituted interpreter and guardian...
>
> It is the province, then, of the Church Hierarchy to decide authoritatively whether political social and economic theories are in harmony with God's law, but it is outside of their sphere to determine amongst *approved* theories and systems, which is best calculated to promote the temporal welfare of the community.

In May 1953 the episcopal committee which dealt with health matters met Eamon de Valera and Dr Ryan in Cashel, Co

Tipperary. The detailed notes of this fascinating meeting are at last available. De Valera and Ryan outlined the new amendments demanded by the Bishops and already accepted, but the hierarchy now reconsidered the earlier amendments. Once again re-shaped to their joint requirements, these were in turn accepted meekly by de Valera.

The joint episcopal and cabinet committee also discussed a proposal to establish a new national health council. The episcopal committee laid down that half of this council must consist of members of the medical profession, nurses and members of voluntary institutions. This proposal was also readily accepted. All pretence at being independent members of the Cabinet of a sovereign parliament had been abandoned.

The Bill finally became law in October 1953.

14

In Fianna Fáil

PUBLIC life for me has rarely been free of controversy. Possibly my decision in November 1953 to cross the floor of the House to join Fianna Fáil was never clearly justified by me, nor understood by many. I was going from one republican party, Clann na Poblachta, to another, Fianna Fáil. In the context of the tribal loyalties which divide those who revered de Valera and those who respected O'Higgins and Collins, and who maimed, jailed and even killed one another in the subsequent civil war, the political solecism of which I was accused seems trivial. I had no blood links with either side in that civil war and could not share their loyalties or cold hate for one another.

My experience during the mother and child controversy had been a disappointment. The petty-minded fear of Rome gave little hope for conscientious debate on sophisticated ideological grounds. My natural instinct was to turn my back on politics. There was my profession as a doctor, with the prospect of rewarding work anywhere in the world. The new Minister for Health, Dr. Ryan, had given me to understand that there was a particularly attractive senior appointment in my own speciality at one of the new major regional sanatoria just being completed. It was suggested that my qualifications must give me a good chance of being appointed. I had the option of a financially secure future with a stable home, the perfect basis for a happy family life.

In the long talks we held on such matters, Phyllis shared my own inability to contemplate accepting that attractive option so long as others whom we could help might continue to suffer. As a solitary and introverted person I have always actively disliked public life, with its aggressive gregariousness and loss of privacy. At the same time, I have felt unable to tolerate life in a society in which there has been so much palpable suffering and injustice

all around me. I felt compelled to remain on in politics as long as
the public chose to elect me, and Phyllis strongly supported me
in this belief.

I could have continued as an Independent deputy for Dublin
South-East, but it was clear that an Independent was helpless to
make the fundamental changes in state policies needed in the
Republic. Our first decision was to turn to the Labour Party, in
spite of an atrocious record of its leader, William Norton. With
its socialist origins, it had a clarity of objectives absent from
Fianna Fáil or Fine Gael. In any case, to gain membership of
these parties without a civil war pedigree was nearly as difficult
as gaining membership of the exclusive Kildare Street Club. My
earliest attempt to join Labour on coming back from England
had apparently been opposed by Jim Everett. Everett later
refused to consider my application for membership of the Irish
Transport and General Workers' Union after the defeat of the
first coalition Government. Subsequently I joined the Amal-
gamated Transport and General Workers' Union.

The immediate reply from Norton to my suggestion that I
might now join was that he 'would never sit around a table with
me'.

This left Fianna Fáil. To their credit was the achievement,
mainly that of Lemass, of keeping our people fed during the
Second World War. I had got more help from Fianna Fáil in my
troubles as Minister of Health than from anybody else. Martin
Corry and Tommy Walsh in Kilkenny took risks when the
Labour man, Patterson, would not, in the dispute over my
policy of obliging empty fever hospitals, run by nuns, to take in
some TB patients. The early radicalism of Fianna Fáil had led to
a certain amount of slum clearance; they had introduced the
widow's pension, the orphan's pension and sickness allowances,
none of which had been available to my mother's generation.
This was a seed that could be developed within Fianna Fáil.

It was a measure of my innocence that I stood as the second
Fianna Fáil candidate, with Sean MacEntee, in Dublin South-
East when a general election was called in June 1954. Fianna
Fáil could not have won two seats out of three in Dublin South-
East at that time, particularly as MacEntee had just reneged on
an arbitration agreement with the civil service. MacEntee's
people dominated the party organisation in the constituency

and I could do nothing about it; I knew I wouldn't be allowed to win. And I wasn't, although I came within 382 first preference votes of taking the third seat from MacEntee. The votes were: Costello, 11,305; John O'Donovan (Fine Gael), 2,598 (elected on Costello's transfers); MacEntee, 5,971; Browne 5,489; V. McDowell (Labour), 1,455. Costello returned to power at the head of a second inter-party coalition comprising Fine Gael with 50 seats, Labour with 19, and Clann na Talmhán with five. Clann na Poblachta's three deputies agreed not to oppose it.

My membership of Fianna Fáil was to be brief and interesting. I was close to topping the poll in the subsequent rank-and-file voting for the election of officers in the governing bodies of the party, and was elected a member of the Committee of Twelve and joint treasurer. It was part of my responsibility to speak at public meetings down the country. At our public meetings the speaker was expected to discontinue his speech during the sound of the Angelus. He must then bless himself, move his lips piously, bless himself again, and when all present had blessed themselves, continue with his speech. The Protestants present simply waited at our convenience. The level of political consciousness was negligible.

All my life I have enjoyed the company of the rank and file of Fianna Fáil: they are refreshing, mildly iconoclastic and independent, and given any chance at all would be first-class material for a properly developed society. But they are not given that chance by the leadership. For instance, an attempt by me to have a motion for discussion at the Ard Fheis (annual conference) on the advantages of the co-operative movement was deleted from the Agenda. Shortly after joining Fianna Fáil I had made a speech in the Dáil advocating a massive land division so that the unused land could be given to the landless by forming co-operatives all over the country. There was a tirade from Dr Lucey, Bishop of Cork, claiming that I was a Communist. A Maynooth theologian had said that if the land wasn't being used you had a right to divide it, and that a citizen had a right to steal if he were hungry. I wrote him a letter, asking if his abuse of me applied to the theologian as well. I was hauled over the coals in Fianna Fáil for this. A big discussion went on which I ended by looking around the table and saying 'Well, I am the only one amongst you who has not been excommunicated'. And Dan Breen, always a great friend of mine, smiled thoughtfully.

Another thing that I fought very hard on was prisons. I used to say to de Valera and the rest of them, 'You people have been in the damn places, I've never been in one. They're terrible, why don't you do something about them?'

As a member of the Fianna Fáil Executive I was to have close contact with Eamon de Valera. Lemass once claimed that de Valera relied on the force of physical exhaustion to get agreement. He had a capacity to sit at the head of the table, patiently listening, and remain unimpressed by what he heard from those who dared to disagree with him. I submitted a memorandum which dealt with the many serious defects, as I saw them, in our educational system. For instance, only 47,000 of the 450,000 children who attended primary school went on to secondary school. Sixty thousand went to technical schools. There were a mere 2,000 scholarships to schools and colleges, and a minuscule thirty-five free scholarships to universities. This meant that 90% of our children were leaving school at fourteen. It was not surprising that the one-in-three forced into exile by the failure of Fianna Fáil's government policies did so as semi-literates and were fitted only for the most menial of jobs. Under the influence of Tone, Fitzgerald, and Emmet republicanism in Ireland was democratic, revolutionary, and opposed to Rome. For a time we felt the effects of the social upheaval in Europe after the French revolution. With the ending of the predominantly Protestant influence, as well as later with the death of Parnell, Ireland became intensely Catholic and ceased to be republican. During a period of extraordinary activity churches were built, seminaries established, priests ordained, and clerically-controlled schools built. The lax social behaviour of the priests was subject to a new rigid discipline. A carefully trained élite of religious teaching and nursing orders of nuns and brothers was established, controlling education and the health services. In 1851 there were 1,160 Sisters of Charity among the religious orders. By 1976 there were 13,938.

A continuous recruitment and indoctrination process for the Irish spiritual missions abroad was initiated. At home there were missions, novenas, masses, benediction, holy hours, sermons, confraternities, sodalities. But most important of all were the schools, under the exclusive control of religious teachers. New well-stocked libraries with carefully-chosen books became available. A printing press, run by the Catholic Truth Society, was established. Comparative study of alternative religions or political cultures was not tolerated. The function of the press, in simplistic language, was to pour out Catholic apologetics.

The end effect of all this I saw as a child in my own home. Both my parents, while literate, had been taught little except a blind unquestioning faith in Rome. The passive, credulous formula, consistently repeated to us by my mother, justified the meanest of tragedies — 'It is the will of God, and his holy mother'. I saw little of faith in the power of love or compassion. Fear of hell and an angry God motivated their lives and determined their behaviour.

The new provisional government of the Republic supported Rome against the final British attempt to upgrade educational standards for the Irish under the McPherson proposals, which sought to end denominational teaching in schools. In a masterpiece of rhetorical hyperbole, Rome accused McPherson of 'forcing Irish children into the Irish school system at the point of a bayonet'. Cardinal Logue used all methods open to him to keep control of education. The peak of that clerical campaign against better education ended with the threat by Rome to withdraw Irish children from the schools. The Bill was dropped, and McPherson resigned. Quite cynically, Rome had used ill-educated but well-tutored Irish parents to deny access to better education for their own children.

With the establishment of the new state, the influence of Rome was seen everywhere. The Irish state's first Minister for Education, Eoin MacNeill, said that 'state involvement in education was not contemplated', John Marcus O'Sullivan followed MacNeill as Minister for Education, and said that he was unwilling to encroach on Rome's control of education, in any way. As Minister for Education Eamon de Valera had once advocated special recognition for Latin: 'We like to know it as the language of the Church'. What church? Seán T. O'Kelly had the phrase 'the republic will encourage the most capable men to devote their talents to the education of the young' eliminated from the proclamation of the Republic. Its implementation would have threatened Rome's domination of education. As to mass illiteracy, the Catholic Headmasters' Association claimed, 'over-much education totally unfits the Irish, if only making them discontented'.

During my period as Minister for Health General Mulcahy proclaimed his vision. 'As Minister for Education, I am the plumber who is only called in when something goes wrong'. When compelled to accept lay teachers in schools, the Church insisted, successfully, that all teacher training colleges were under its control. The first non-denominational teacher training college in Marlboro Street was closed.

With the development of the Irish trade union movement steps were taken to prevent its infection by radical socialist ideas. The Jesuit order established their workers' training college, complete with diplomas and certificates. Irish trade union leadership has been as conservative and as politically dependable and loyal to traditional class attitudes and sectarian beliefs as any middle-class product of Clongowes, Belvedere, or Blackrock.

Lemass and de Valera, faced with my memorandum, defended this educational system with all its obvious 'warts', and denied that anything needed to be improved. This, presumably, was a manifestation of their standards. Was it not de Valera who had said that nine out of ten would have to be satisfied with primary level education? He went on to say that primary education should concentrate on the basic essentials; there should be no room for anything else.

Having considered the memorandum, the executive voted for the establishment of a committee of enquiry into the educational system. De Valera did not oppose this suggestion. The committee contained, among others, Charles Haughey, Brian Lenihan and Eoin Ryan. We held a number of meetings and in the end produced a good report, the greater part of the credit for which must rest with Michael Yeats, the conscientious and hard-working secretary. We made a number of radical proposals for improvement. Naturally I was pleased, but I reckoned without de Valera. The committee report was duly considered and its recommendations readily accepted for implementation. It was then that I was confronted by the inestimable skills of which I had heard so much in committee: 'There is one small addendum which I am sure you will accept, that the recommendations will be implemented when financial considerations permit'. With that handful of words, our valuable and useful work had come to naught; the recommendations were not to be implemented so long as de Valera remained leader of Fianna Fáil. I understand that they formed the basis of the later valuable improvements made by the Fianna Fáil Minister for Education, Donough O'Malley, under Lemass as Taoiseach, in the 1960s.

Early in 1957 the second coalition government fell on a vote of 'No Confidence' proposed by Seán MacBride over its handling of the new outbreak of IRA violence in the North. Seán MacEntee, remembering how close he had come to losing his seat to me in 1954, prevailed on the selection conference in Dublin South-East to reject my nomination as the second Fianna Fáil candidate in favour of Seán Moore. When I refused to accept this decision, and announced my intention of standing as an Independent, I was expelled from Fianna Fáil.

I polled 6,035 first preferences, behind John Costello (6,918) but ahead of MacEntee (5,916). Sean Moore polled 2,473 and the other unsuccessful candidates were John O'Donovan (Fine Gael), 1,332: P. J. Bermingham (Republican), 1,291 and G. Callinan (Clann na Poblachta), 396. Fianna Fáil, with 78 seats and 48.3 per cent of the poll, formed a government with de Valera as Taoiseach. They were to remain in power for the next sixteen years.

Once returned to the Dáil I was able to renew my old alliance with Jack McQuillan, who had been returned as an Independent in Roscommon. Our purpose was to harry the government by making radical proposals for all the unresolved issues in society. We put down questions on everything from public ownership of the whiskey distilling industry to gay rights. Lemass described us at one time as 'the only real opposition'. We were even the first to advocate the boycott of South African goods. We ran a very powerful anti-apartheid movement; there was a wonderful march, a tremendous tribute to the people of Dublin, which started at Parnell Square with a band, and ended up filling the Mansion House, with Dan Breen and Peadar O'Donnell on the platform.

It has been said of politicians that we act a lot. Actors and politicians have this in common; their lives are lived in public, and they share the experiences of acclaim, failure, excitement, or the misery of defeat. Above all there is the insecurity of employment and sudden loss of a job.

But in politics everyone, government and opposition, makes up both the cast and the audience in the parliamentary theatre.

The shrill bell rings at ten minutes to three, and from all parts of the House deputies make their way to the Dáil chamber, which fills with ministers in varying degrees of unconcern and apprehension, all of them fresh from their departmental briefing.

To protect the minister on 'the day', civil servants comb every available source of information about every question. The Dáil Reports, those great green volumes stretching back to 1922 and the Treaty Debates, are leafed through for useful ammunition. If an ex-minister is now the questioner, the civil servant obediently changes sides. He collates every word, every promise, every refusal or dismissal as 'impractical', of the present idea made by that previous minister.

Soon there is nothing more to be done; the politician is as much on his own as is the actor with a new play, but the politician always performs before a predominantly hostile audience. At least half of it will not approve of his performance, no matter how good his act. The parliamentary opposition must always be hostile; it is their job to prevent the minister from appearing to do his job well. No matter what you say, you will be told, 'you could have done more' or 'done it sooner', or 'why wait to be asked?' No minister can ever win. The opposition must convince journalists, and through the journalists the electorate outside, that in Leinster House, in helpless frustration, quite wrongly and unjustly in opposition, there sits a group of men and women who could do the job infinitely better than the present lot.

Such is the dynamic of parliamentary politics. It is accepted by both sides, yet it doesn't make performing on that stage any more pleasant. 'Will I get confused, or flustered?' 'Will my store of information suffice?' 'Have they information which we have not got?' In those carefree days in opposition, did you make wild promises about what you could do, and of greater importance, *would* do when you came to office? Now those easily-spoken words come back to haunt and humiliate you.

The suddenness with which you can lose your job hangs over both the actor and politician. With a handful of exceptions, for whom life must be pleasantly dull, your political existence can end at any time. For the actor there is the empty theatre and no audience. For the politician there is the empty public hall, no-one interested in what you have to say.

While I never came to enjoy question time as minister, I certainly enjoyed it from the backbenches with Jack McQuillan. It is a valuable feature of parliamentary democracy; its suppression must be a cherished objective for an impending dictator. Yet question time had become subject to abuse by government deputies 'flooding the question paper', thus slowing up the production of replies from ministers. In the past the Order Paper was cleared by the end of each week. Every minister could expect to answer questions, and the real questioners, the outside public, would be certain of a quick reply.

But it is hard to get more information from an experienced minister than he chooses to give. Dr Tom O'Higgins was a master of the pleasantly evasive answer. Dr Jim Ryan specialised in practically monosyllabic mumbling replies. He did not seem to mind whether he had satisfied you or not; looking across the floor over his spectacles in surprise at your persistence, he gave the impression that you'd no right to be bothering him. Each of these ministers, especially when they dealt with each other's party members, could introduce savage, angry and bitter recriminations about the civil war. As a young politician in Leinster House, I recall my shock at the white-hot hate with which that terrible episode had marked their lives. The trigger words were 'seventy-seven', 'Ballyseedy', 'Dick and Joe' and, above all, 'The Treaty' and 'damn good bargain'. The raised tiers of the Dáil chamber would become filled with shouting, gesticulating, clamouring, suddenly angry men.

McQuillan and I together could batter on the doors of Leinster House until kingdom come and go unheard. It was the only question on which all three parties agreed. Readily they combined all their forces to be rid of us so that they could continue with their prolonged parliamentary squabbles about who started, who won, and who lost the civil war. We were considered to be irrevelant and tiresome interlopers. With no

wounds to display and no blood on our hands, we were represented as intruders by both sides. Between them they had
created a fantasy world of myths, ballads and questionable
statistics, at the heart of which each one of them was a Jack the
Giantkiller, yet of that time Kevin O'Higgins was to say to all
the bombast, 'We have not been able to drive the British from
anything beyond a good-size police barracks'. Marvelling at the
thousands of IRA pensioners I heard MacEoin, himself the
genuine article, smilingly wonder, 'Where were all these brave
warriors when we needed them?'

Throughout our years in parliament, there was no serious
mature informed debate on the causes for our chronic misuse of
land, labour and capital in the creation of wealth, either in
industry or agriculture. Nor have we seriously attempted to
understand the causes or deal with the gross maldistribution of
wealth and the mass suffering and chronic poverty of so many.
For all the influence that our generation has had on that fos-
silised fly in amber which is Irish public life, we might as well not
have tried. Too old to fight now, undisturbed, they were content
to pester one another about each other's motives for the rest of
their lives. They had no interest whatever in the outside world.

Finally the curtain falls for the last time on a parliament. The
transient, ephemeral fate of the actor can also be seen in the
politician's brief life. Following his defeat in the House of
Commons, the British Prime Minister Harold Macmillan soon
afterwards was photographed at a bus stop; he had been
deprived of his state car. He spoke whimsically of the speed with
which 'they roll up the red carpet'. On the night of my own resignation as Minister for Health the driver of my state car, Joe
Shanahan, was compelled to tell me that from that moment he
had no legal right to use the state car to drive me home. However,
Garda Joe Shanahan never ceased to be the kindly man I and my
family knew him to be, and he drove me home regardless.

It was not the unpredictability of public life that most
impressed me. It was the ritual preceding the change of government, the purest of all theatre. The last speech in defence of the
government is over. The opposition has ended its tirade of
criticism and abuse. All sides have exhausted their rhetoric. At
last there is a call for a vote. As the vote is taken, each deputy
passes slowly up the steep stairs out of the debating chamber. At

the head of the nearly vertical stairway to the voting lobby, those in favour of the government go to the left, and those against go to the right. The last remaining deputies, uncertain as Independents how to vote and survive, move reluctantly past the two tellers. They could be voting themselves out of parliamentary life for ever. There is a Government teller and one for the Opposition at each gate into the voting lobby, and a deputy for the Government and for the Opposition supervising the tellers; *nemine crede* operates here as in Maynooth. They see that the count is correct, and so recorded. With the proliferation of the smaller parties and independents, even the shrewdest of tallymen may get their sums wrong. The last vote is verified by the tellers. Then comes the verdict for which all anxiously wait. The usually noisy chattering monkey house of the Dáil Chamber falls silent. The bleak prospect looms in all our thoughts; a general election, with all its worries, expense and uncertainties, especially for the marginal seats. Some are about to take their last lingering look around the Dáil for ever. All eyes await the appearance of the teller at the top of the steps. Here is the first crucial indication; whichever party teller is entrusted with the tally paper tells the waiting deputies their fate, and the result of the count. Cheers, from one side only, welcome the trot, sometimes breaking into a run, of the teller down the steps, I have seen hopeful shadow ministers ingratiate themselves with fervent hand-clasps of congratulations for the Taoiseach to be. The unconcealed dismay, the brave smiles, the silence of the government benches, tell all.

Yet for me easily the most moving moment occurs in the solemn ritual which follows the voting: the statement made by the Ceann Comhairle following his formal notification of the result of the count to the House. In 1948 de Valera and his government, after sixteen long years in office, were still seated slightly stunned on the government benches. That strange mixture of parties, a coalition of novices, sat opposite. Following the receipt of his slip of paper Frank Fahy, old Fianna Fáil veteran, slowly came to his feet. He read out the result of the tellers' count, as verified by the clerk of the Dáil; there erupted the usual one-sided cheers. As they subsided, the Ceann Comhairle made his simple statement. He declared, 'The government motion has been defeated. The Dáil will retire for two hours, and resume at 6 p.m. On resumption, the government will move to the right, and the opposition will move to the left'. With the declared authority of a majority of the people, that formula peacefully stripped all power from a government of men and women. With these words, they had lost control of the generals, the army, the police, the courts and the jails. Taken from them was control over education, health, agricultural policies, the power to create and distribute wealth.

For the immature and the bully the world over, violence is the easiest way. For the mature and the civilised, a peaceful solution, though more difficult, is, in the end, inevitable. If only representative democracy could be permitted to work within a mature, literate, well-informed electorate! It is the preservation of this peaceful transition which is the basis of my dogged resistance to the usurpation of this ultimate authority by a non-elected extra-parliamentary body. Most of us believe that while parliamentary democracy is not an ideal form of government, there are others which are worse.

The propaganda against Jack McQuillan and myself throughout our years on the backbenches was blatant, widespread and insidious. I do not complain about that; it is part of the mechanics of politics. We had to be silenced. It is a great tribute to the electorate that they kept putting both of us back in spite of the lies. That is the beauty of the secret ballot. Once I was at the polling booth at an election and a lady came in pushing a pram, with one child in her arms and another holding onto the handles. Through gritted teeth she said 'It won't be our fault if you don't get in'. Women were very oppressed at the time, but they knew somehow or other that even though I was a 'Communist' and an 'atheist', 'anti-clerical' and 'anti-Christ', everything you could think of as far as propaganda was concerned, I was still somebody who was anxious to help ordinary people.

Jack McQuillan and myself moved probably the last motion to which Mr de Valera replied. Many believed that it was probably instrumental in prompting him to leave office.

By accident, we were to uncover the true extent to which de Valera exercised personal control over the Irish Press group of newspapers. These newspapers influenced a substantial number of the Irish people and created and kept unchallenged the awesome charisma of Eamon de Valera. They also contributed to the formation of the unique Fianna Fáil ethos of Irish republicanism, particularly in rural areas. Independent Newspapers were just as conservative and Catholic, though not 'republican'.

Those of our citizens who would not conform to this society could not get work and were forced into exile. Britain, the US and the Commonwealth were de Valera's parallel to Stalin's Siberia. Compulsory exile afflicted many of our writers and artists. Pressure to conform was exercised in a hundred variants of my own, my wife's and our children's experience after the mother and child row. Emigration was an indispensable policy plank for all parties. The 'hated John Bull' would look after us and feed us. Our leaders meanwhile ranted on about the iniquity of the British and felt no shame whatever about the jobless unwanted Irish exiles.

How many letters did Jack McQuillan and I get from young exiles in the four corners of the world, saying 'Keep up the good work'. What a solution to a nation's unsolved social evils!

Somewhere, anywhere, just get out of sight, out of mind except for the grieving families. It is little wonder that Irish society wore that well-known contented look on the faces of the survivors, who enjoyed an entirely fraudulent prosperity under de Valera's benevolent rule. In the *Irish Press* the pattern of Fianna Fáil election strategies was developed between the 1930s and 1950s, shamelessly fostering the cult of the warrior and the soldier and typified by the nation's bellicose national anthem, the Soldier's Song. Having been a soldier of the republic was enough to ensure Dan Breen's success at the polls; having been a soldier and wounded was enough to last him a lifetime in Leinster House. De Valera's most telling sobriquet for years was 'the last surviving commandant of 1916'. I have no wish to denigrate the achievements of that generation of soldiers or the intelligence of the electorate. But this uncritical blind loyalty to the soldier was no substitute for a discernible ideology or serious political policy.

For years I have been pilloried for my beliefs about Irish republicanism and its conservative sectarian nature. It is asserted among republicans that 'while good on social matters,

Browne is bad on the national issue'. My reply would be that many of my republican comrades are both confused on the national issues and bad on social issues. To me, nationalism without social aims is akin to fascism. Republicanism without pluralism and secularism is a contradiction. As one of his devoted admirers, I have always been puzzled by Connolly's actions in 1916 in the face of his then clear-headed assessment of the objectives of Irish nationalism. He had defined his concept of narrow Irish nationalism which would follow the 'rising' in his memorable and perceptive essay on the 'Whoop it up for Ireland' green nationalists of the period. It would 'change nothing... The cap badges of the Corporation officials, evicting the pauper tenants from their council houses, would have a harp instead of a crown... The pillar boxes would be painted green'.

During the hunger strike carried out by the Provisional IRA in Northern jails in 1981, a number of young republicans starved themselves to death in the vain hope of achieving prisoner of war status with civilian clothes. As a Dáil deputy I was called to support the campaign. I agreed to do so. There was but one condition: that the campaign for civilian clothes for prisoners be extended to all prisoners in all our jails. As a socialist I believed that the majority of persons in our jails were products of broken homes, unemployment, illiteracy, poverty and hunger. The reply from those in charge of the hunger campaign was that the Provisionals would not accept my socialist analysis of the origins of criminality.

Hundreds of these confused republicans over the years have killed or died most painfully in order to re-establish Rome rule all over Ireland. As late as the mid-sixties, I recall that the most noisy protest of all made by young imprisoned republicans was because they were 'not permitted to attend Mass on Sundays, when in prison'. They also complained that 'their rosary beads were taken away from them, on their arrest'. There must be few declaredly anti-imperialist republican revolutionaries any-where else in the world who would protest at such arcane grievances. To extend the ethos of our society to the North of Ireland would not be an extension of freedom. Yet committed left-wing Irish politicians have been divided on this, as was Connolly in the early part of the century. This is one of the reasons why we have failed to build a strong left-wing movement in the Republic.

In 1958 Jack McQuillan came into possession of a number of shares in the *Irish Press*. He made one of these over to me, the only share I have ever owned, and this gave me the right to inspect the books at head office. As I turned the pages of the great volume of listed shareholders and transfers, it became clear that de Valera had systematically over a period of years become a majority shareholder of Irish Press newspapers. Although he was controlling director of the newspapers, the share prices were not quoted publicly. The price paid by the de Valera family to shareholders was nominal. It was clear that de Valera was now a very wealthy newspaper tycoon. Recall the origins of the *Irish Press:* £1 shares were sold to Irish republicans, the poorest section of the population, who bought them in the patriotic belief that their newspaper would be used to penetrate and destroy what Griffith called 'the paper wall around Ireland'. Of greater importance was their hope that through the *Press* newspapers enlightened education would help our people to understand and enjoy the benefits of a pluralist, egalitarian republicanism.

McQuillan and I decided to raise the matter of our surprising discoveries in the Dáil. In spite of our nominally extensive rights under Standing Orders, no matter how we framed the questions to the Taoiseach we were refused permission to table them. The Ceann Comhairle, Paddy Hogan, a Labour deputy from Co Clare, having no wish to antagonise de Valera supporters in the constituency he shared with him, protected de Valera from embarrassing questions. Finally we were compelled to frame a motion for debate in the Dáil. This is a much slower process and had to wait for over a year, but finally the debate took place. It is of interest to note that since that episode the three main parties have deprived private deputies of this valuable right to table a motion on an important issue. Instead, at least seven signatories to the motion are needed.

The Dáil chamber was crowded for the debate. The opposition appeared to be surprised and shocked by the disclosures made by us about de Valera's questionable behaviour in accumulating majority share holdings of the newspapers in this way. We made the case that it must be onerous to the point of impossible for Mr de Valera to carry out his duties as Taoiseach and at the same time be responsible for the day-to-day control of three national newspapers. Somewhat extravagantly, since we had a mere handful of shares, we claimed that there was a danger that if he continued in these posts, either the newspapers or the country must be mis-managed.

A much more compelling argument concerned de Valera's notorious ambivalence about the illegal use of force. The whole of the back page of the *Sunday Press* carried gruesome scarlet colour cartoons illustrating the valorous deeds of republican violence during the Anglo-Irish and the civil wars. There were the bombed and burned-out buildings, the dead civilians, the dead soldiers, the dead policemen bleeding in the gutters. Meanwhile the brave killers disappeared with smoking revolvers to their own greater glory and safe seats in Leinster House for life. De Valera could not disown personal responsibility for these warlike pictures; under his carefully drafted articles of association, he was personally responsible for all editorial and administrative policy.

We went on to claim that these cartoons and their contents constituted a direct glorification of war, and were an indirect incitement to murderous IRA killings and bombings in the North of Ireland and Britain. An even more grotesque feature was that on the front pages of the same papers were lists of names of young 'republicans' interned without trial by de Valera in the Curragh.

De Valera left the chamber soon after the start of the debate, leaving the case for the defence to be made by MacEntee. He later returned and, as reported in the Dáil records, put forward a limp defence for his anomalous position.

Possibly the most significant event of that night's debate was the behaviour of Fine Gael, in particular Richard Mulcahy. Ever since the bitter civil war split, nothing had united de Valera and Mulcahy more consistently than their determination to resist the pernicious doctrine of radical French republicanism preached by McQuillan and myself; invariably and consistently they united to vote down our radical proposals. Not so tonight, however.

Mulcahy and his followers could not ignore this shameful betrayal of shareholders' trust by de Valera. For the first time, and no doubt hating it, Mulcahy and Fine Gael decided to join us in the voting lobbies. It was a considerable triumph for us, especially since de Valera was heard to complain to Mulcahy, 'I did not believe that you would do this to me'. The national press, as is their wont, closed ranks behind their 'leader'. The public, while they couldn't crown him 'King of Ireland', instead sent him up to the Vice-Regal Lodge as President in 1959. As far as McQuillan and I were concerned, he was out of harm's way at last.

15

Psychiatric Practice

SIDE by side with my political life, with all its uncertainties, I had to consider the question of my medical career. Tuberculosis was no longer a disease of significance in the Republic, and those of us who worked in sanatoria necessarily became redundant. The inadequacy of our personal financial position now became both frightening and precarious. Throughout the years during which I had worked in Ireland, it was correctly assumed by my employers that I was content to work for nothing in the care of those suffering from pulmonary tuberculosis. On principle I would not take private patients. Yet although I had completed my postgraduate years of study in two famous English chest hospitals, both before and following my period as Minister for Health I found it impossible to get work in tuberculosis in Ireland in any hospitals other than Newcastle, which was a small voluntary hospital.

It was now imperative that I commence to train in a new and different speciality. The Marine Port and General Dock Workers' Union had offered to accept me as a general practitioner within their trade union service. Once again, with regret, I declined, because neither Phyllis nor I believed that we should work within the 'fee for service' form of medical practice inseparable from private medicine in Ireland.

It was clear that the only other form of medical practice for which there was a considerable state sector in Ireland providing for the non-paying poor patient was in psychiatric medicine. In my late forties, I returned to university to begin life again as a student. Following over eight years of study and work in the most menial of medical posts I finally qualified with a Diploma of Psychological Medicine and membership of the Royal College of Psychiatrists. Once again I was qualified to work in medicine, and was appointed as consultant psychiatrist to the Eastern Health Board in 1972.

The years of training were to be particularly lean ones for myself and my family. The small lump sum of money given to us following the final closure of Newcastle Sanatorium was completely absorbed in my own studies at university and the maintenance of my family.

On hearing about the impending closure of the sanatorium our bank manager foreclosed on a loan of £800 with which we had bought the semi-derelict house in Bray in which we lived. With no money and no credit, and with all our furniture on the lorry of our kind neighbour Mr Costelloe, we limped off to occupy a condemned two-room national school. It had neither running water nor sanitary facilities, and the roof was riddled with woodworm. Worse still, we did not have the £300 needed to pay the caretaker to whom the school had been given by its former owners. By some kindly sleight-of-hand our sympathetic solicitor made some loan arrangement with the owner, who himself at one time had been under my care. With Phyllis, Ruth and Susan, I began to make a home in that derelict outhouse.

With moving and unselfish generosity, a number of craftsmen friends of ours from the Newcastle area combined to make the place habitable. Sitting around a fire of scrap garden timber, the concrete blocks, baulks of timber and barrows of cement criss-crossed between us, we drank our tea in our primitive sitting-room. Windows, doors, gutters, slates, all bought by myself and carted home, came from scrapyards around Dublin. Our half-glass front door had once opened into the ancient Apothecary's Hall in Holles Street. The insignia was faintly etched on the glass, making an elegant entrance to our new home.

I now began a long and searingly painful training in the tragic environment of our grim and cheerless mental hospitals. I attended lectures and courses, but needed in addition long periods of residential hospital training at the level of house physician. This poorly-paid, much exploited and shamefully overworked job I had last left behind me nearly twenty-five years earlier. The transition from Minister for Health to house physician was in itself a considerable shock for myself and my family.

Knowing that it was reputed to be the hospital with the

highest standard of mental care for its patients, I first called on Dr Norman Moore at St Patrick's. Dr Moore gave me to understand that he had no work for me but would help me to get work in England, but I declined his offer. Work in an English mental hospital at that time was easily found, but we had no intention, if it could be avoided at all, of being driven out of Ireland.

My medical colleagues of all denominations made it clear that no matter what my qualifications, they would not permit me to practice medicine in Ireland again at any level. I was even rejected as unfit for one job whose only responsibility was to distinguish between the abnormal and normal chest X-ray picture, work at which I had spent all my medical life; instead a former student of mine was appointed.

The ugly peculiarity about a boycott is the measure of moral cowardice which it induces. Individual value judgements are suspended. An uncritical consensus takes over. Without doubt there were clerics, doctors, politicians and others who, though silently in sympathy, were too fearful of the boycott to protest openly against the injustice to myself or my family. There is no self-pity in this assessment — I had well known what would be the consequences of my actions for myself. Phyllis and I had no regrets, except for our children, who were innocent of having inflicted hurt on anyone. Ruth and Susan were refused admission to a number of schools, both Roman Catholic and Protestant. Ruth was told that because she lacked artistic talent, she must leave the National College of Art. Within weeks of leaving, she had won first prize in the national Caltex competition, in which there were twenty-two thousand other competitors, and second prize in another.

During the period of greatest hostility to us, I sat waiting to have my hair cut in Prost's hairdressers in Stephen's Green. Nearby sat a well-known Dublin anaesthetist Dr Tom Gilmartin, a friend of ours whom we had last met at a diplomatic cocktail party at the Italian Embassy while I was Minister for Health. There we had held the usual animated and friendly conversation. On this occasion, however, he leaned furtively across to me, momentarily grasped me by the shoulder and gave it a sympathetic squeeze. Without uttering a word, he passed on to his waiting chair. A kindly man, no doubt, he was sorry for me, but at the same time unwilling to be seen saying so.

Finally, as my last hope, I went to see the RMS at St Brendan's Hospital. The last occasion on which I had visited Dr John Dunne had been in my capacity as Minister for Health. Dr Dunne received me again with the same courtesy and anxiety to help. We were now two medical consultants meeting on equal terms, and he was puzzled at the reason for my visit. He was understandably shocked to hear me ask for a job as one of his house physicians, but he quickly recovered his aplomb. A vacancy was available, and I got the job in January 1964. I hurried to tell Phyllis that we had reason to hope again. Shortly afterwards I suffered my fifth relapse with tuberculosis, and once again was put out of action with no pay.

St Brendan's may be all the fearful things which it is claimed to be at regular intervals in the national press. Yet there is another way of looking at it. For the aspirant consultant psychiatrist in his late forties with little time or money, St Brendan's is an encyclopedia of human distress in every possible form and point of development. A weekend duty there was a truly educational yet wounding exposure to intense mass suffering. Of much interest to me too was the effect of that suffering on others, in particular the response of the so-called normal population to that collective despair.

Never before had I heard such a varied litany of adult cries for help which came to me over my house telephone. How useless I felt! These calls went on for most of the day, through the weekend, and much of it at night. A man had broken a window and tried to hang himself from the window bars. A high security ward patient had escaped in his pyjamas with an open razor, and was threatening the staff in the hospital grounds. A deeply depressed young girl had broken glass and cut her wrists. A patient had taken an overdose and was unconscious. There was word of an old lady wandering the streets, talking to herself, at three in the morning. There was a drunken singing pub visitor, suffering from an overdose of alcohol, who needed a bed for the night. A woman patient had barricaded herself behind the sturdy mahogany hospital furniture, and was bombarding the staff with flower pots; could she be given 10 ccs. of chloral hydrate — the usual knock-out drops of that time?

Much later on I was told what such a procedure entailed. A young girl told me of her terror when faced with this injection.

Following a misunderstanding, she had been shocked, frightened and confused. The female nurses, either intent on making an example of the recalcitrant patient, or simply fearful of getting hurt by her, usually called in the male nurses to help them. When all was ready, armed with loaded syringe, they formed a wall of white coated nurses, a threatening sight. Like a cavalry charge they advanced in line to fall on and physically subdue the victim. They then sank the needle into the victim's thigh. Its effect was total swift oblivion. It is difficult to believe that it is not as distasteful a job for nurses as for the patient.

Though being woken by telephone at night to get up and admit someone could never be pleasant, I rarely walked across from the residency to the admission block in driving rain or under a summer moon without a sense of the privilege of my medical calling. On behalf of the people I had been entrusted with responsibility to care for, even if inadequately, the rejects from society. Some had been turned out of their own homes; as 'mental patients' they had been turned away from every other hospital and home in the city. They came to me at any hour of the day or night; we could not give them much but we would not turn them away.

Having chosen to study the problem of mental illness in Ireland, I hoped to understand its social origins and implications. As with tuberculosis, the mentally ill predominantly are members of the poorest social class, the victims of job insecurity, over-crowding, poor housing, over-large families. I had no idea of the infinite canvas of distress that would unfold before me in the years ahead. The one doubtful virtue of mental illness over tuberculosis was that you could die of tuberculosis. With mental illness, though desperately wanting to, you need not die. With a restless mind that cannot find comfort or rest, to know that you are *not* going to die is often the greatest source of distress for man or woman. In addition, the effect of mental illness seems to be all-pervasive, involving thousands rather than hundreds. Mental 'disease' is impossible to categorise as a series of predictable signs and symptoms. The population of a mental hospital reflects the hidden-away, private agony of thousands. They are either under sedation and asleep, or nearly asleep, or restlessly awake and inconsolable. Some, heavily doped for the rest of their lives, bide their time in the benevolent jails we call mental hospitals until their release in death. There is a tacit conspiracy between psychiatrists and the public to imprison without public trial, for months, years, sometimes even for life, our dissident social nonconformists, the misfits or the inconsolably miserable. For the most part they are there simply because we, the 'normal' population, can no longer tolerate their distress, of much of which distress we are the cause.

My introduction to the mental hospital service came at the end of the era of repressive custodial care for the mentally disturbed, following the introduction of powerful new 'mood changing' drugs. Before this, the nurse in a mental hospital was called a 'keeper'. He was dressed in a policeman's style uniform and carried a thick stick. This was the period of brute physical restraint of the patient in the padded cell, naked, wild-eyed, clothes ripped, squatting in scattered food and filth. For the most intractable there was also the unthinkable awfulness of the straitjacket. The new drugs stupefied their victim into an inert conformity, creating the effect of a 'no touch' benevolent straitjacket. By their means human beings were transmuted to non-resisting, remote, mindless automatons.

Within the main hospital at St Brendan's there was the desolate 'hospital' sector, a special unit in which passive dummies lay under heavy sedation, a long line of misery-ridden human beings who already unsuccessfully had tried to end their tragic lives by suicide and if given a chance would try once again. It was sufficient simply for the doctor across the telephone to command that a patient 'be put on the line'. There was an aura of congealed misery hanging over that line of silent men and women, linked by their common despair and the will and intention to kill themselves. No flowers, no books, no photos, simply a reluctant resignation to the agony of living.

It was to this ill-lit Dickensian hospital that one night I was called out of an exhausted sleep to the real-life nightmare of a middle-aged man who simply wanted to die. He refused to eat in the hope that, no matter how painfully in the end, he could die. He had nothing and no one left for whom or which he wished to live.

The procedure was, that I, the lowly house physician, on the orders of my consultant psychiatrist, would force-feed him. A non-violent man of peace, I would have found it easier to have shot him. I had to ram a semi-rigid inch thick rubber tube down his throat into his oesophagus and stomach. Meanwhile two silent purposeful nurses, suffering no doubt my own sense of revulsion, held our victim by his shoulders, his body, head and neck forcibly thrown back. Revolted at the prospect of so mauling a fellow human being and subjecting him to such humiliation, my face must have disclosed my feelings. A sympathetic experienced nurse who, no doubt, had had to become hardened to such experiences, intervened to release me from my ordeal. Briskly and expertly he passed the tube down into the stomach. A great white enamel funnel was put into the end of the tube, and down through this was slowly poured a cement-coloured mix of gruel, designed to keep that wretched man alive. It seems that one other purpose of force feeding is the intimidating crude deterrent of fear. But do the victims not resolve that at the earliest opportunity, 'cured of their depression', they will leave the hospital so that alone in peace and with dignity, they will kill themselves?

Yet another treatment procedure comparable in repulsiveness was the use of electric shock so as to alter an individual's vision of his unhappy life. To the end of my days in psychiatry I could not accept that an electric shock would transform the parent mourning for a dead child, or the spouse for a lost partner, from being deeply depressed to being the classic 'happy man'. To me it was wholly reminiscent of the many futile, sometimes dangerous, procedures used in desperation by us in the 1930s to save the life of the dying consumptive.

The procedure was carried out in a long, low-ceilinged, barn-like ward, divided into a waiting space and a smaller operating centre. My job as house physician was to provide a completely purposeless ritual presence. I would stand at the head of the patient as he was anaesthetised and then apply an electric terminal to each side of the sleeping patient's skull. It was the anaesthetist's job to apply a plier-like instrument, so as to force open the mouth, into which he inserted a thick rubber biting pad. A series of standard shocks was then applied through the terminals. The effect on the sleeping body was both disturbing and repellent to watch; the whole body sprang into a tense involuntary series of jerking spasms. Meanwhile the patient was forcibly held down, to avoid self-injury, by an attendant nurse.

The patient was revived with oxygen inhalations, then wheeled out. Later, as consultant psychiatrist, under no circumstances would I submit a patient to that procedure. What is more, I found that they had no need for it. The unexplained rationale of the procedure was much too reminiscent of the use of cupping, blood-letting and the application of leeches.

The anaesthetist I worked with was Dr Gilmartin, the same man who could not resist the sympathetic pat on the shoulder in the barber's shop. Through those long afternoons, with their hours of waiting and watching, we discussed every conceivable aspect of life, society and medical practice in the Republic. One afternoon he went on to express radical opinions about the ideal organisation of medical practice in an enlightened society, ideas with which I could agree. Suddenly, aware of the dangerous talk of which he had just been guilty, he concluded abruptly, 'I must give up that kind of thing. If I were to express those kind of ideas publicly and freely I would soon find myself like you, on the outside in our profession, doing a boring badly-paid purposeless job, such as yours. I wouldn't like that'.

I came to know well the many faces of that great hospital, its out-patient clinics, the over-crowded wards, the bare pictureless walls, the narrow-fretted prison windows, the uncarpeted floors, the absence of colour or flowers except in the show-piece admission unit. In the back wards the grey-suited, sallow-skinned, tired yet restless men and women padded around and around like prisoners in an unending circular death march to nowhere. Then there were the wards for the aged, row after row of neatly packaged humanity, for the most part unwanted at home by their 'loved ones'. Yet another side of the 'closely-knit' Irish family was represented by the featureless, cattle-penned wards for the recalcitrant young, the once well-loved but now mis-understood, rebellious and unwanted adolescents, all victims of broken family relationships. What went wrong after that glad newspaper birth notice, 'the gift of a child'? Who was to blame? Within all this for me was my own equivocal custodial healing role as jailer/physician. It was my unenviable job to untangle the complex vortex of emotions that had engulfed the tormented victims of these disturbed relationships.

For over a century we doctors have manned our mental hospitals. Over these years, each of us in our different communities has structured and moulded our mental hospitals according to our cultural ethos to serve the needs of our communities. In western societies the recent use of the Thymoleptics mind-moulding drugs has rescued us from the ugly violence of bedlam. In contrast to our own uncaring concern for the aged in their homes, county homes and mental hospitals, I recall the brightly decorated and furnished old persons' flats which I visited while Minister for Health in 'godless' Sweden. We have such homes here in Ireland too, but as with so much else in our society they are reserved for that privileged few who can pay.

In mental illness diagnosis and treatment are both culturally determined, varying in time, place and community. Does this variety in both diagnosis and treatment not establish the age-old truth in medical practice? Where there are many cures, we know there is none. For the most part the mental hospital service is that great black rarely-upturned flat stone lying at the heart of every modern society, under which no one readily cares to look or, once looking, lingers over for long.

In any of our Irish mental hospitals, consider the number of derelict men and women who for the remainder of their lives, once committed to a mental hospital, are never again written to, visited or released. They may be so imprisoned for life without having committed any known criminal offence. They are committed without benefit of a public trial, the presence of the newspapers, the help of defence counsel, the facility afforded to the meanest or most brutal 'criminal'. As a psychiatrist, my signature on a piece of paper effectively was the judge, jury, and whole judicial process, and the sentence of the innocent one was for life.

I have sat opposite to a mother and father who had come to tell me that they never wished to see their otherwise healthy eighteen-year-old son Paddy home again. The origin of that boy's illness had been the father, a senior civil servant with a serious drink problem, who with drink taken became uncontrollably violent. On one of many such night, he had beaten his wife unmercifully and then turned on his three young children. At that time Paddy was aged six; he had pushed his younger sister into the only available shelter, under the stairs, while he remained, as a pitifully inadequate guard over them, on the outside. He had been badly beaten by his father, and still suffered in consequence. Surprisingly, he still loved both his parents, and greatly missed his now grown-up sisters. One of the sisters was now getting married. With no remembrance of what she owed to Paddy, she did not wish her husband-to-be to know that she had a brother in a mental hospital. The father, now cured of his drink problem, was at liberty. If they had their way, with my connivance, Paddy would become a prisoner for life. The father, a highly intelligent man, made it clear to me that were Paddy allowed home, he would deliberately set out to provoke him so as to ensure that Paddy would react violently. He could then call the police and Paddy would end up in prison. I asked the mother if this was also her wish; she replied, 'Yes, it is'. So Paddy, the most innocent victim of all, was to become a prisoner for life, an unthinkable sentence to impose on what society in our courts of law is pleased to call 'the most incorrigible and brutal of criminals'.

Equally was I a prisoner of my demeaning job as psychiatrist jailer. I had come to understand my true role; we are an élite, authorised by law to deprive a fellow citizen of liberty for life. Society pays us well and buys our compliance, and with it our silence. I was not proud to be a consultant psychiatrist.

Increasing experience of mental hospital practice left me with the belief that our mental hospitals are occupied by categories of inter-related groups of unhappy men and women in conflict with one another. There are the troublesome children, victims of their inadequate parents and now unwanted by these parents. There are the aged and difficult parents unwanted now by their children, with whom earlier the parents have created disturbed relationships. Their children, who may want the land or the home or the flat for themselves, are exacting their own reprisals on the parents. There are the wives who for many reasons are unwanted by their husbands. There are the husbands, possibly inadequate or alcoholics, who are now unwanted by their wives.

What I found most surprising was that there are few in our community who know as much as psychiatrists know about the emotionally-damaging results of defective social living and working conditions, or broken marriages. Yet rarely does the psychiatric profession individually or collectively intervene in support of remedial legislation.

Psychiatrists are by no means immune to the melancholy for which we claim to know the cause, and presume to advise the cure. In my short few years at St Brendan's, one consultant woman psychiatrist poisoned herself, and a male consultant, married with a family, blew his head off with a shotgun. Of all professionals, suicide is highest among psychiatrists. Least of all do psychiatrists enjoy the secret privileged 'happiness' pill. I too was to suffer an experience which I had not known through the years of my care of those suffering from tuberculosis. Shortly after becoming consultant psychiatrist as a clinician in a high-rise flat area in Dublin, I found that by the end of each week I could listen to no more. In the end, to restore my peace of mind, I was compelled to ask for twelve months' leave of absence without pay, as a relief from my work.

I provided a consultant psychiatric practice for one of the city's densely populated high-rise flat complexes, my role being to delude young newly-married men and women, most commonly the women, into believing that I could help them in their distress, amounting at times to near-suicidal misery. For the most part they suffered from, and that is the correct verb, their uncontrolled fertility, with rapidly growing, largely unwanted families. Because of our archaic laws and their religious upbringing, effective fertility control, although readily available throughout the civilised world, was not allowed in Ireland until 1979. In addition, these young couples had been removed from the inter-dependent support of the extended family they had once enjoyed in their former city centre homes. Within the now acknowledged planning disaster of their high-rise bins, they suffered total isolation. In addition both were subjected to the multiple strains of newly-married life.

An interesting feature of their lives, told to me by the priests, was the apparent desertion of the obsessional religious practice normally seen among such young people in centre-city housing schemes. The chaplains expressed the same sense of helplessness that I as a psychiatrist also felt. The psychiatrist must listen to tales of the unrelieved frustration of young men and women, and to their futile attempts to sublimate, understand or exercise the unexpected venom and explosive hate of their conflict-torn disturbed relationships. It was hard to believe that acts of ugly, painful violence which they claimed were uncontrollable could be used by one young person on another. Why and what were their origins in these two recently-loving human beings? How had they been so damaged by their life experience at home, at work or in their marriage? To the young girl with the bruised nose and eye, my question, 'Why not leave him?' expressed my own futility and inability to help her. Her reply was, 'How can I?' She already had one infant and was expecting another; she had nowhere to go. She was captive and caged, for life. The sadistic husband realised that his new young bride had become his helpless plaything. Recommending recourse to the police, I was told that in our society 'the gardai will not interfere in a marital domestic quarrel'. Such a defenceless mother and her children have no refuge. Each baby for her becomes one other helpless dependent, a trap for the conscientious mother, and well does the husband come to know this.

Some years ago a young psychologist, the late Ian Hart, carried out a survey on behalf of the Department of Psychology at the Eastern Health Board. Its purpose was to establish projections for probable criminality, among children born in poor circumstances. I recall a senior psychologist assuring me that the conclusions disclosed in the paper proved that, without doubt, 'because of increasing criminality among Dublin working class children from such areas, in five to ten years' time Dublin will become as lawless as New York, they'll march on Dublin'. Characteristic of the deceit among those who lead our society was the fact that this revealing survey, with all its frightening human and social implications at so many levels, was suppressed. In spite of repeated parliamentary questions by myself, as far as I know it was never publicised. Certainly no attempt was made to take successful remedial action on its implications or to change that poisonous environment. Now crime reports in our daily papers validate that young psychologist's grim forebodings and the findings of his survey.

16

The Left in Ireland

IT WAS difficult for people of left-wing political views to gain public support in the Ireland of the 1950s and early 1960s. Since the Communists could make no progress because of the active opposition of the government, they were compelled to adopt three broad stratagems. One was for certain members to fade into various key activities in society, and 'wait'. They infiltrated the Labour Party, the trade union movement, radio, newspapers and similar sources of influence. Then there were committed Communists, entirely ineffective people, such as Mick O'Riordan, Seán Murray, Nicholas Boran, Seán Nolan, Peter Connolly, Tom Waters, and Betty Sinclair of Belfast. They remained on the surface but were so harassed by the authorities that they could not hope to form a mass movement. They did launch the valuable New Books in 1942, leading to the publication of Connolly's writings as well as those of Marx, Engels, Lenin and other socialist works.

There was a third Communist group whose function was to enter emergent and even competing left-wing groups as 'sleepers' to practice 'fraction work', to cause a split in the new group and so eliminate it. From my memories of a small book which circulated to certain members of the Cabinet, I knew that nearly every active Communist group was either infiltrated by or was well known to the police. It came as an embarrassment, for instance, to Seán MacBride to find that the Special Branch had a sixteen millimetre film of Peadar Cowan, a Clann na Poblachta deputy, entering the Communist bookshop in Pearse Street. The camera was clearly in a permanent position and used strictly for surveillance.

May Keating was one of the most valuable supporters in the small group of like-minded people who worked with me for many years on the left in Ireland. She was a marxist, and a dedicated worker for revolutionary change in Irish society. She held the belief that western society had entered into a post-Christian phase, and that control of education must be taken from the Church as an indispensable first step towards revolutionary change.

It was May Keating's job with our group to make sure that the practice of 'sleeper' members of the Communist party should not jeopardise my position as a politician in Leinster House. My opponents in all three parties in Leinster House frequently accused me of 'being a Communist', a politically damaging charge. Those who used this tactic most frequently were Seán MacEntee, Charles Haughey and Brian Lenihan, and some rank-and-file members of Fine Gael. The Fine Gael leadership at no time made such a claim. It clearly carried its own invalidity; if unwittingly I became associated with a Communist known only to the police, then the Fianna Fáil minister in the Dáil would have been glad to give the House chapter and verse about my 'Communist allies'.

In 1958 I was told that May Keating's son, Justin, who at that time was associated with the British Young Communists, had been nominated to act as editor of a small left-wing paper, *The Plough*, with which I was associated. I resented the fact that I had not been consulted about the advisability of giving her son a piggy-back into Irish public life. Justin, having sown his political wild oats in the Communist Party, now wished to 'repent' and find his way into the Labour Party. Like young Jim Larkin before him, he became its most notorious 'right wing' disciplinarian. Life under unending pressure from the right was hard enough, without this troublesome harassment from the left. I made a speech in November condemning the use of 'sleepers' by the Communists, and broke with May Keating.

One man who worked with much enthusiasm in support of our joint causes was David Thornley, who had canvassed for me as a student. Thornley became impatient of my independent role; he saw no hope of a political career for himself. It was agreed that Jack McQuillan and I should establish a small radical group to provide a rallying centre for dissident groups in the country. When I did not initially favour the idea, Thornley accused me of thinking only of myself and wanting to go on as an

Independent forever, which was quite untrue; I felt that I was not leader material. However, since Jack wouldn't be leader and there was nobody else, I became leader of the National Progressive Democratic Party (NPD), which was founded in May 1958.

There are those who dismiss politicians as an easy-living, self-indulgent breed of parasites. Generally, that is a misconceived belief; whatever their motives, there are those who suffer. David Thornley was eventually to offer his fine talents and many gifts of intellect to that party which claims to be the most caring of the three major parties, the Irish Labour Party. During his time in that party, working class, aristocrats, intellectuals and rural deputies alike combined to shred and then pulverise that fine intelligence with a special competence which only the Irish Labour Party has acquired over the years.

What was the irresistible force which compelled Thornley to desert his role as a talented university teacher, a stimulating public affairs broadcaster, and a contented family man, for the painful disappointment and tragedy of his subsequent life in politics? It would seem that the attraction of being an historian was not equal to that of the prestige and power of a successful politician and statesman. At one stage, to judge by his reading, he became fascinated to an unusual degree by the development of Hitler and the Nazi movement in Germany. It later transpired that the equally messianic romantic, Patrick Pearse, was his special hero. For a boy educated in an English public school, Thornley was surprisingly obsessed with the cause of Ireland's freedom, denied to her by the 'perfidious British'. Pearse, Brugha, MacBride, Larkin, de Valera and others, all more Irish than the Irish, would well repay a separate psychological study. Thornley was a passionately patriotic Irishman. Although increasingly he came to protest his left-wing socialist beliefs, he was never more than an old-fashioned liberal. As with so many liberals, under pressure Thornley was capable of ruthless beliefs and practices where his opponents were concerned.

Thornley was a non-Marxist; he had made a thorough study of Marxist writings, and remained unconvinced. In spite of diligent attempts to do so, he rarely succeeded in empathising with the working classes whose cause he professed to espouse. He disliked the sordid milieu of working-class life, and with a strange lack of logic, he appeared to attribute to the working classes themselves a measure of the blame for their social conditions.

It is conceivable that Thornley's instinctive alienation from the working class was reflected by the powerful barrier created by the way he spoke. Although gifted with a fine musical talent, he made no attempt to rid himself of what even in the British House of Lords would have been considered a striking upper-crust accent. Could it be that he affected the accent to antagonise those whom he instinctively wished to ignore or drive away?

Thornley wrote an illuminating monograph on Pearse, from which there is no doubt that he believed he and Pearse had much in common, with their half-English origins, their sexual ambivalence and their shared obsession with violence. Incredibly for a man of his sensitivity and intelligence, Thornley was proud of his boxing skills; a study of his later life would suggest that he even shared the strange driving death-wish of his admired hero. Following the funerals of dead republican comrades, he was always prepared to sing in his fine baritone voice. His favourite ballads were either the lachrymose dirges for our patriot dead or the aggressively militant jingoist battle songs of the Republic.

Thornley was fascinated by guns, particularly hand-guns. Once during a blood transfusion session at Leinster House, he caused much embarrassment when a large loaded revolver fell from his pocket as he lay on the couch to give his pint of blood. Therein lay the paradox of the generous but violent child that he was. Thornley was later to be in trouble with the Labour Party over his appearance on a 'Provo' platform during the bogus hunger strike of the presently hale and healthy half-English romantic republican, Sean MacStiofáin. At a Labour parliamentary party meeting, I well recall him making an impassioned appeal to us about the problem of eating his Sunday chicken dinner while MacStiofáin lay alone on his bed in the Mater hospital. It was wasted on that roomful. Thornley was a devout practising Catholic, and proud of his faith. Irreverently he would claim, 'I am prepared to wave my rosary beads with the best of them'. He had limitless personal charm. Though frequently I knew he was in the process of attempting to survert my political career, I found him to be an entertaining and likeable person. He was ambitious but his ambition was turned inwards on his own clamouring need for reassurance and recognition. With his family he worked with unselfish efficiency in Dublin South-East to secure my election and re-election.

More and more, however, his sole preoccupation became his own political future. In the distinction which I make between those who 'need politics for themselves', and 'those who enter politics for others', David needed politics and his obsession with his neurotic needs precluded concern for anyone who might, in his pursuit of these needs, get hurt. In time I came to appreciate his inability to control his blacker side, and the driving compulsion of his pursuit of power.

Thornley was annoyed when the NPD submitted Noel Hartnett instead of himself as a candidate in a Dublin by-election. Soon after Noel's failure to win the seat David, with the help of right-wing allies, made an abortive attempt to take over the party. Unsuccessful, he resigned, and publicly declared his disgust with our politics. In the process he did much damage to our new small group.

Though we parted for a time following the NPD's eventual collapse (both Jack McQuillan and I had held our seats in the 1961 general election won by Fianna Fáil) we were to meet once again as members of the Labour Party.

Because of a further flare-up of my tuberculosis in 1964, in spite of many invitations to campaign throughout the country, I was compelled to discontinue both active politics, and my job as a house physician at St. Brendan's. The new young party could not be nurtured as it deserved, and slowly disintegrated. However, this was for me a fruitful period of political development. I met with a group of like-minded radicals at least once a week in a Kildare Street basement. Prominent among them was John Byrne, a member of an old Donnycarney family, whose father had been a driver for a coal merchant in the early years of the century. John had set out to become a self-educated, widely-read authority on socialist Marxist and Trotskyite literature. He had been deported back to Ireland, while working on the left in Britain, because of his anti-war activities. We first met during the mother and child crisis; since then we have continued to remain close friends and political associates.

We were visited on occasions by left-wing comrades from Britain; these meetings were of value for the interchange of ideas about Anglo-Irish left-wing politics. At the beginning of one such meeting, which was to be addressed by one of our visiting speakers, an incident occurred that was to have serious results for me politically but showed at the same time a refreshing side of liberal-minded Dublin people's sense of justice.

This happened during the Kruschev-Kennedy confrontation over Fidel Castro. In what became known as the Bay of Pigs invasion, the United States threatened to abort Cuba's socialist revolution. In defence of Castro, Krushchev moved missiles to Cuba in October 1962. We now know that the world was closer to nuclear extermination that night than ever before or since. As our meeting began that night, 23 October, we all shared a restless foreboding of impending danger. Worse still was our sense of helplessness before it. John Byrne pleaded the futility of our sitting in a basement discussing the future when there was a good chance there might be no tomorrow for any of us. He moved that we take to the streets in Dublin to try to create a public awareness about the possible imminence of world catastrophe.

For an Irish politician in Dublin to protest in defence of a Marxist revolution, even thousands of miles away, was asking for trouble. As we walked up the steps from our basement head-quarters, I murmured to him 'John, this is going to cost us Dublin South-East'. We marched up Kildare Street, around Stephen's Green, down Grafton Street, along Nassau Street towards Merrion Square and the US Embassy in Ballsbridge. It was our intention to protest formally, leaving a message to that effect at the embassy.

As we marched down Grafton Street calling out our message and asking for support, a few good-humoured young boys and girls from the cafés and ice-cream parlours decided to join us. The rest ignored us or patronisingly smiled at our foolishness, remaining in their queues for whatever makebelieve dream world was to be presented to them on the cinema screens. We were eventually met by a solid blue line of gardai. As a parliamentary representative in a peaceful protest march acting as its spokes-man, I asked permission to protest formally at the embassy. Seconds later I was violently hurled through the air, victim of some kind of street-fighting artistry favoured by a notorious policeman who specialised in brutality and was proud of it. This was followed by a general assault on our small group. Slowly we were driven back towards Clare Street. Many of the gardai were patient and did not use brutal methods. Our resistance, was finally crushed, however, by the use of savage alsatian dogs, which had arrived in a police van. The assault, the strange animal sounds, the snarls, excited barks and whimpers, were all so unexpected and unthinkable that it was hard to know what was happening. There was the sudden realisation that a large and angry animal with sharp teeth was furiously tearing at your clothes, your body, your head, face, and arms. My first reaction was one of incredulity. Fear was blotted out by emotions closer to despair and disgust. As in most Irish homes, we have always kept dogs. I experienced a sense of hurt revulsion that men could pervert the age-old friendship of man and dog. Someone had trained these dogs to savage a fellow man instead of serve him, to deliberately pervert a generous instinct into a fearsome hurting one.

By this time a crowd had gathered in Clare Street. While being mauled by the dogs, I tried to tell the public that the men setting these dogs on us were the men whom we as citizens paid to keep the peace. Finally the press arrived, among them a photographer. He got a particularly spectacular picture of one alsatian jumping at my head, a record of the event which could not be controverted. Some of the young men and women needed hospital treatment for their bites. I treated my own.

There were a number of sequels. There was a court case in which it was implied that it was we, the marchers, who had provoked the police dogs. There was even a suggestion of irritation that I did not look frightened in the photograph, the implication being that I had enjoyed the whole revolting episode. Those who went to court were given no sympathy. But a worthwhile result was that the police may no longer use alsatian dogs to disrupt protest marches. Credit for this must go to the distinguished short story writer, Frank O'Connor, one of the early republicans in the Anglo-Irish struggle. He wrote to tell me of his sympathy because of the attack by the police dogs. While disclaiming any interest in the subject of the march, he went on to invite us to take part in another march, to be led by him to establish without question any citizen's right lawfully to march anywhere, without molestation by police dogs, in the city of Dublin. It was for such a freedom that earlier, as a young man, he had risked his life.

It was a dramatic occasion. That march duly took place, silently and peacefully. Nothing was said; there were no partisan flags, no scrolls or banners, no political slogans. No note or letter was handed in when finally we arrived at the American Embassy. The march completed, all of us, citizens of differing shades of political and religious beliefs and of all ages, departed our different ways. It was comforting to see the citizens of Dublin validate of their own accord, in the streets of Dublin, that liberal thesis, 'I don't agree with what you say, but I will defend your right to say it'.

Several years later a member of the gardai with whom I had become friendly told me of that incident as seen by him that night. He said that inside the American Embassy a number of embassy staff were armed, and prepared to use arms against us. The gardai had been for *our* protection; it was essential that we be prevented from reaching the embassy.

For ourselves, the sad sequel was as we had feared. The McCarthyite smear that our march had been a gesture of pro-Communist solidarity was used ruthlessly in the 1965 general election. Our protest march had indeed 'cost us Dublin South-East'. I lost my seat to Fianna Fáil's Seán Moore, although increasing my vote from 4,717 in 1961 to 5,348.

With the demise of the National Progressive Democrats in 1964, Jack McQuillan and I concluded that our contributions in the Dáil, while valuable, remained limited in their long-term effect without the support of a political party. Inevitably and reluctantly we were driven to accept the need to work within the least objectionable of the three main parties. With equal reluctance the Labour Party finally accepted us as working members in October 1963. Surprisingly, the conservative Jim Tully voted for my admission while, unsurprisingly, Brendan Corish fought against it.

All went well for a short few years. I was even elected vice-chairman of the party in 1967. Then, as the pact-making between Fine Gael and Labour intensified, we became effectively isolated and silenced. It is possibly true that we had been mistaken in not appreciating quite how effective what was euphemistically called party discipline could be. Parliamentary questions were permitted only with the authority of the shadow minister. The use of motions, and bills on the order paper, which had been so effective and valuable in elaborating radical policies by initiating debates in the Dáil up to now, was forbidden. Frank Cluskey, the party whip, was an enthusiastic member of the inner cabal, determined to form yet another coalition with Fine Gael and so win ministerial office. For this reason, none but those chosen speakers who preached harmless banalities unlikely to ruffle Fine Gael were tolerated as speakers in the Dáil, especially on contentious issues. It was Cluskey's practice to promise permission to speak on a subject, but at the end of a long list which appeared miraculously to elongate further just as soon as I asked permission to speak. I began to wonder whether we had been deliberately permitted to join the Labour Party so that we could be silenced.

In the late sixties and early seventies, for the first time, there was talk of liberal, even socialist, thought in the Republic. Politics began to ease its way from the monosyllabic, catch-cry rhetoric of anti-British republicanism to a more creative, mature political mould. Much of this may have resulted from marginal access to world opinion through international travel, the extension of television through the country, and the access to technological education needed to accommodate the new multi-nationals now beginning their ritual transitory flit to the favourable tax concessions of the gullible Republic's Ministers for Commerce.

Back in the fifties, the nationwide enthusiasm for our cause during the mother and child election have been a truly memorable but fleeting experience. The exuberant spirit of youth in the 1969 general election now came as a new and encouraging element in Irish public life. What an opportunity was to be missed by the Labour Party to harness this into something lasting. By this time I myself was more consciously radical politically than I had been in 1951. Young people poured into the election rooms in Margaret Gaj's restaurant in Baggot Street, all anxious to fight the Labour Party cause. The potential then for social and political change was considerable.

Whatever its origins, there had been an exciting resurgence of interest in Labour Party politics. From the national schools to the universities, debates on socialist ideas among the young were common to an extent never before seen, or indeed, permitted, by the authorities. For the first time I was to hear Marx and Com-

munism referred to and discussed by young students at Synge
Street School debating society. Socialist ideas began to compete
with the limited rhetoric of republicanism. The new influx of
well-known names into the Labour Party, supported by an
improved administrative machine, appeared to have relieved
the traditionally conservative Brendan Corish of his normal
dislike of socialist ideas. In the United States, Conor Cruise
O'Brien had been associated publicly and courageously with a
number of radical issues, such as apartheid and the peace movement. This had given us hope that in turn he might, when the
opportunity arose, help similar causes in his own country.

In a well-publicised speech, we were surprised to hear Corish
promise 'Socialism in the Seventies'. Growing more daring, he
went on to cause raised eyebrows by taking an oath declaring
that, under no circumstances, would he take part in any future
Fine Gael coalition. Even more recklessly he promised that he
would go into the backbenches, sooner than go into a coalition.
These were brave empty phrases, as time would show; they
meant nothing either to Corish or to his speechwriters.

Within the Labour inner cabal it was perceived that, with the
radical spirit of youth during that era, socialism was a possible
password to office. The captive Corish, like any well-trained
circus pony, simply went along in the expectation of a lump of
sugar at the conclusion of his act.

With a well-equipped head office, for a change, and more
money than usual, we set out to fight the 1969 election. Though
I was as anxious as anyone for radical change, I was uneasy
about such an over-optimistic estimate for the promised socialist
millenium. It seemed to me to be wrong to promise, in the
context of our still predominantly conservative Irish society, the
unattainable ideal of socialism in the 'seventies.

Just in time for the annual Labour Party Conference, I felt
compelled to write two articles, which appeared in the *Irish
Times,* questioning the socialist protestations of the Labour
leadership. I proposed an alternative prospect for an entirely
new left, arising from within the three existing parties. In the
Labour Party, our sole claim to be a rallying point for a radical
re-grouping was the reality of James Connolly, our socialist
founder. Outside that, there was little we had to offer in the form
of left-wing radical or socialist thought. Though all three

political parties were predominantly conservative, there were among the rank and file men and women who would have joined a liberal or socialist party had such a party existed. Increasing literacy had bred young people who recognised the dangers of taking their politics with their nationality and religion as compulsory parental birthrights. A genuine alternative to civil war politics was needed. A new re-grouping on conscious ideological lines was suggested by me as a pre-condition to the creation of new political structures in the Republic along western European lines.

I was promptly condemned for my temerity in questioning the analysis of the Labour Party leadership. I was to find myself in trouble for making these somewhat obvious proposals as a counter to their irresponsible claims for instant socialism. I was damned for my pessimism, yet such a re-grouping on ideological lines still remains to be achieved as an essential pre-condition to a genuine ending to civil war politics in the Republic.

17

Leaving Labour

FOLLOWING the general election in 1969 — Fianna Fáil were returned to power with 75 seats, Labour winning 18 and Fine Gael 50 — the unjustified demoralisation and disillusionment of the Labour leadership was reminiscent of what had happened earlier in Clann na Poblachta. The leadership had anticipated being swept to power in the new wave of socialism, just as Seán MacBride had hoped for success in an earlier wave of republicanism. Without a backward glance at their socialist Republic, their oaths against coalition, or their threat to go to the backbenches, they prepared to seek office otherwise. Standing for Labour, I was re-elected in Dublin South-East, with 5,724 first preferences to Garret Fitzgerald's 8,412 and Seán Moore's 4,979. I continued to advocate a socialist solution to the economic problems of unemployment, poor housing, and neglect of the aged.

From 1969 to the mid-seventies it became noticeable that our Labour Party policy statements were being carefully orientated to dovetail with the conservative thinking of the Fine Gael party. I realised that I was wrong in my earlier assumption that the new leadership of the Labour party genuinely shared my political commitment to socialism. I had believed that it would be possible for them even to enter coalition and survive with suitable safeguards. The almost total defection of the Labour Party from socialism between 1969 and 1975 soon cleared up that mistaken belief. For the second time in twenty years a radically-minded generation of young Irishmen and women felt betrayed. Not surprisingly, they became sadly disenchanted with politics and the parliamentary system.

Isolated in a party which had only one objective, office at any price, I felt a hopeless sense of entrapment. There appeared to be

no worthwhile political action open to me. I decided that I
should try to remind Irish society, the unions and the political
parties, that parliament was not simply a sterile bureaucracy
concerned solely with ward-heeling activities. Traditionally it
was the function of a Labour Party to articulate the needs of the
underprivileged and down-trodden. Yet the Labour Party
appeared to avoid such issues deliberately. It had set out to
ingratiate itself with the power institutions and the financial
groups. Politically it appeared to wish to merge into Fine Gael.
Connolly's Labour Party had simply become a political trading
stamp for use in exchange for a handful of Cabinet seats in a
coalition government.

At a public meeting of the Labour Party held in Tramore on
23 April 1971, I made a comprehensive statement calling for an
alternative set of objectives and policies for the Labour Party. I
dwelt at some length on the powerful influence of the Catholic
Church, which I described as being comparable to the influence
of the Orange Order in the North of Ireland. If we were to change
Irish society in ways appropriate for Connolly's socialist labour
party, then this control of education by the church must be
altered radically.

I numbered the most obvious ways in which the church interfered with political decisions — the powerful influence of the
confessional, the use of the pulpit and the pastoral letter, and
finally, the perennial secret and undisclosed interference by the
bishops in political matters. I put it to those present that the
Labour Party must show that we in the south were free to
debate, discuss, and decide on all matters which concerned our
people's lives, issues such as coeducation, interdenominational
education, inter-church marriages, homosexuality, abortion,
capital punishment, corporal punishment, contraception,
divorce, socialism and Marxism.

'It is time', I concluded, 'that our people got off their knees,
and our people, both in the north and in the south, finally took
on the responsibility of governing themselves, uniting our unhappy divided nation, under the common name of Irishmen'.

This was the occasion on which I finally came to understand
the remarkable poverty of spirit within the Labour Party. This
fear of the church affected all classes in the parliamentary
Labour Party in an identical manner as it had affected my

Cabinet colleagues in the coalition twenty years before. Consciously or not, it was the last serious move I was to make in what John Whyte correctly described as my attempt in 1951 to 'break the mould of Irish society'. Undoubtedly it failed. The meeting of the parliamentary Labour Party on the following day verged on the hysterical. Indeed, the whole nation, to judge by its newspaper headlines, equally verged on the hysterical. With the single exception of deputy John O'Connell, all those present shared the conviction that I must be disowned without delay.

As expected, the deputies from rural Ireland were mystified by much of the substance of my criticism and shocked by my suggestion of sexual ambivalence among celibate clergy, and its consequences through clerical control of the schools. All of them favoured the commonly-held simplistic appreciation in the Republic: 'If it were not for the Christian Brothers, I would never have got an education'. They believed that my critique of the true dynamics of power in Irish society was unfair.

I was subjected to varying forms of abuse. Echoes from Clann na Poblachta recurred: 'You can't afford to fight the Church'. In twenty years, nothing had changed. What did surprise me was that the intellectuals and academics competed with one another to dissociate themselves from me and all that I had said. Conor Cruise O'Brien joined with Keating and Thornley in a mixture of shock and disbelief. Each in his own way hurried to dissociate himself from such sacrilegious and dangerous ideas. At the same time, each carefully signalled to the rural deputies and to Corish that they need have no fear of a revolt by the intellectuals or academics in the submissive 'battery hen' conditions of what passed for politics in the Labour Party.

Brendan Corish was genuinely shocked; he was a devout practising Catholic. At the other extreme was Conor Cruise O'Brien, who in a short essay, 'The suspecting glance,' had written, 'we philosophers and free spirits feel consciously irradiated as by a new dawn, by the report that the old God is dead'. He was a declared agnostic, and in the US he had been associated with a number of civil rights activities; he must have agreed with all I had said, yet under minimal pressure he succumbed to the most sordid kind of domestic politics.

Until I read Cruise O'Brien's strange confession in the *New*

York Times in 1985 about having been 'liberated' from the
political process, 'from having to say things which I did not
necessarily believe', it was hard to understand his strange
reaction. I was among those who had gladly and publicly welcomed him into the Labour Party. With his liberal record in the
United States, we had hoped he would help to broaden and
rationalise our way out of the unthinking sectarianism of Irish
public life. Instead, regrettably, O'Brien and Keating, the two
most polished and talented politicians I know, failed our society.
Their behaviour well illustrated the phrase used by my wife in a
comment on an optimistic claim made by Michael McInerney,
political correspondent of the *Irish Times,* following the formation of the disastrous 1973 coalition. 'Now we have a government of all the talents', wrote McInerney. 'Yes', was her
comment, 'Undoubtedly, but how will they use them?'

Thornley dismissed my intervention as a typical piece of blundering foolishness. What could they expect from me? His main
concern, however, and much to her surprise, was for his wife,
Petria. A fine lady, respected by all of us, she was a teacher in a
convent school. Now in a voice on the edge of tears that did not
conceal a wickedly smiling eye, the artist Thornley drew us a
picture to melt a heart of teak. There was the hushed, silent,
embarrassed Petria. Eyes downcast, properly penitential,
swathed in sackcloth, near to tears, she stumbles her way into
her classroom to face not only her open-eyed, shocked young
pupils but also her equally stunned teacher-nun colleagues,
headed by the Reverend Mother, all of these ladies in voices of
murmured horror reading the dread abuse of them by the
Labour Party spokesman, Dr. Noël Browne. Thornley pleaded,
'What is she to say, what is her defence? What is our defence?'
Thornley chose to fasten on that subject which, with socialism,
causes the most anxiety in the Republic, that is sex. He said I
had created in the public mind the idea that these good ladies,
with their brother and priest colleagues, were a band of homo-
sexuals and lesbians who cavorted around their nun-
neries, convents and monasteries in wild orgies, not to mention
what went on with their under-age pupils in the garden sheds of
our national schools. All this tirade was because I had dared to
refer to the possibility of ambivalent and confused sexual
attitudes among some of those who choose voluntary celibacy in

religious orders, and had asked whether there might not be undesirable repercussions for our children.

At this stage Conor Cruise O'Brien intervened with a crisp denunciation of the impropriety of the speech, and the political foolishness of the speaker. His theme echoed Cosgrave, de Valera and MacBride before him: 'You can't afford to fight the Church'.

That was my last attempt to drag the reluctant Republic out of the nineteenth century. On 30 April 1971, speaking on TV, radio, and in the newspapers on behalf of all the members of the parliamentary Labour Party, none dissenting, Corish gladly denounced and disowned my speech and its contents.

Happily I have lived to see many of the proposals which I made in the Tramore speech either accepted into the law of the land, or becoming subjects of mature deliberation and discussion throughout the Republic. One of my most vituperative critics, Barry Desmond, no doubt for his own sound political reasons as a deputy in a predominantly Protestant liberal constituency, now freely promotes and advocates ideas that he, with Cluskey and others, anathematised in 1971 as an 'insult to the Church' when I first expressed them. What if Labour had chosen to give that radical leadership then?

It is important to distinguish office and power. They are by no means synonymous. From his earliest experience in the first coalition government, watching Norton's helplessness in office and without power in formulating a comprehensive social insurance scheme, Corish must have learnt this simple truth, as had I. Because the Labour Party was predominantly composed of conservative rural deputies, it was a Labour Party as such in name only.

With other intellectuals such as Conor Cruise O'Brien and Keating, David Thornley worked tirelessly to assume leadership of what Keating behind their backs called 'the culchies' of the Labour Party. These were the cute rural deputies, Spring, Coughlan, Michael Pat Murphy and others who could, with a practised ease, 'build a nest in your ear, while minding mice at a crossroads'. Whereas Cruise O'Brien simply concentrated on flattering and supporting Corish in his beliefs and policies, Keating and Thornley appeared to concentrate more on assuming leadership of the rural deputies. Keating simply weighed in on their side, at the appropriate time, and with effect. But David set out to shed the impression he might have given that at any time he shared our socialist beliefs. The ease with which the despised rural deputies survived to live on politically and prosper in Irish public life long after the disappearance of the intellectuals tells its own tale of Irish politics.

Thornley was also involved in ingratiating himself with the inner cabal of Cluskey, Halligan, Keating, Cruise O'Brien and others to bring the parliamentary Labour Party and Fine Gael together, in anticipation of yet another coalition with Fine Gael. Brendan Halligan was the puppet-master extraordinary who master-minded the 1973 coalition that ended ten years of Fianna Fáil government. It became an essential condition, laid down, I understand, by Fine Gael, that before any coalition was entered into the Labour Party must 'get rid of Noël Browne'. In pursuit of this objective Thornley was to play his own eager part in bringing about my expulsion. The activities of that close-knit inner mafia contributed to the decline of the Labour movement in the Republic to its position today — a fall of electoral support from between 18 per cent and 20 per cent to a mere 5 per cent.

Thornley was to do his most useful and valuable educative political work while involved with Muiris Mac Conghaile in the popular RTE current affairs programme 'Seven Days'. Thornley made no attempt to invite me to take part in this programme, until I made a speech in Leinster House which they appear to have misunderstood, believing that I favoured a coalition government. Knowing David somewhat better by now, I knew that it was to be my function in the programme discussion to which I was invited to promote his idea of a coalition. I agreed to take part.

I was happy to collaborate with the Thornley-Mac Conghaile plan until just before the conclusion. It was then that I decided to call a halt, by the use of a seemingly spontaneous 'political blunt instrument' remark. Asked about the true function of the minority in coalition, I replied, 'Just as soon as we achieve our political objectives in any coalition with a conservative party, it is the responsibility of a smaller radical party to "pull the trap" on the other parties.' While no one was or is prepared to say that this is so, inevitably it must be the objective of each party in the coalition to increase their representation, even at the expense of the coalition government. During my period as member of the first coalition, I felt no sense of corporate loyalty to the other members of the government, with the possible exception of the Labour Party, nor they to me. Understandably, none of this inbuilt battle for votes inseparable from a coalition relationship was contained in the Thornley script. For myself, I hoped that the effect of my candid exposure of the reality of coalition politics would help at least to slow down the inevitable coalition which I saw ahead. I did not re-appear on 'Seven Days' thereafter.

Thornley yearned for Cabinet office at any price and on any terms, preferably in a Fine Gael coalition. As his speeches have shown the nation lost in him a fertile, innovative and original mind. Together with Cluskey, Cruise O'Brien, Keating, Halligan and the others, he now worked with a manic dedication for a coalition with Fine Gael. Well I recall seeing his head bounding along behind the delegates' seats at the Labour Party conference in Cork in 1970 as he went from one to the next in a frenzied attempt to win their support for a coalition. His dedicated zeal was to help achieve this objective for all of that cabal, with the exception of Thornley himself, who was shed by the Labour leadership with chilling indifference when they failed to appoint him to a ministry.

It is important to apportion fairly the responsibility for this. O'Brien, Keating, Desmond, Tully, Corish, the rural deputies, the intellectuals and urban working-class alike — all shared equally in this mean act. While such a political defeat is a commonplace occupational hazard of public life, the effect on a man of Thornley's delicately-balanced psychological make-up was catastrophic. He simply could not credit the duplicity of those within the Labour leadership with whom he had ingratiated himself in order to promote and help their joint ministerial ambitions. He had deserted all his formal radical postures and friends in their interests. Those of us who retained our affection for him, and for his self-sacrificing, devoted and loyal wife, Petria, shared their distress.

Thornley appeared to have resolved to bury himself and to disappear within a grotesquely altered human being. Rapidly he became the direct opposite to the mildly vain, impeccably dressed, scintillatingly intelligent young Trinity don all of us had known. We were at the Labour Party Conference in the Leisureland centre in Galway sometime after this. We had already passed this hideously distorted creature when my wife, shocked, murmured 'That was David'. Between heavy drinking, illness and neglect of his appearance, David had taken on the form which in psychiatry is known sometimes as a variant of the 'Pickwick boy' syndrome. His eyes were scarcely visible, buried as they were in the great distended blubber of a once handsome face.

In spite of the attempts of many of us, still his friends, who desperately wanted to help, David was unhappily inaccessible to reason. Shortly he was to gain the only relief and peace open to him, dying at a very young age in June, 1978. Characteristically, all the Labour Party leadership turned up at his funeral, as they had to the funeral of yet another talented young man who had been expelled from the Labour Party, the incomparable Brendan Scott. Within the Irish Labour Party, there was no place for such men.

The Labour Party refused to nominate me as a candidate in the 1975 general election because I would not sign a pledge supporting a coalition agreement with Fine Gael. A lot of my supporters were annoyed and left the party, but I saw no point in resigning. Dr Ryder, of Cork, suggested that I should stand for the Senate on the Trinity College panel and I won the seat left vacant by the death of Owen Sheehy Skeffington.

I was able to use the Upper House to criticise the government on various social issues, in particular contraception; before resigning as Labour spokesman on Health the previous year I had attempted to introduce a bill on contraception.

The National Coalition's period in office coincided with the oil crisis and a period of inflation which saw many prices increase by over 100 per cent. The Fine Gael Taoiseach, Liam Cosgrave, had shrewdly allocated Labour the more vulnerable money-spending ministries without any money to spend. Michael O'Leary was to find himself blamed for the unprecedented unemployment figures, Justin Keating for the sell-out of our natural resources and the collapse of price controls, Jim Tully for the recession in the building industry and Brendan Corish for the total stagnation and inaction on social welfare, while Conor

Cruise O'Brien's mis-management of his Department of Post and Telegraphs.

Having been elected to the Senate, I declined to take the Labour whip. To my mind there was a matter of principle involved. In 1977, when the coalition was finally forced to go to the country, I stood for the Dublin Artane constituency where I was now living. The Labour Party refused to endorse my candidature. They used as their reason my failure to take the Labour whip in the Senate.

That being so, I stood as an Independent, and was easily elected with 6,600 first preference votes. As I had warned the Labour party in 1974, at the final parliamentary meeting at which they decided to go into coalition, the general election in 1977 was a total debacle for the party. Though they had won 17 seats, their share of the poll had dropped from 17% in 1969, to 11.6% in 1977. Thereafter, nothing could stop the continuous, inglorious slide of Connolly's labour party into oblivion. Its current miniscule 4% of the poll tells its own tale. Both Justin Keating and Conor Cruise O'Brien, powerful and influential advocates of coalition, were defeated. Meanwhile, the Labour country deputies whom Keating had contemptuously dismissed as the 'culchies', survived to take over what was left of the party, and finished it off.

Regrettably, for the second time in my political career, in 1981, on being returned in the new constituency of Dublin North Central, I found myself holding the balance of power in the Dáil. With Hobson's choice, FitzGerald or Haughey, I supported FitzGerald despite my own doubts about his capacity to realise his hopes for a liberal crusade.

Because, among other influential people, Garret FitzGerald continuously dismissed the possibility of Catholic hierarchical interference in government as 'a thing of the past', I decided to test the assumption. In 1979, I put down about forty amendments to Haughey's blatantly sectarian Family Planning Bill. It was my intention that were the amendments accepted, our family planning facilities would be comparable to those available now throughout the advanced world. It was as if I had had the plague. No party, no individual deputy, made any attempt to debate those possibilities, during the long period in which I was involved along in the Dáil. There was no woman deputy prepared to support my proposals. Equally I moved a Private Members' Bill on divorce in 1980. There is no divorce in the Republic, because of a Constitutional ban included in De Valera's 1937 Constitution. Though both the Labour Party and Fine Gael annual conferences had voted to investigate the matter of divorce in the Republic, not a single deputy in any of the parties rose to support even the proposal that the matter be debated. My proposal was defeated by default. The same was true on the question of both gay rights and abortion. Though there were at the time six women members in the House, none were prepared to claim for women that in such a matter as important as an unwanted pregnancy, women had a 'right to choose'. Neither were the men or women deputies prepared to support the plea made by the minority churches in the republic that, in their opinion, in case of rape with consequential pregnancy, or where the birth of an anencephlic monster was inevitable, or in case of pregnancy following incest, the right to terminate pregnancy should rest with the woman. I was the only member of the House who, on behalf of Irish womanhood, claimed their 'right to choose'. It was on the issue of divorce that the minority churches were also ignored, when they claimed that, in their belief, divorce should in carefully limited circumstances be permissible.

It was soon after this, with the 1982 budget introduced by John Bruton, that the government fell, on the proposal to impose VAT on childrens' shoes. Considering the multi-million pound size of the budget involved, it was a particularly silly proposal. Yet, FitzGerald and Bruton proudly claimed to have discovered a serious source of tax evasion. As the debate concluded, FitzGerald enormously pleased with his vigilance showed me a piece of paper, cluttered with figures. He claimed that the figures proved that women with small feet could buy childrens' shoes, to wear themselves. So, since childrens' shoes were not rated for VAT, the women could avoid paying tax. Helplessly and hopelessly, I turned away, murmuring, 'Who cares?' Of such imbicilities are the trivia which determine issues in public life in the Republic — even to bringing down governments. That government, could find its way into the *Guinness Book of Records* as the shortest living administration government in the history of the republic.

Nevertheless, Garret FitzGerald went on to the even greater and much more serious misjudgement in, unilaterally with the British, drawing up the infamous Anglo-Irish agreement, with all its blatantly unenforceable guarantees to the Northern Protestant Unionists.

After his defeat by the church on the Constitutional amendments needed to introduce divorce in Ireland, FitzGerald must at last be convinced, that, on the really important matters affecting the whole community in the Republic, 'Bishops' rule still O.K.', as I said in the Senate some years before.

18

Reflection

NOW in the seventh and final of Shakespeare's ages, impeded by increasing frailty, there is time for reflection. No longer may the patronising elders, envious yet critical of the young, tell them 'it was so much worse in our time'. Bad it may have been, but today's children must endure the all-pervasive shadow of a grim nuclear nemesis seemingly beyond their control. Sameul Beckett's bleak truth: 'the tears of the world are a constant quantity. For each one who begins to weep, another stops. The same is true of the laugh'.

On the credit side, the Marxists claim that with mixed enthusiasm and success, one third of the world struggles on towards the socialist millenia. The capitalist world, to a great extent casualty of its own unique scientific ingenuity and greed, is in total dissary. Yet in a stagnating and bankrupt Ireland there is no politics. Both North and South voters uncritically cheer on their team, like schoolboy football supporters, swearing blind loyalty to their leaders.

For a member of the medical profession and a conscientious radical, the problem always was how best to rationalise political involvement in a society where primitive superstition replaces the mature political ideologies of the outside world. My three years as Minister for Health was a committment to political involvement. Lives were saved, suffering and pain were avoided or reduced. Fine modern hospitals and clinics were built all over Ireland. The elimination of tuberculosis was achieved and the infra-structure for a good health service was established. Progress at that level was possible through politics until I was overwhelmed by an obscurantist tide at its high spring. By relegation to the back benches, it was hoped that I could be rendered harmless.

Why was it that, after such an experience I neither returned to medical practice exclusively nor emigrated to a satisfying job in the British national health service? Again Samuel Beckett put it well:

So offer it up, plank it down,
Cancer, angina, it's all one to us.
Cough up your TB, don't be stingy,
We'll put it with the rest.
It all boils down to the blood of the lamb.

That being the form of Irish medical practice why waste time as a doctor in Ireland?

Is there not another side to that argument? Medical practice being thus, how could a conscientious doctor leave a whole community to the depredations of medical practice of the time? To remain a constant critic was to me a valid option.

There is however beyond the visible achievement of my three short years as Minister, my conviction that the failure by society in the Republic to distinguish between the profession of politics and its practitioners is a grave mis-judgement by the Irish people of the proper function, scope and potential of politics. Just as my own brief period in charge of a minor department, and as Sean Lemass also showed in industry and commerce, major achievements could not have been recorded other than through political action. I could have worked for a lifetime as general practitioner or consultant and not achieved any advance in hospital care or welfare. Is it not extraordinary that in advanced western society, in its education of the professions, elaborate institutions are built at enormous expenditure from public funds to equip avowedly and inevitably elitist universities and colleges?

At the same time, education for the individual who is to be responsible for the successful creation of a prosperous community in which university graduates will work at their various professions, is virtually non-existent. The archane art and skill of politics is left to untrained, unskilled and whimsical 'do-gooders' who choose to designate themselves as politicians. Overnight they are entrusted with the phenomenally difficult task of designing, building and administering the elaborate structures of a modern society in which the creation of wealth and its enlightened distribution is ensured. In its potential for society the profession of politics transcends the separate and individual wisdom and skills of every component of that society. Above all other questions, society must ask should politics be left to the amateur? There is no aspect of our lives, in education, in health or sickness or recreation in youth or in old age where individual human happiness is so crucially dependant on the professional skills of adequately trained politicians.

As to my thirty years soujourn on the backbenches my friend Paul Campbell recently commented in wry commiseration: 'You're the watchdog, Noël, to whom nobody listened!' It was a dismissive observation on backbench politics. Yet in recent times, new and contentious arguments on subjects so long forbidden are now widely debated and championed by one-time conformist and fearful political colleagues. Maybe from the backbenches I helped in that enlightenment. Despite the confusion of political parties with their misleading republican rhetoric and primitive loyalties there was a re-assuring accolade at the end of my political career. Generously and unanimously, our parliamentary correspondents united in their citation: 'Consistently he has pursued his socialist objectives'.

Because of my unique life experience in Ireland and England in both working and middle class milieux, there is one inescapable conclusion. With few exceptions it is as difficult for a member of the working class in the Republic to leave that class, with all its limitations and penalties, as for a camel to pass through the eye of a needle. The question needs to be posed as to how in a society where the working classes constitutes the vast majority of an electorate they continue to elect politicians who maintain an educational system which so blatently discriminates against them and their children? Such discrimination persists in the health services, in employment, in housing, in recreation, against women and in living conditions among the aged. Because of this obvious anomaly, the thoughtful have long since shed the fiction that through our system of parliamentary democracy do we have an effective instrument of popular will. As in the Aesop fable of the Fox and the Crow, the middle class continues to hold power and to use it so that it is retained.

Possibly one of the greatest disappointments has been that the leadership of the Irish trade union movement has made little serious attempt to use its resources and the network of its contacts among working people to protest against, or to displace this carefully constructed discriminatory feature of the Irish educational system against its members.

Saddest of all are the daily television images of countless millions of starving children, including those of the one million of our own people on the poverty line, while food surpluses accumulate that few can pay for. In the failure by politicians to resolve this obscene dilemma, could there be a more compelling defence for the role of a properly educated and enlightened politician as a first step towards justice in modern society?

Index